The Story of
THE ROYAL FAMILY

THE STORY OF THE ROYAL FAMILY

Text by DON COOLICAN

FOREWORD BY

THE EARL OF LICHFIELD

Designed by Philip Clucas MSIAD
Produced by Ted Smart and
David Gibbon

COLOUR LIBRARY BOOKS

FOREWORD

In this age of holograms and wholefoods, Concorde and computers how can we explain the enduring appeal of the British Royal Family? For there can be no doubt that they are popular, despite the ritual complaints of republicans and radicals. Anyone who has heard the roaring approval of the crowds massed outside Buckingham Palace on state occasions knows that there is more to the Monarchy than their role as central pivot for pageantry and pomp.

The crowd's attitude to their Queen is unique, compounded of respect, a certain healthy curiosity, but above all affection, a very special kind of admiration that seems particularly British.

Perhaps the most noticeable aspect of the relationship between crown and commons is the fact that it endures, remaining constant through thick or thin, in times of national sickness and of health, something that's almost entirely due to the resilient flexibility of the institution.

As times have changed so has the Royal Family, not suddenly or dramatically, not running after passing fads or fashions, but moving slowly, steadily, like a great ocean liner responding to the helm. Fifty years ago it was literally unthinkable that television cameras would be allowed to film the Royal Family's private moments, that the grandson of the Sovereign should start his life without a title, or that the names of members of the family should appear in the Divorce Courts. In the last few years all these things have come to pass and still the family survives unscathed.

As guardians of a long and continuous tradition the Monarchy cannot afford to take change lightly, but traditions cannot be regarded as a substitute for clear thinking and in recent years the Royal Family has demonstrated its healthy respect for both. In this, as in most other things, it is the Queen herself who has led the family.

It is of course the Queen that we first think of when we think of royalty: dignified, serene, perhaps at times understandably pensive, but always unmistakably royal. Having served her apprenticeship in public she now provides the unshakeable sense of leadership that has helped to establish her family as a still strong centre in the storm of contemporary life.

But above all it is surely the family itself that accounts for the Monarchy's enduring appeal. For in the Royal Family there is something for everybody, a gallery of types and characters that mirrors the national characteristics of the British people. We have a truly loveable grandmother, a sister who's determined to live her life the way she wants to, and a son who shows great promise. Now, with the wedding of that son to a fairy-tale princess, we have another valuable addition to the family and another set of pictures to stick into our family album.

RT. HON. THE EARL OF LICHFIELD. F.I.I.P., F.R.P.S.

At the time of the celebration of Victoria's Diamond Jubilee her rule over the British Empire and her influence throughout Europe had both reached their peak. The celebrations in London were seen by some as not just the sixtieth anniversary of the old Queen's accession but also as a massive public display of the powers of Majesty world wide. The date was 22 June 1897.

A contemporary writer was able to say with much justification: "Happy is the nation which has a sovereign like our Queen, who uses the great power of her exalted position in the interests of her people.

"How wise and experienced the Queen is in all matters of state as her ministers have often testified. One Prime Minister succeeds another, but the Queen has continued in office without a break for 60 years. It may, indeed, be fairly said that she has more knowledge of the business of governing nations than any of her Prime Ministers . . . more insight into the mysteries and intricacies of foreign affairs than any of her Foreign Secretaries . . .

"More influence in European Courts from her personal character and kinship than any other Crown Head.

"By this personal influence she has often been able to promote the interests of peace, and by the knowledge, derived from private intercourse with other Monarchs, she has often been able to guide the councils of her ministers. At the same time she has never tried to impose her opinions upon them, knowing that theirs is the responsibility and theirs, accordingly, the right to act as they think best.

"But, whilst the Queen has won golden opinions as a wise constitutional monarch, paying at all times her loyal and willing obedience to the declared will of the nation, she has enthroned herself in the hearts of her people by her home life and motherly character.

"Her influence for good over her people on account of the love and purity that had always reigned in her home has been simply inestimable . . .

"While our most sovereign lady is the most queenly of women, she is also the most womanly of Queens. The two predominant feelings in her breast are the love of home and the love of her people."

Victoria was by now a slow-moving, crusty, intolerant old woman of 78 years of age, not taking easily to the realisation that not only Britain but the entire world was changing. The idea of a truly democratic parliament had become fully accepted in Britain and these ideas were now spreading elsewhere in the world. Already there were movements in some of her colonies demanding independence from London. Britain's industrial lead, once so profitably exploited, was beginning to be taken over by new techniques and energy in Germany and the United States.

Gladstone, the Liberal, was her Prime Minister for the fourth and last time – still without ever achieving any sympathy or co-operation from Victoria. His views were too liberal for her liking. She once threatened to abdicate (in 1880) when Gladstone was returned for his second spell in office.

When he died in 1898, the Queen refused to have Gladstone's death mentioned in the Court Circular. "I am sorry for Mrs G," she wrote. "As for him, I never liked him, and will say nothing about him." She reluctantly allowed the Prince of Wales, much against her better wishes, to act as a pall bearer for the funeral of a man whom the *New York Tribune* referred to as "the world's greatest citizen".

Reluctantly, very reluctantly, and after many battles with her political advisers, Victoria began to realise that the men at Westminster were no longer just her parliamentary servants. With the Reform Acts of the early part of her reign they represented now the people of Britain and had to act according to the wishes of the population.

She lived long enough to see the start of the crumbling of her empire. In 1899, when she was 80 years old, the Boer War broke out in South Africa. The next two years brought her nothing but sad news of her army's misfortunes against the Dutch settlers. Opening telegrams from the colony made her ill.

She was beginning to go blind, and on one occasion she cheered up briefly when she misread a defeat for a victory. Her joy lasted only until breakfast, however, when she learned the truth from others.

Victoria died at Osborne at 6.30 on a gloomy winter's evening, 22 January, 1901. She kept in touch with both her family and empire's affairs to within a few days of her death – suffering from indigestion, insomnia and general exhaustion.

The Prince of Wales, on the brink of becoming Edward VII, wept when she uttered her last word to him: "Bertie".

There is a bitter irony about her last two-and-a half hours alive. During this time her head was cradled in the right arm of her grandson Willy – Kaiser William II of Germany – who was soon to lead Europe into a war that would end the monarchial achievements of her age forever.

With the death of Queen Victoria the man who was the least favourite – until her latter years – offspring took over the throne for which he had been waiting for 60 years. King Edward VII gave his name not only to an era but to a racy lifestyle that Britain had been waiting for throughout the staid reign of his mother.

The fun loving, girl chasing, champagne drinking gourmet shamelessly made it clear to his subjects that widow's weeds were out and the enjoyment of life to the fullest was back in fashion . . . mistresses and all!

Of all her nine children, Edward, christened Albert Edward and called Bertie, had given Victoria the most heartache. As a teenager she considered him to be idle and lazy with "a disregard for everything". Through the later years of his life, when his mother had given him very little say in the affairs of the State he would one day rule, he was to her invariably "Oh that boy!"

The prince certainly had a record of wild ways to justify the old queen's worries and those of her more sober and properly behaved subjects, most of whom had considerable reservations about his suitability to rule.

Opposite *The frozen, imperious features of Queen Victoria, Britain's revered matriarch, almost sanctified by her millions of subjects spread over a quarter of the globe.*

Victoria and Albert always harboured doubts about their eldest son's suitability for the crown because of the waywardness he had displayed from so early in his life.

Albert had tried very hard to shape his son into the mould of a worthy constitutional monarch, but with little success. Wenching and generally enjoying himself with his risqué set pleased the feckless Edward more. Horseracing, gambling and the pleasures of fashionable society on both sides of the English Channel were the

Opposite page King Edward VII and his Danish born wife Queen Alexandra: she remained faithful to him throughout their 47-year marriage, even though he was several times unfaithful to her. Above Edward in tweeds, personifying the Edwardian preoccupation with the pleasures of the country. Top right A house party during a shooting weekend, with the King in the centre of what critics called "his vulgar friends". More respectfully regarded were members of his own family, many of whom attended a gathering at Windsor in November 1897: among them above right his niece Queen Victoria Eugenie of Spain, his nephew Kaiser Wilhelm of Germany with his Empress, Queen Amelie of Portugal, King Alfonso XIII of Spain, and King Edward's daughter, Queen Maud of Norway. Right The King was the first British sovereign to be driven by motor car.

sort of pursuits that shocked Victoria but gave the headstrong Edward no end of fun.

In his late twenties the scandal of his goings on included being cited in a much-publicised divorce case. His string of beautiful mistresses eventually included the actress Lillie Langtry – known as the "Jersey Lily" to her admirers, but the "Jersey Cow" to Edward's enemies.

His bedroom activities earned him the soubriquet "Edward the Caresser".

Because Albert and Victoria had seen Edward's penchant for the wilder side of life from early on, they had been determined to get him married, and

King Edward VII's successor, King George V (bottom picture, with his wife, his eldest son, and his sister Princess Victoria in 1907) was the first sovereign of the House of Windsor. With his dutiful wife, Queen Mary **left** he reigned, soundly if unimaginatively over the country for one of the most tumultuous two and a half decades Britan had ever witnessed. Though his qualities as a parent may be doubted, he was the epitome of the Edwardian family man: **below** his four eldest children – Princess Mary, Prince Albert, Prince Henry and Prince Edward, in 1902.

hopefully settled down, as soon as possible. They had searched among their European relatives for a suitable bride who would keep him in check. A good, moral, high-minded German girl was what they had in mind from among their Teutonic relations, but, shades of the problem until recently faced by the present Prince of Wales, princesses who fitted the bill were in short supply.

They eventually chose Princess Alexandra Caroline Marie Charlotte Louise Julie of Schleswig-Holstein-Sonderburg-Glücksburg, the 16-year-old daughter of Prince Christian of Denmark. She was "spotted" by Edward's elder sister, Vicky, who had been instructed by her mother to keep her eyes open in the urgent bride-hunting stakes.

Vicky, by now married to the Crown Prince of Prussia, had written to her

As a young naval officer **above** *King George (then Duke of York) married Princess Mary of Teck* **above right** *in 1893. It was an arranged marriage, but the early obliged friendship eventually blossomed into love.* **Right** *King George as Prince of Wales with his children at Sandringham in February 1902.*

mother after hearing about Alexandra: "I have seen several people who have seen her of late and who give such accounts of her beauty, her charm, her amiability, her frank natural manner and many excellent qualities. I thought it right to tell you this in Bertie's interest, though as a Prussian I cannot wish Bertie should ever marry her."

Victoria did not wish to offend the Prussians either, who at the time were

attempting to make the Schleswig-Holstein area of Denmark part of Germany. The British Queen also disapproved of the Danish Royal Household, whom she considered to be a cut below her own standards – a form of regal snobbery. She replied to her daughter's letter as follows, therefore: "The beauty of Denmark is much against our wishes. What a pity she is who she is."

Daughter Victoria looked elsewhere among her European relatives but still could not come up with anyone better than the Danish contender. She had inquiries made as to the young girl's morals, manners and character and was able to satisfy her mother that Alexandra came up to scratch.

Princess Victoria discussed the possibility of a match with the prospective bride's father Prince Christian and a meeting was arranged between Edward and Alexandra. He seems to

The family of King George V and Queen Mary. The eldest child (opposite page, with his father and grandfather in 1903) succeeded as King Edward VIII on King George's death. **Left** Prince Edward as a midshipman in the Navy in 1908; his father was determined that his sons should follow in his footsteps. **Above** Princess Mary, the King's only daughter, later to become Princess Royal and mother of the present Earl of Harewood; here seen in Coronation Robes in June 1911. She died in 1965. **Above left** King George and Queen Mary's first five children in 1903 – including Prince George, later Duke of Kent, as a year-old baby.

have displayed neither enthusiasm nor apathy at the prospect of marrying her. He merely talked gushingly about her beauty and accepted that she was to be his wife in an arranged marriage. He

felt he had no say in the matter and continued with his women chasing.

The delicate, dark-haired Alexandra was certainly an attractive creature. When Prince Albert saw a picture of her he said: "From that photograph I would marry her at once." The Prince Consort was never to meet her in the flesh, however, because he died shortly after the matchmaking began.

A year later Queen Victoria took the trouble, in the midst of her orgy of widowly misery, to meet the bride-to-be during a visit to her beloved Albert's old

Opposite page *The shy but conscientious Prince Albert, second son of King George V, in 1920. A model of reliability, he assumed the Crown as George VI in the most difficult and appalling circumstances of his brother's abdication, and in his quiet way helped to raise it to a new peak of popularity and respect.* **Far left, above** *On his wedding day in 1923: his bride is now Queen Elizabeth the Queen Mother – though she wouldn't have been if he had not asked her a second time for her hand in marriage.* **Left** *Prince Albert at Balmoral in 1910.* **Far left, below** *As a naval cadet in 1909.* **Overleaf** *King George V and Queen Mary with their children on Prince Albert's wedding day – 26th April 1923. (Left to right) Edward, Prince of Wales, Prince Henry, later Duke of Gloucester, Albert, Duke of York and Prince George, later Duke of Kent.*

congregation as one would normally expect of the mother of the bridegroom.

Instead she looked down on the white-crinolined bride and Bertie, dressed in the uniform of a Knight of the Garter, from behind a screen on a balcony above the nave of the church. Fortunately the cheering crowds outside, who took the shy new Princess of Wales to their hearts, lifted the gloom from what should have been a happy occasion.

Edward found his bride to be intelligent, a happy spirit and a loving spouse, but this was not enough, it seems. As soon as their honeymoon at Osborne was over he returned to his old ways of womanising. Queen Victoria, disappointed that even marriage could not bring her wayward son into line, brought up the subject with him several times . . . but he would not change his lifestyle. The Queen once wrote of Alexandra: "I often think her lot is not an easy one, but she is very fond of Bertie, though not blind."

Alexandra soon had to get used to a lonely life, never expecting her husband home until the early hours of the morning, or putting up with him going off with his racy friends to country house parties without her. When she was going through one of her difficult births Edward ignored three telegrams

home in Coburg. She immediately gave her approval and was determined to get her troublesome 20-year-old son married off and settled down as soon as the days of mourning were over.

Nine months after the death of his father Bertie proposed to Alexandra while walking in the gardens of his Uncle Leopold's palace in Belgium and six months later, on 10 March 1863 the couple were married in St George's Chapel, Windsor. It must have been a bizarre affair, because Queen Victoria insisted on wearing her widow's black dress, and refused to sit among the

pleading with him to be at her bedside. Instead he went steeplechasing at Windsor.

All told she bore him six children, though one died in less than 24 hours. The surviving five were Albert Victor, the Duke of Clarence, who was to die at the age of 28, George, the future King George V, Louise, Victoria and Maud.

Despite his not very discreet womanising Edward was a popular figure at home and abroad. He was constantly travelling to his mother's far-flung outposts and dominions, before he came to the throne. With Victoria enjoying

Lower left *Princess Elizabeth, aged 18 months, in October 1927: she was then third in line of succession to the Throne.* **Below** *Riding her tricycle in St James's Park in 1931, when she was living at her parent's town house at 145 Piccadilly.* **Below left** *In celebration of King George V's 68th birthday, his granddaughter Princess Elizabeth rides with* her mother the Duchess of York, her grandmother Queen Mary and her aunt, the Princess Royal, to witness the Trooping the Colour ceremony on Horse Guards Parade on 5th June 1933. **Opposite** *An official photograph taken by Marcus Adams in July 1928 at 145 Piccadilly: a delightful study of the future Queen.*

being the Widow of Windsor after Albert's death it was up to Edward to keep the royal family in the public eye and carry out many of the duties of pomp and circumstance that would normally be expected of the monarch.

Having been brought up in an atmosphere of disapproval from both his mother and father he was determined to start his reign in 1901 with a clean sweep of the past. He cleared all the palaces of pictures and treasures that had been acquired by his parents, especially the room where Albert had died 40 years earlier. This had been preserved exactly as it was on the day the Prince Consort died – a gloomy mausoleum that Victoria had regarded virtually as her private shrine.

His mother had always wished that Osborne should stay in the family, but he quickly got rid of this as well, giving it to the Royal Navy as a training college and convalescent home. He also

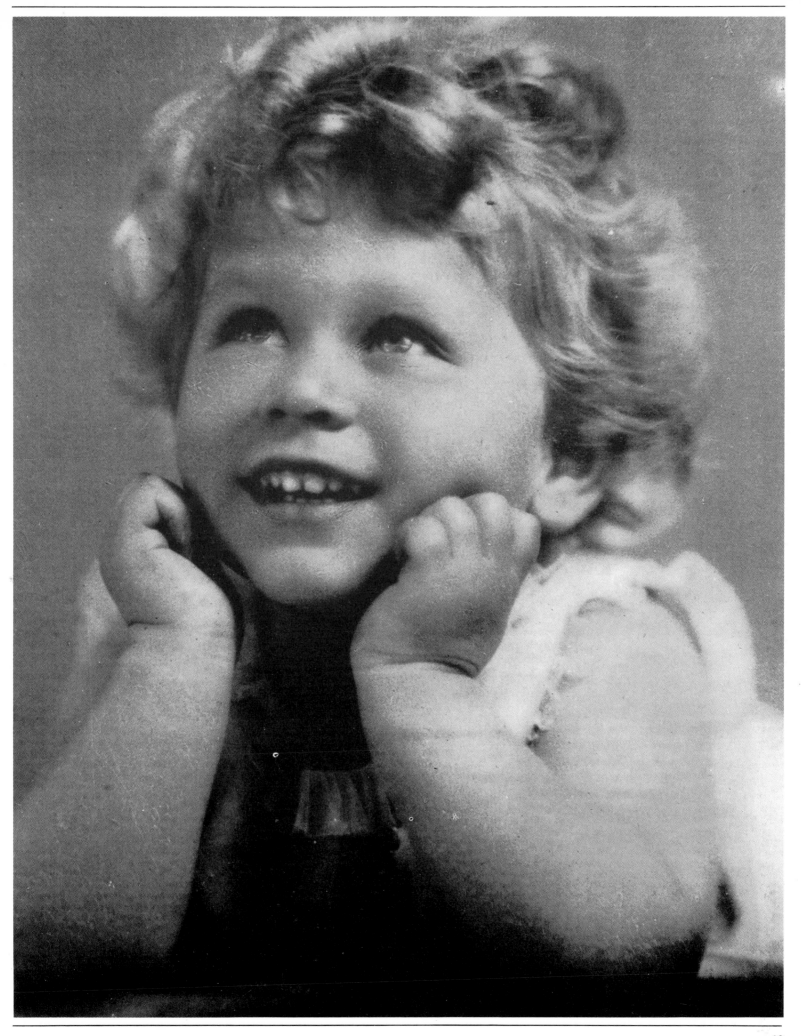

Above *Princess Elizabeth and Princess Margaret with their mother, the Duchess of York in an official portrait by Marcus Adams in 1934.* **Right** *Prince Charles held by his grandmother Queen Elizabeth, on 15th December 1948, the day of his christening at Buckingham Palace. The pictures on the opposite page show* **top left** *an official portrait of Princess Elizabeth taken for her 18th birthday, April 1944* **Top right** *Princess Elizabeth with her first child, Prince Charles, in April 1949.* **Bottom left** *King George VI with his two daughters at Royal Lodge Windsor in 1943.* **Bottom right** *The Royal Family at Buckingham Palace in the summer of 1939.*

ordered the disposal of statues, paintings and mementoes of John Brown, the old queen's close companion in widowhood.

At the end of this hectic removal of as many memories of his past as possible,

Edward almost failed to survive long enough to be crowned king. Forty-eight hours before his coronation, fixed for 30 June 1902, he became seriously ill with severe appendicitis, which required surgery in an age when this type of operation was rarely carried out.

The final dress rehearsal for the coronation at Westminster Abbey became a service of prayer for the life of the uncrowned sovereign.

Either the prayers or a surgeon's skill worked, because he recovered rapidly and was, at last, able to go ahead with the ceremony a few weeks later on 9 August.

If Queen Victoria had been the "Grandmother of Europe", Edward became the "Uncle of Europe", constantly making State visits with Alexandra to their various relatives. It was an era in which Britain was still at the peak of her power and influence, and only just about to begin losing her com-

manding position in the world.

Relations with nephew Kaiser William of Germany began to sour, however, because "Kaiser Bill" thought Uncle Bertie was patronising. Edward encouraged greater friendship with both Russia and France instead and he was the powerful force behind the signing of the Entente Cordiale which, on paper at least, declared undying friendship between two neighbours who had both fought and been suspicious of each other for centuries.

At home he was popular with his people as "King Teddy". His matchless energy for the good things in life and generally jolly demeanour suited the mood of prosperous Edwardian England. He made horse-racing the "sport of kings" and his enthusiasm for it was such that one of his last demands before collapsing into a coma and dying on 6 May, 1910 was to ask if his horse had won at Kempton Park. It had and he is said to have died a happy man.

Such was his popularity that more than half-a-million people filed past his coffin when he lay in State in Westminster Hall for three days. And such was the character of the man that not only nine reigning monarchs walked behind the gun carriage carrying his body in the funeral procession . . . but also his favourite fox terrier.

Old King Teddy's successor, George V, was a "second-son" monarch. He became next in line after his elder brother, Albert, Duke of Clarence, died, following what was reputed to have been a fairly dissolute life.

George not only inherited the throne, but also the fiancée of the deceased – Princess May of Teck, better known as Queen Mary.

The new king was born on 3 June, 1865 and blessed with a more than usually happy childhood. This was because his father was determined that his children should not suffer the mistakes of his own upbringing. As a result all of the Prince of Wales' offspring led boisterous, indulged lives mainly at Sandringham.

The Princess of Wales, Alexandra, having had to make a life of her own

*Left The Queen, then Princess Elizabeth, with her mother, then Duchess of York, in about 1935. With heavier responsibilities after the abdication of her uncle King Edward VIII in 1936, Princess Elizabeth stands on the balcony of Buckingham Palace **below** with her sister Princess Margaret and her grandmother, Queen Mary, and her parents King George VI and Queen Elizabeth after their Coronation on 12th May 1937. **Bottom right** The two princesses and their grandmother at the Royal Tournament on 22nd May 1939.*

In July 1939 the Royal Family visited the Royal Naval College at Dartmouth **right.** It was on this occasion that Princess Elizabeth first met in public her distant cousin Prince Philip of Greece, who became her husband in 1947. **Below** Two pictures reflecting different moods as Princess Elizabeth attends Sir Robert Mayer's Coronation Concert in Westminster in 1937. Little did she imagine that forty-two years later she would, as Queen, meet Sir Robert Mayer again on the occasion of his 100th birthday!

while being neglected by her philandering husband, had a particular need of a happy family around her. The effect of this was that she lavished affection on her children.

George having reached his early teens, the Royal Family's sea traditions were firmly established when George and his elder brother Albert – known

as Eddy – went to naval college. Queen Victoria had opposed the idea because she thought that a rough and bawdy life on the ocean waves was unsuitable for the heir-presumptive and his brother.

In fact George thoroughly enjoyed his time in the Royal Navy. He spent 15 years in the service, which encouraged a devotion to duty that served him well in later years. His love of the sea also earned him the title of "Sailor King".

Above *The Queen Mother, then Duchess of York, with Princess Elizabeth at Bertram Mills' Circus in January 1934.* **Top left** *Princess Elizabeth rehearsing for her first broadcast on 13th October 1940, at the height of the London blitz; Princess Margaret joined in at the end* **opposite page, centre.** *VE Day celebrations in May 1945 included an appearance by the Royal Family on the balcony at Buckingham Palace:* **left** *the King and Queen, with their daughters Princess Elizabeth (in uniform) and Princess Margaret.*

In much the same way that three generations later, Prince Charles was to get closer to his future subjects because of his life afloat, George got to know about life away from the palaces and strict royal protocol.

His tours of duty included being stationed in Australia, South Africa, and West Indies and the Mediterranean. There was every indication that while brother Eddy looked after the throne, George would have a successful naval career ahead of him. It never turned out that way, however.

Eddy seems to have been too much of a chip off the old block, showing all his father's tendencies for wine, women and song. Whereas the father indulged his exotic tastes for the most part in smart salons in London and Paris, the son preferred the low life of cheap East End brothels.

There was talk at the time that he was a homosexual, and even today there are students of criminology who say he could have been the notorious "Jack the Ripper" who slashed to death Victorian street-walkers.

Murderer or not, his behaviour so shocked Queen Victoria that she insisted something had to be done about the boy. At first it was decided to send him away from England on a tour of the Far East, but then the Queen's familiar solution for troublesome young men was suggested – marriage.

The unfortunate girl chosen for the role of wife and future consort to high-living Eddy was Princess May of Teck. Her mother, Mary Adelaide, was the daughter of the Duke of Cambridge, an uncle of Queen Victoria. So the Queen's choice of a bride for her grandson followed the tradition of keeping romances as near to the family as

possible.

Princess May – christened Victoria Mary Augusta Louise Olga Pauline Claudine Agnes – was born on 26 May 1867 at Kensington Palace. By the time she was 24 years old, and been suggested as a royal bride, her earlier pampered life at Kensington Palace had come to an abrupt end because her father, Prince Franz of Teck, started to run out of funds. The entire family, including her three brothers, went to live in Florence, where the cost of a style suitable to their rank proved cheaper than in London.

The poor girl did not have much choice in the matter, therefore, when Victoria decided May would marry her grandson. With a family almost on the royal breadline, she had to take whatever, or whomever, was offered to her.

The engagement of Princess May

Below *In the final years of the war, Princess Elizabeth became a Second Subaltern at an Auxiliary Territorial Service Training Centre in Southern England: here, in 1943 she joins the Motor Transport Unit and learns how to change a wheel during a visit by the King and Queen.* **Top** *Princess Elizabeth in her study at Buckingham Palace in the summer of 1946, the year she began to take on a heavy and regular round of royal duties.*

and Prince Albert in December 1891 pleased the old Queen, both families of the couple, and the cheering crowds in the street when the announcement was made. But a love match it certainly was not. This was a strictly arranged coupling, with neither party having any influence at all on the planning of their future.

The rejoicing over the match-making was not to last for long, however. A month after the engagement, Eddy died

from pneumonia. He had, at first, contracted influenza, but his condition is said to have deteriorated in part because of the years of debauchery among his low-life friends which generally affected his health.

His death is reported to have shattered Princess May, though whether her mourning was over the loss of a husband or the loss of a more comfortable life-style we shall never know. A solution to her problems was already on the way shortly after Eddy's death. May's family began indicating to Victoria that perhaps the second son and now heir to the throne might be interested in taking the distraught ex-fiancee as a bride?

The Queen approved of the idea, so George was told propose to May. Unlike his late brother, George was very fond

Left *The widowed Queen Mother, with Queen Mary and the new Queen Elizabeth II wear heavy mourning as they await the arrival at Westminster Hall of the body of King George VI for his lying-in-state in February 1952. Only three months earlier, Queen Elizabeth had attended the wedding of her niece, Mary Bowes-Lyon, at St Bartholomew's Smithfield* **above. Top** *The Queen Mother brings smiles all round as she chats to the Wellington Highland Pipe Band from New Zealand who visited her at Clarence House in June 1958.*

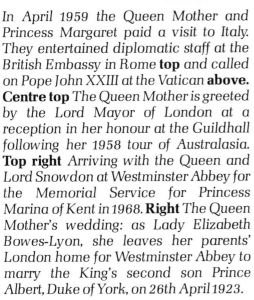

In April 1959 the Queen Mother and Princess Margaret paid a visit to Italy. They entertained diplomatic staff at the British Embassy in Rome **top** and called on Pope John XXIII at the Vatican **above**. **Centre top** The Queen Mother is greeted by the Lord Mayor of London at a reception in her honour at the Guildhall following her 1958 tour of Australasia. **Top right** Arriving with the Queen and Lord Snowdon at Westminster Abbey for the Memorial Service for Princess Marina of Kent in 1968. **Right** The Queen Mother's wedding: as Lady Elizabeth Bowes-Lyon, she leaves her parents' London home for Westminster Abbey to marry the King's second son Prince Albert, Duke of York, on 26th April 1923.

Above left *Prince Charles at his christening at Buckingham Palace on 15th December 1948: he is held on the lap of his great grandmother, the 82-year-old Queen Mary.* **Above right** *The Prince with his mother waves from a wall of Buckingham Palace to a passing procession in the Mall in 1951.* **Right** *The scene on the balcony of Buckingham Palace after the Queen had returned from her first State Opening of Parliament on 4th November 1952: Prince Charles, almost 4 years old, with his two-year-old sister and their parents.*

of the girl. He was delighted to take her as his bride and they married one scorching hot July afternoon in 1893 at St James's Palace . . . 18 months after the death of the first suitor.

After the wedding, George was so moved with love for his bride – now known as Princess Mary – that he used to write tender letters to her. The strict Victorian influence on their emotions prevented them from showing too

Memorable moments from the early years of the Queen's reign. **Above** *An official picture taken in the Throne Room of Buckingham Palace: the Queen wears the Star and Collar of the Order of the Garter, after opening her first Parliament in November 1952. After her Coronation in 1953, she returns resplendent in her robes and bearing the royal regalia, to the Palace. Her first Prime Minister, Sir Winston Churchill, resigned in 1955, and as a farewell gesture, gave a dinner party for the Queen and Duke of Edinburgh that April:* **right** *Sir Winston, with Lady Churchill, greets his Sovereign on her arrival at 10 Downing Street.*

openly what they felt about each other, so they preferred to use the written word to say "I love you" rather than declare it out loud.

George's feelings for Mary were beautifully described in one message:

"I saw in you the person I was capable of loving most deeply, if you only returned that love ... I have tried to understand you and know you, and with the happy result that I know now that I do love you, darling girl, with all my heart, and am simply devoted to you. I adore you, sweet May, and I can't say more than this."

Mary shared her feelings one day with her former governess. She said: "George is a dear. He adores me, which is touching . . . I am very glad I am married and don't feel at all strange. I feel as if I had been married for years and quite settled down."

George proved to be a responsible family man with none of his father's wild ways. Happiness to him was a

The Queen's reign began with a painful journey from East Africa to London on 7th February 1952 after the sudden death of her father the previous day. She was greeted at London Airport **above** *by her Prime Minister, Winston Churchill, and the Leader of the Opposition Clement Attlee. In contrast, the following year brought the dignified solemnity and triumphant rejoicing of the Coronation:* **right** *the Queen crowned and enthroned in St Edward's Chair in Westminster Abbey on 2nd June 1953;* **above right** *she exchanges smiles with the Duke of Edinburgh on the Palace balcony after the Coronation, while their two children, the Duke of Cornwall and Princess Anne, watch the RAF flypast;* **top right** *a final wave from the Royal couple before they leave the balcony.*

country life at Sandringham with his family, shooting, gardening or helping to run the estate. In the evenings he wanted nothing more exciting than a game of billiards or reading to his wife.

He had no desire for foreign travel like the late Prince of Wales. He once made it clear: "England is good enough for me. I like my own country best, climate or no, and I'm staying in it. There's nothing of the cosmopolitan in me."

Sixteen years after their marriage George and Mary came to the throne.

They did so during a constitutional crisis. The Liberal government had tried to get its budget through a House of Lords that was dominated by Tory peers. The Tories persisted in rejecting the budget proposals and, as a result, two General Elections were held in one year for the first time ever. The outcome was a reform of the House of Lords, but by this time, the King was deeply involved in politics.

The Liberal Prime Minister, Herbert Asquith, persuaded the King to agree to create new peers to counter-balance the Tory dominance in the House of Lords. Before this highly unorthodox step had to be taken, though, the Liberals managed to push through their legislation.

George wrote in his diary: "I disliked having to do this, but agreed that this was the only alternative to the Cabinet resigning, which at the moment would be disastrous."

He was saved from this embarrass-

Stages in the long Coronation ceremonial and its aftermath. **Below** *A canopy is raised over the Queen before the private and solemn moment of the Anointing as the Choir in the Abbey sing Handel's stirring Coronation anthem "Zadok the Priest".*

House of Windsor.

George and Mary had to take these steps despite strenuous war years in which they came closer to the people than any previous sovereigns. They both travelled throughout the country among the relatives of the fighting men and munitions workers. They toured hospitals full of wounded troops and George went over to France to visit his soldiers at the front.

On one excursion in 1915 he became a casualty when the cheering men frightened his horse. It fell and rolled on top of him breaking his pelvis in two places and causing internal injuries that were with him to the end of his life.

Peace in 1918 saw the end of Victoria's European dynasty. States, kingdoms, dukedoms and princedoms that dominated the map at the start of the war were no more – gone for ever in the aftermath of war, revolution and

Above *The Duke of Windsor attending the farewell performance of the French entertainer Maurice Chevalier at the Champs Elysées Theatre, Paris on 1st October 1968. The previous year the Duke and Duchess paid their first official visit to England to attend the unveiling at Marlborough House of a plaque commemorating his mother the late Queen Mary who had been born 100 years before:* **right** *the Duke and Duchess waving cheerfully to crowds at Southampton harbour as they arrive for the occasion on board the liner United States.*

ment, but not a more serious one when the First World War broke out five years later after his accession. Because of European family links, especially ties with Germany, many of the kings and princes on the enemy side were relations. Kaiser Bill was George's first cousin.

Although the Royal Family's loyalties were completely British, there was hatred at home for anyone with German connections. Their very names were objected to . . . Saxe-Coburg-Gotha, Teck and Battenburg, for example. The King thought the attacks on his family ancestry were ludicrous, but in July 1917 he had to make a Royal Proclamation changing the Battenburgs into Mountbatten, the Tecks to Cambridge and the creation of the

the democratising of their homelands by angry returning soldiers.

The Romanovs disappeared with the Russian Revolution of 1917 and the Kaiser and Austrian Emperor, together with scores of dukes and princes, were overthrown. Most of them were related to the couple at Buckingham Palace.

Even during peacetime, George seems to have been doomed to a troublesome reign. There was Civil War in Ireland . . . social unrest and unemployment in Britain . . . and the world-wide Slump following the Wall Street crash. In the midst of all this, however, George and Mary continued to grow in popularity with their subjects; a great tribute to their obvious

The Queen invariably attends the annual Badminton Horse Trials at the home of the Duke of Beaufort in Gloucestershire: **above right** *taking photographs of the event in April 1973, when Princess Anne was competing. Although the Queen spends most of her weekends at Windsor, she also relaxes occasionally at Sandringham after the week's duties.* **Above** *leaving Heathrow in May 1970.* **Right** *An unusual, but now famous, photograph of the Queen leaping ashore at Delmabehoe harbour during her State Visit to Turkey in October 1971.*

care and concern for the people during a period when the existence of Royalty was disappearing all over Europe.

Typical of the subtle awareness he had of his people was a gesture by George when he received Ramsay MacDonald, the first British Socialist Prime Minister in 1924. He wore a red tie.

By the time George and Mary celebrated their Silver Jubilee in May 1935 affection for them was immense. As he drove through cheering crowds in London, the King said to his Queen in a surprised manner: "Do you know, I really think they like me for myself."

Less than a year later he died at Sandringham from a lung infection and bronchitis. By the time of his death he

IN LOVING MEMORY

FROM

PHILIP AND LILIBET

Britain and the world paid solemn tribute to Lord Mountbatten on the day of his ceremonial funeral, 5th September 1979. **Top left** *The Prince of Wales and Prince Philip, with Prince Michael of Kent, walk in procession to Westminster Abbey.* **Above** *The cortege passing the statue of Sir Winston Churchill in Parliament Square.* **Left centre** *The Queen and Prince Philip watch tensely as the coffin is brought into Westminster Abbey.* **Top** *The Prince of Wales, deeply moved, with his midshipman brother Prince Andrew and Prince Edward, after the funeral.*

was already disturbed by the affair that was going from strength to strength between his eldest son and the American divorcee, Mrs Wallis Simpson. He confided to Mary: "After I'm gone the boy will ruin himself in 12 months."

George V, who had come to the throne at the age of 45 in 1910, was considered to have "no personal magnetism, no intellectual powers. He was neither a wit . . . well read nor well educated." He was, in fact, like most of his subjects, and he demonstrated his common link with them by a genuine and deep feeling for Britain's unemployed. In 1921, he wrote to the Prime Minister, Lloyd George, to say that men wanted work not "dole" (unemploy-

Above One of the last photographs taken of the Royal Family's "Uncle Dickie", Earl Mountbatten of Burma. On 28th July 1979, just a month before his assassination, he attended the Rundel Cup polo match at Tidworth, Hampshire, in which his great-nephew Prince Charles played. **Right** In 1975, Lord Mountbatten and the Prince of Wales went to Katmandu to attend the coronation of King Birendra of Nepal, a close friend of Prince Charles. The photograph **right** shows the royal guests in the grounds of the King's palace at Hanuman Dorha.

As well as his years of service in the RAF and the Navy, Prince Charles has maintained close connections with the Army as part of his public duties and private pastimes. The photographs on this page show him taking part in a commando assault course in January 1975 as part of his naval training at the Royal Marines Training Centre at Lympstone, Devon: this included wading down a stream **above right,** passing through a half submerged pipe **above,** and tree-walking **right.**

ment benefit) money, and that this money was in any case pitifully inadequate. Then, when a Conservative minority government was defeated in January 1924, the King sent for Ramsay MacDonald as the Leader of the next-largest party, Labour.

This was an amazing move in a traditional Right Wing society. MacDonald was not only a socialist, he was also the bastard son of a Scottish peasant farmer. Yet the King came to admire him. Nevertheless, Labour was thrown out in that October's election.

Despite the turbulent social conditions of the 1920s, George trusted his people. At the time of the General Strike in 1926, Lord Durham, a coal-owner, told him that the striking miners were a "damn lot of revolutionaries".

"Try living on their wages," came the royal reply. The King saw plenty in the state of Britain to justify the anger of the poor.

Between the two world wars, Britain was still one of the great powers, and the centre of the world's largest empire. George V was proud of his title of "King Emperor". As he lay dying in 1936 he enquired: "the Empire?" "It's absolutely all right, Sir," came the reply of a courtier.

After his death Britain was to go through one of its greatest constitutional crises with the decision of the Duke of Windsor to abandon his right to the throne – by abdicating – to marry

Mary died at the age of 85 on 24 March 1953, two-and-half months before the new Queen's coronation.

They were sad years, displayed by her taste for black clothes. She was unhappy not just because of widowhood, but also because she felt that Edward, the Prince of Wales who rejected the throne, had not only let her

Left *During a visit to the Gurkha Rifles in Norfolk in October 1980, Prince Charles prepares to fire a self-loading rifle.* **Lower left** *The Prince at RAF South Cerney in April 1978 at the conclusion of his parachute training as Colonel-in-Chief of the Parachute Regiment. The two photographs below show him taking part in a shooting match between the Lords and Commons at Bisley in July 1980. He took part, as Duke of Cornwall, for the House of Lords, who lost the match by a narrow margin.*

an American divorcee, Mrs. Wallis Simpson.

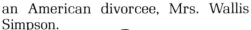

Queen Mary survived the death of George for another 18 years. Eventful years in which she witnessed her eldest son throw away a throne for the woman he loved... the hard and bitter years of the Second World War... and the death of her second son, George VI.

Throughout this period she was a pillar of strength to the son who had taken over the crown and she lived long enough to see the accession of her granddaughter, Queen Elizabeth II.

Left Fun and games at Olympia as Prince Charles takes part in a camel race during the International Show Jumping Tournament on 13th December 1979. **Below** More high jinks when he danced to soul music after opening a multi-ethnic exhibition at County Hall London in June 1978. **Bottom left** Prince Charles and his shipmates on HMS Minerva take on HMS Sirius in a tug-of-war at Hamilton, Bermuda in February 1973. **Bottom right** He watches with mock disbelief as one of the Queen's horses helps himself straight from the bucket during a polo tournament at Windsor in May 1979.

and the family down, but also the nation and Empire.

Yet there are some historians who claim that Edward's need to be constantly surrounded by admiring friends of both sexes could have been caused, to some degree, by his early childhood. His father was of the school that children should be seen and not heard, while his mother, with her Victorian reticence, never exuded the love and affection that a child normally needs for a rounded emotional development.

One of the results of this was that as a young man the dashing, stylish Prince of Wales was always seeking admiration and the love he had missed in childhood.

His flamboyant manner made him popular with the people and he tried even harder than his father to get to know how his future subjects lived, undertaking a series of tours around Britain and overseas. He was especially worried about the social injustices of the workless Twenties and Thirties and tried to use his influence in government and business circles to provide help for the unemployed, particularly

Above left *Prince Charles has to cope with a troublesome microphone when opening an engineering conference in London in October 1980.* **Above right** *He enters into the spirit of a Ukranian folk-dance during his tour of ethnic communities in Derby at the end of February 1981.* **Left** *More clowning on the polo field as the Prince rides in a horse-drawn buggy.* **Above** *Prince Charles meets a favourite comedian, Harry Secombe, at a Variety Club show at the London Palladium in April 1969.*

the Welsh miners.

The other side of his character, however, was one of holidays in the smart watering holes of the Continent, dancing the night away in London clubs and endless flirtations. He truly became the world's most eligible bachelor, with a string of girl-friends – though none of them managed to catch the light-footed devotee of the Charleston.

He tended to have long-running affairs with mature married women, the sort who could give him the warmth he had missed in his childhood. His favourite was Mrs Freda Dudley Ward, a well-known London hostess, who he first met in 1918 when he was 24 years old. Their romance, which included his intervals with other women, lasted 16 years. It survived her divorce, when it was discreetly ensured that the heir-to-the-throne's name was never mentioned.

There was some semblance of approval even from King George and Queen Mary, because Mrs Dudley Ward was of the sort of social strata that knew exactly what being a royal mistress entailed... not causing a fuss and being the soul of discretion. In any case she was devoted to her two daughters and would never have contemplated abandoning them and running off with someone else. Edward – David to his family and friends – used to enjoy playing "father" to the girls.

Among the prince's other well-known liaisons was an affair with Lady Furness, the wife of the British shipping millionaire. He landed himself in hot water with his family over his more public carryings on with her, especially when the two of them went on safari together in East Africa. Holidaying with another man's wife was definitely frowned upon in those days, unless discretion was assured. In this case it was not, and the royal parents made it clear to Edward that he had to mend his ways.

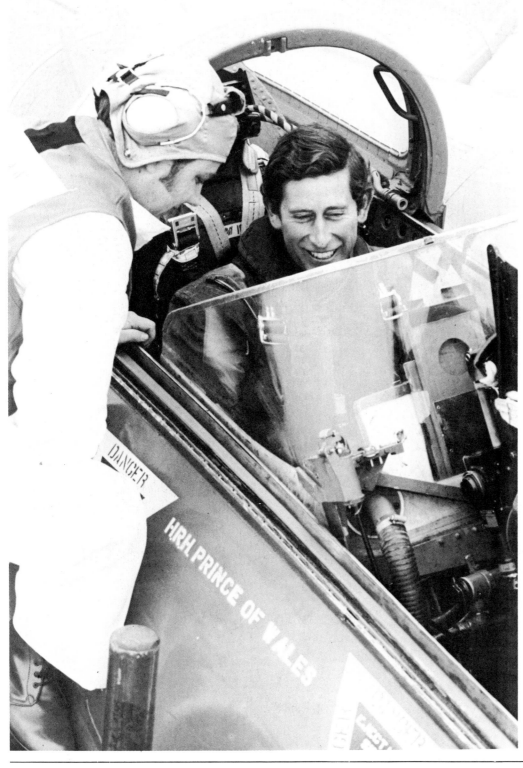

Promoted to Wing Commander early in 1977, Prince Charles paid a visit to RAF Wittering in July of that year and took over the controls of a two seater Harrier jump jet **top** *for a familiarisation flight before undertaking a simulated operational mission over Wales. The photographs on the opposite page show him* **far right** *about to board the Harrier and* **top left** *inside the aircraft before the flight. In September 1977 he visited the Royal Naval Air Station at RAF Culdrose, where he inspected a Royal Navy Buccaneer aircraft* **left.** *During a visit to France in July 1980, he was shown over a Mirage III aircraft at Colmar* **opposite page, bottom.**

This advice he did not take very seriously, because it was via the salon of Lady Furness that he met the woman who was to topple him off the throne, Mrs Wallis Simpson.

Born into a prosperous Baltimore family, the Warfields, Mrs Simpson had already been divorced once from her United States Navy officer husband, and was in the midst of a shaky second marriage to British businessman Ernest Simpson when she met Edward in 1930. She was then 42-years-old, a year younger than the Prince of Wales.

He quickly abandoned all other

women, including Lady Furness, who had acted as an unwitting "cupid", to devote his time to the striking dark-haired American sophisticate. The Simpsons were frequently his guests in nightclubs and private parties and he accompanied the couple on a holiday in the South of France. Ernest Simpson soon got the hint that he was a hindrance, so he found excuses not to be around when his wife and Edward wished to be together.

Six years after their first meeting, Wallis was divorced for the second time in a quiet hearing at Ipswich, Suffolk. By this time their friendship had become a scandal in London society,

In the course of her 30-year reign the Queen has officially visited many countries which had never before received a British sovereign. In February 1979, for instance, she undertook a lengthy tour ·of the Arab countries, including the Persian Gulf state of Qatar **centre left** with Emir Khalifa of Qatar. More recently, she visited Tunisia, Algeria and Morocco: her state visit to Morocco at the end of October 1980 was memorable both for the unpredictability and the variety of its programme. **Top left** The Queen is entertained by King Hassan II of Morocco and the Crown Prince at a formal banquet at the Royal Palace at Rabat. The pictures left and above show the Queen with King Hassan, enjoying an equestrian tournament in the desert near Marrakesh.

was making headlines abroad, and causing no end of heartache for George and Mary. The British Press, feeling the affair was endangering the monarchy, studiously kept what it knew off its pages until only a few weeks before what became known as the Abdication Crisis began.

Society's view of Mrs Simpson was expressed by the gossip diarist of the time, "Chips" Channon, who wrote: "The Prince is obviously infatuated and she, a jolly, unprepossessing American, witty, a mimic, an excellent cook, has completely subjugated him. She is madly anxious to storm Society while she is still favourite so that when he leaves her (as he leaves everyone in time) she will be secure."

But leaving Wallis was out of the question. With the death of his father

Above *The Queen being greeted by President Tito of Yugoslavia at a State banquet given in her honour on the first day of her visit there in October 1972. The Queen was the first British monarch to visit Yugoslavia. She has paid two State Visits to Italy;* **below right** *she attends a banquet given by President Pertini at the Quirinal Palace in Rome during her second visit in mid October 1980. Prince Charles is also much travelled, both privately and officially. In April 1980 he attended the Zimbabwe independence ceremonies, and met Zimbabwe's first Prime Minister, Robert Mugabe* **above left.** *In November 1980, he met Mrs Indira Ghandi, Prime Minister of India at New Delhi* **left,** *and* **bottom left** *spent three days walking in the foothills of the Himalayas.*

the new, but uncrowned King Edward VIII, felt he had even more freedom to carry on his affair. To critics and friends alike offering advice he would protest: "I am the King, after all."

He ensconced Wallis in Fort Belvedere, his private house near Windsor, where she would always be waiting for him at the end of his days of official duties. He caused undying resentment among his family, especially his mother and sister-in-law, the future Queen Elizabeth, the Queen Mother, by arranging for her to be present at the announcement of his accession. He showered her with jewellery, including some diamonds from the family vaults that were considered royal heirlooms. She was said

to be "dripping in new jewels and clothes".

Edward further upset the family and court advisers, when, while the court was still in mourning after the death of George VI, he abandoned public engagements in Aberdeen, including a visit to a hospital, to be with Wallis, who had been sneaked into nearby Balmoral.

By this time the Royal Family, courtiers, leading politicians and church leaders were beginning to realise that Wallis was not just one of the King's passing affairs. The nation faced a turning point in the history of the monarchy.

In November 1936 the new King spoke frankly for the first time to his mother about his devotion to a twice-divorced woman. Not only a divorcee, but a commoner and foreigner to boot. He told her he would either marry Wallis and keep his throne or abdicate. She turned down his proposals out of hand refusing to tolerate anything but Edward carrying out his inherited duty.

He then spoke to his three brothers, the Duke of York (soon to be George VI), the Duke of Gloucester and the Duke of Kent. Their reaction was the same as their mother's

A possible solution was floated by some of Edward's political friends. Edward and Wallis could have a morganatic marriage – one where she would never be Queen and any children would have no claims to succession. The Prime Minister of the day, Stanley Baldwin, a Tory, put the suggestion to his Cabinet who gave it a resounding turn-down.

As pressure built up, Wallis went to the South of France, where she said she would be willing to give up the King and end their affair, but Edward would not hear of it. He always hoped that one day she would be accepted as his wife while he still retained the crown.

But those around the court, from the Prime Minister to the bishops, from members of the House of Lords and the Commons to influential figures of the day, refused to accept such an idea. The inevitable end came on 10 December, 1936 when he signed the Instrument of Abdication.

*Before her engagement to the Prince of Wales on 24th February 1981, Lady Diana Spencer worked as a teacher at a kindergarten in St George's Square Pimlico. In September 1980, when her name was first linked with Prince Charles, she was pictured **opposite page, above,** in the grounds of the school. By November she was persistently photographed leaving her flat **left and lower right** or arriving at the school, and complaints were made about the way in which the everyday life of this 19-year-old girl was being affected by the constant publicity. **Far right** Three days after her engagement, the future Princess of Wales leaves Buckingham Palace and drives back to Clarence House, her home until her wedding.*

The following rainy evening, a Friday, he broadcast to the nation: "At long last I am able to say a few words of my own. I have never wanted to withold anything but until now it has been not constitutionally possible for me to speak.

"A few hours ago I discharged my last duty as King and Emperor, and now

Like the previous Prince of Wales, Prince Charles has in the last two years taken an increasing interest in steeple-chasing, but his efforts have brought indifferent results to date. In his first race **opposite, bottom left** *in March 1980, he finished last at Sandown on Sea Swell: in February 1981, his promising horse Allibar (the Prince is seen riding him –* **opposite, top left** *– in October 1980 at Ludlow) suddenly dropped dead after a training gallop: in March the Prince got a bloody nose* **right** *after falling from his horse Good Prospect at Sandown; and a few days later fell again from Good Prospect at the Cheltenham Festival* **below.**

that I have been succeeded by my brother, the Duke of York, my first words must be to declare my allegiance to him. This I do with all my heart.

"You all know the reasons that have impelled me to renounce the Throne. But I want you to understand that in making up my mind I did not forget the country or the Empire which as Prince of Wales, and lately as King I have for 25 years tried to serve. But you must believe me when I tell you that I have found it impossible to carry the heavy burden of responsibility and to discharge my duties as King as I would wish to do without the help and support of the woman I love.

"The Ministers of the Crown, and in particular Mr Baldwin, the Prime

Above right Prince Charles taking one of the jumps on Good Prospect at Sandown shortly before his fall. His nose still bleeding, Prince Charles rejoins his fiancée **right** who accompanied him to Sandown for the race. **Left** Lady Diana visiting the Gloucestershire Constabulary's HQ at Cheltenham at the end of March, 1981. The police here were already responsible for security at the homes of Princess Anne, and Prince and Princess Michael of Kent: and would assume resonsibility for guarding Highgrove, where Prince Charles and Lady Diana would live after their wedding.

*Formal and informal: official engagement photographs of Prince Charles and his fiancée – some **opposite page and left** taken at Highgrove House – by Lord Snowdon.*

Minister, have always treated me with full consideration. There has never been any constitutional difference between me and them and between me and Parliament. Bred in the constitutional tradition by my father, I should never have allowed any such issue to arise…

"I now quit altogether public affairs, and I lay down my burden. It may be some time before I return to my native land, but I shall always follow the fortunes of the British race and Empire with profound interest, and if at any time in the future I can be found of service to His Majesty in a private station I shall not fail.

"And now we all have a new King. I wish him, and you, his people, happiness and prosperity with all my heart. God Bless you all. God Save the King."

Then, stripped of his titles except one

created for the occasion "His Royal Highness the Duke of Windsor", Edward bid farewell to his brothers and sailed to exile in France. Six months later, on 3 June, 1937 he and Wallis were married at the Chateau de Cande near Tours.

One of the guests at the wedding, Lady Alexandra Metcalfe recorded in her diary: "It could be nothing but pitiable and tragic to see a King of England only six months ago, an idolised King, married under those circumstances, and yet pathetic as it was, his manner was so simple and dignified and he was so sure of himself in his happiness that it gave something to the sad little service which is hard to describe. He had tears running down his face when he came into the salon after the ceremony."

With the approach of the Second World War, the Duke hoped he would be

given some useful job back in Britain, but both the royal family and the Government were anxious to keep him out of the country. A visit to Hitler by the Windsors in late 1937 did not help their image at home and gave rise to speculation that they were Nazi sympathisers, but this was never adequately proved.

After the fall of France in 1940 the Windsors had to flee the country. They were still not wanted back home so a job was found for Edward as Governor of the Bahamas for the duration of the War. With peace they settled for ever in a house alongside the Bois de Boulogne in Paris, which began to resemble a miniature palace with royal crests and coats of arms on the walls and attendant liveried footmen.

Their main source of income was supposed to be around £60,000 a year, which was an allowance agreed at the time of the abdication with King George VI in exchange for the sale to him of Balmoral and Sandringham. Over the years it was always said that further funds reached Paris from London by private means.

The Windsors never healed the wounds completely with the British Royal Family. When, in 1945, he saw his mother for the first time in nine years she would not allow Edward to present his wife to her. One of his few other official visits was seven years later when he attended the funeral of his brother George and some months later the burial of his mother.

Fourteen more years were to pass before he was officially invited to Britain again. That was in 1967 when

On 20th November 1947, Princess Elizabeth married her third cousin, Prince Philip of Greece, in Westminster Abbey. He had previously renounced his Greek title, taken the surname Mountbatten, and been created Duke of Edinburgh by King George VI. **Below left** *Husband and wife leaving the Abbey.* **Above left** *They later appear on the Palace balcony with the King, Queen and Queen Mary, as well as Princess Margaret who was her sister's chief bridesmaid. The photographs on the opposite page are official portraits of the royal couple taken inside Buckingham Palace after the wedding.*

he attended the unveiling of a memorial to his mother. By this time he was a haggard-looking man of 73 and showing signs of ill-health. What might have been a last attempt at a family reconciliation never happened in the summer of 1972, when the Queen and the Duke of Edinburgh went to the Windsors' home during a State visit to France. Although the Queen met the Duchess for the first time, she was unable to be received by her uncle because he was lying in bed upstairs, too ill for visitors.

Shortly afterwards the Duke died. His widow was, at last, invited to Buckingham Palace when she accompanied his body from Paris to Britain for the funeral. He was buried among other members of the House of Windsor... with a space left alongside his grave for the woman he lost a throne for.

It was King George VI who said: "We're not a family, we're a firm." Yet a long-serving member of the Royal Household once told me: "I never feel as if I'm working at Buckingham Palace – it's like being part of a very busy family."

Is Queen Elizabeth II merely the managing director of a company called

"Royal Family Ltd" promoting Britain and the monarchy? Or is she the head of a group of kinsfolk, leading lives cut off from the rest of us, but who occasionally pop out of their palaces to wave to the masses?

To many people the royals seem to be slightly plastic figures from the world of glossy magazines, television newsreels and gossip columns: apparently protected from the problems of living that lesser mortals face; superstars who exist only in a world of pomp and privilege.

In 1952, a Coronation Committee was established to decide, amongst other things, on the design and construction of decorations for the streets and public buildings of London. The result helped to transform London into a showpiece of colourful traditional symbolism. These triumphal arches **above and top left** hung with coronets and surmounted by lions and unicorns, bestrode the Mall. **Top right** A simple but effective banner straddled a London street, whilst **left** a deep sense of indebtedness to the past and hope for the future found expression in the selected statements of the first and second Elizabeths.

The aura which surrounds them at all times tends to cut them off from most men and women. They either hold, or will inherit, great titles; there is little uncertainty in their lives, and the problems of paying the monthly bills never bother them.

Yet with our tendency to hedge them in behind gold-painted gates, we can overlook that the House of Windsor is above all a family: wives, husbands, sons, daughters, aunts, uncles, grandfathers, grandmothers, and cousins – a group of relations like any other family, which shares both joy and sorrow.

The Queen was never destined for the throne from birth. Her father and mother were the Duke and Duchess of York, and it was never thought likely that they would become King George VI and Queen Elizabeth. Her uncle, the popular Prince of Wales, was destined to succeed to the throne. That he would

The world famous statue of Eros in Piccadilly Circus was highlighted by a decorative cage **below,** *whilst in Oxford Street, Selfridge's festooned its pillars and balconies with tasselled hangings and flowers* **right. Lower right** *The State Coach, originally built for King George III in 1762, stands in the Royal Mews ready for the Coronation procession.*

abdicate to marry the woman he loved was a dramatic gesture never imagined by the family of the uncrowned King Edward VIII.

Elizabeth, therefore, never anticipated being trained for the life of a monarch. She was "Lilibet," a cheerful child, not too serious, enjoying a privileged existence in a smart Mayfair house, outdoor fun at Royal Lodge, Windsor, and playing among the heather at Birkhall near Balmoral.

All this changed for her, and for her sister Margaret, when they were ten

and six years old respectively. Their uncle David gave up his throne and their father had to step into his shoes. From then on life took on a more serious aspect because now Elizabeth had to be trained to become a sovereign. Private lessons became more purposeful and a little of her lightheartedness disappeared as she became more involved in protocol and learning about the affairs of State. Until then she and Princess Margaret had grown up in a blissfully happy home, without any of the pressures of impending responsibility

that, for example, Prince Charles has had to face.

Elizabeth spent her teenage years during the austerity of the Second World War, when she soon learned about the obligations of being a monarch as she shared the dangers of the Blitz in London with her father's subjects, and toured the war-torn areas of the country with her parents. When she was old enough she joined the Army, wearing khaki as an officer in the Auxiliary Territorial Service, the predecessor of today's Women's Royal

Left *A spectacular view for the Queen, accompanied by the late Emperor Haile Selassie during her tour of Ethiopia in February 1965.* **Below** *A proud moment for the Queen Mother on the day when Viscount Linley, son of Princess Margaret and Lord Snowdon, was christened – 30th November 1961. This picture was taken as the Princess and her husband and baby left Clarence House.* **Below left** *Princess Alexandra of Kent in the early 1960's:* **left** *attending a Disabled ex-Service-men's Sale of Work, and* **right** *an informal moment on her arrival at the Royal Opera House, Covent Garden in October 1960. The Duke of Kent is in the background.*

Army Corps.

Few people who meet the Queen when she is in silken and bejewelled finery realise that those well-manicured hands have suffered their fair share of broken nails, cuts and oily bruises while servicing lorries. The Sovereign can count among her many talents that of a trained motor mechanic, a skill she acquired during her Army days.

The Queen was only 25 when her

father died in February 1952. He died while Princess Elizabeth and Prince Philip were in Kenya on the first leg of a royal tour of East Africa, Australia and New Zealand.

His death did not come as a surprise to the Princess and the rest of the family. He had been ill for more than three years, a grim piece of information that had been kept quiet from his subjects and the world at large. In March 1949 he underwent an operation to im-

prove the circulation in his right foot. Two years later, the Queen Mother and the two Princesses had confirmation of their worst fears – King George, a heavy smoker, had a cancerous growth in his left lung.

Surgeons did their best and after an operation the King seemed to make a bright recovery. It was not to last. Less than a year later the illness took its toll. Few who were present or saw newsreel and newspaper photographs will forget the haggard expression on his face as he waved farewell to his elder daughter and her husband at London Airport when they set off on their world tour. It was a harsh winter's day. He was so ill that he should not have ventured out – yet it almost seems as if he sensed it might be the last time he would see his "Lilibet".

A week later he was at the royal estate of Sandringham, enjoying one of

An almost carefree atmosphere pervades these pictures of two of the Queen's early trips abroad. **Right** The Queen meets the Mayor of Hamilton as she visits the Bermudan House of Assembly during her Commonwealth Tour of 1953-4, in December 1953. **Below right** Leaving the House, with Prince Philip wearing tropical naval uniform. **Below** The Queen leaving a concert house in Amsterdam during her State Visit to the Netherlands in March 1958: she has a smile and a wave for the waiting crowds.

his favourite sports – shooting pheasant. At the end of the day he had dinner with his queen, listened to radio reports of Princess Elizabeth's tour in Africa, then had a cup of cocoa while he read a magazine. He went to bed and died in his sleep from a coronary thrombosis. The King was found dead by one of the valets, who drew back the curtains, turned round to say "good morning" and faced a stilled body. At 56 years of age the man who had never sought the throne, yet became one of Britain's greatest loved monarchs, had passed away.

"Long live the Queen" was the shout from town hall steps throughout the

the hotel on stilts which was known as "Treetops". A father had died and all his daughter wanted to do was to cry and mourn his passing, comforted by her husband. The harshness of the responsibility of her new role, however, became clear to her as the day progressed.

From "Treetops" they returned to a nearby royal hunting lodge at Sagana where they had been spending a few days' holiday. By the time they arrived news agency reports were confirmed by official telegrams and messages from London that made clear where her duties now lay. They were couched in courtly politeness, but it was evident that she was not to suffer her grief in private like a member of any other family. She was now Elizabeth the Queen, and, as such, she must be seen to rule as soon as possible. The public needed evidence that the majesty of monarchy would continue. The new Queen Elizabeth II therefore, in the days before Concorde, made a tiring night and day flight back to England with Prince Philip.

All the Royal Family carry around with them while they are on tour, at home or overseas, a suitcase which they hope they will never have to open containing mourning clothes. Smartly tailored, they are included in the luggage ready to wear should they have to dash back to London on receiving news of a royal or a statesman's death. The proprieties of public death have to be observed, and Elizabeth changed on the last leg of her flight into a long black coat and cockaded black hat from that neglected suitcase.

As if to signify the loneliness of her new role, she walked down the aircraft steps by herself – a shy, almost timorous young woman, who had left London only eight days earlier as a carefree wife, and now returned to face the task of being one of the most significant personalities of the twentieth century. Waiting to greet her at the bottom of the aircraft steps was her Prime Minister, Winston Churchill.

Elizabeth had always hoped that she would never have to take the throne so soon after her marriage. She and Philip had been married for four years and were just beginning to settle down to enjoy the marvellous experience of being a young couple with children. She

The first of the Queen's two State Visits to Denmark took place in May 1957, when she and the Duke of Edinburgh were the guests of the late King Frederick IX and Queen Ingrid, both of whom are indirectly related to our own Royal Family. **Above** *The Queen and her husband being driven to one of their many engagements in Copenhagen.* **Right** *In the previous month the Queen had paid her first State Visit as Sovereign to France: she arrives, followed by the Duke, at the British Embassy in Paris, where she gave a reception for the French President.*

Commonwealth as the official announcement of his death was made. A new Elizabethan Age had begun, four hundred years after the previous magnificent period in British history during the reign of the first Queen Elizabeth.

Above the muddy pond where lion and zebra drink in the Aberdare Forest of Kenya there was no rejoicing for a new golden age. Princess Elizabeth was told that she was now Queen, after she and the Prince had spent the night in

had wanted to go through the experience of being the wife of a naval officer, a mother of two growing children, and build a home and family life, just like any other woman, before accepting the duties of the Crown.

The fact that she had to assume royal duties so early in life, depriving her of so much of the freedom that others in their twenties can expect, has influenced, to a certain degree, the Queen's attitude towards Prince Charles. She knows what it is like to have to bear so early the monarchial chains of office. For this reason she wishes that Charles should have the chance to marry, set up a home and lead an undisturbed domestic life before it is his turn to take over the throne.

Right *Passing before a battery of cameras, the Queen attends an opera at Covent Garden during the State Visit of President de Gaulle to Britain in April 1960.* **Top** *The Queen waving to crowds after another evening engagement in November 1962.* **Above** *All smiles again as the Queen drives through London in public in May 1961.*

Prince Charles frequently says that it could be as long as 30 or 40 years before he becomes king, pointing out how healthy and keen for the job his mother is. Waiting for so long would mean Charles reaching his sixties before he has the chance to rule. The Queen and her advisers would, nevertheless, like the heir to the throne still to be young and full of vigour when his time to don the kingly mantle arrives. Should the Queen, as some people say, decide to abdicate in favour of her son, it will certainly not be until he has had a better chance than she had of being just a parent first and a monarch second.

Her full duties began in earnest 16 months after her return to England as Queen, when Elizabeth was crowned in Westminster Abbey on a rainy 2 June, 1953. The country, which was beginning to recover from the Second World War, still had the might of a major power and the coronation gave Britain the opportunity to demonstrate her imperial vigour to the world.

More than ten thousand servicemen – a quarter of them "soldiers of the Queen" from the Commonwealth – marched in the coronation procession. Two thousand bandsmen, making up nearly 50 bands, provided the music.

The Queen opened Parliament twice in 1974: on the first occasion, following the March General Election, she had to break her tour of Australia at short notice to return to Britain, but there was no time to arrange a full ceremonial State Opening. After the October General Election, the usual tradition was resumed and the Queen **opposite page** *was to be seen travelling to the Houses of Parliament in the Irish State Coach. Other carriages carried the Imperial State Crown* **below left** *and the Parliamentary maces* **bottom left.** **Bottom right** *Inside Parliament the procession leads the Queen and Prince Philip towards the House of Lords.* **Above** *Princess Anne driving to the Opening of Parliament in 1976.*

Fellow sovereigns and rulers from all over the globe came to pay tribute to the girlish figure who was now the head of the greatest group of nations in history. A hundred thousand people braved the wet weather along the streets. Such was the length of the procession that it took 45 minutes to pass any one spot.

On the morning of the coronation there had been ructions at Buckingham Palace, because four-year old Charles was allowed to attend the ceremony while his sister, two years younger, was told that she would have to stay at home. There were tantrums, but the Queen insisted that Anne was too young to go to Westminster Abbey. As it turned out, the four-hour-long service proved too much for the satin-suited Charles, anyway. He watched the crowning standing alongside his grandmother, but then he became impatient and noisy, so he was obliged to leave early.

When the Queen and Prince Philip returned to the palace they were hugged and kissed by the children, who were greeting their "mum and dad" – not a newly invested sovereign and her consort. Princess Anne, wearing a pretty white party frock was allowed to take part – at last – in some of the day's

been called the "sport of kings" that the publishers send a copy by messenger straight from the presses each night.

Until lunchtime the Queen concentrates on reading State papers, dealing with official correspondence, and discussing the running of the household with her staff. She holds audiences at noon and after a light lunch she leaves for afternoon engagements. At 4.30 in the afternoon she feeds her corgis – distributing the food into several bowls with a silver fork and spoon.

The Queen, Prince Philip and now Prince Charles have an enormous amount of paperwork to deal with each day. No matter where they are in the world, dispatch boxes, carrying parliamentary or diplomatic documents, State briefings, letters – official and unofficial – and statements of house-

Following the Conservative victory in the General Election of May 1979, the Queen opened the new Parliament on the 15th of that month. **Above** *Her Majesty leaving the Houses of Parliament after the ceremony, during which she had worn the Imperial State Crown, seen* **right** *being borne into the Chamber.* **Far right** *Princess Anne, wearing the Sash and Star of the Victorian Order, leaving the Houses of Parliament after the State Opening.*

excitement. She and Charles came onto the balcony to wave to the crowds and see the fly-past by the Royal Air Force.

The family of Elizabeth and Philip had become truly royal. They were under great pressure in a changing world and faced public curiosity even into their most private moments.

In the years since her coronation the demands on the Queen have been enormous. With jet aircraft speeding up global travel, she, together with Prince Philip, has undertaken more tours abroad than any previous monarch. She has had to maintain stately calm and continuity during a period of industrial, social and political change. She has had to ensure the smooth transition of a Colonial Empire into a Commonwealth and yet, despite this hectic life, she has achieved a happy family existence with her husband and children.

The Queen's day when she is at Buckingham Palace usually begins with a

call at eight every weekday morning. At around eight-thirty she joins Prince Philip and the rest of the family – if they are at home – in a first floor breakfast room overlooking the gardens and lake at the back of the building.

Morning newspapers are read during breakfast, with shared laughter if one of the family spots something written about them that appears to be distinctly outrageous. The first paper the Queen turns to is *The Sporting Life* – the horse-racing fraternity's "bible". Such is her enthusiasm for what has

hold accounts, arrive daily. In London the official papers reach Buckingham Palace during the night and early morning by car or horse-drawn carriage from Whitehall. When the family is abroad they are flown out, no matter whereabouts in the world they are staying.

Among the official letters the Queen has to deal with daily there is always a large batch of personal letters from friends – or warm, usually handwritten, greetings from ordinary people all over the world.

Above left *The arrival at the Houses of Parliament of the Duke of Edinburgh, the Prince of Wales and Princess Anne.* **Above** *The Queen waits for the Prince of Wales to join her as they prepare to leave Parliament.* **Left** *The Irish State Coach about to leave, bearing the Prince of Wales and his sister.*

Every letter is answered, and those sent out from Buckingham Palace are typed on special thick paper called "Original Turkey Mill Kent". They are easily recognised as they pop through postboxes because the envelopes bear no stamps; instead they are marked with E.R., the royal insignia, on front and back. Such is the amount of mail handled at the palace each day that it has its own post office, which is tucked away in the left-hand corner as one looks at the building from The Mall.

A staff of secretaries jets around the globe with the royal family. They tend to be very hard-working and not especially

While the Queen waits in the House of Lords, Black Rod summons Members of Parliament to the ceremony. He first knocks three times on the doors of the Commons **left** which have been closed against him as a symbol of the independence of the Commons. **Top** Having gained entry, he proceeds towards the Speaker to inform him that the Queen awaits his attendance: Mrs Thatcher and the Conservative Members are seen on the left of the picture. **Far left and opposite page** The Speaker, Mr George Thomas, accompanies Black Rod to the House of Lords, preceded by the mace-bearer.

well paid; dictating letters, making phone calls or hammering away at typewriters – more for the enjoyment and prestige of the job rather than for healthy bank accounts.

On overseas tours they can be seen trying to create organisation out of chaos, setting up temporary offices in hotel rooms, or back rooms of palaces as they dash from city to city, country to country. Very often the most they see of their "boss" or the country they are visiting is from a quick glance at local television between handling correspondence and arranging official functions.

The Queen appreciates the strenuous help she gets from her staff, so she usually says "thank-you" with a private dinner party on the last evening of a tour. The next morning they are busy again bundling typewriters, dictating machines, notepaper, files and other office paraphernalia into cases for yet another mad dash to one more airport.

In London the Queen's business day usually follows the pattern of Prince Philip and Prince Charles – except that she has more work to deal with. Her private secretary, Sir Philip Moore, is usually the first person to greet her in her study after breakfast. He will

already have sorted out the more urgent documents and letters that need dealing with and they will discuss the schedule for the day. It would be a rare day when she had no official function in the palace, such as an investiture, or engagements somewhere in the country.

Dealing with correspondence and "the boxes", as the Cabinet and State papers are called, has to be fitted in

between these appointments. As much work as possible is done in the morning, but Her Majesty often has to return to paperwork, which sometimes takes her late into the night, after she has shaken the last hand of the day and given a final wave to the crowds.

Documents in the dispatch boxes come mainly from the Prime Minister, the Foreign Secretary, Home Secretary and Commonwealth governments . . . she is, after all, not just the Queen of England. These papers either inform her of government proposals, fill in the background of events at home and abroad, or seek her signature on legislation. It might be a major bill or a minor overseas reform, but it still needs her signature under the constitution of Britain and the Commonwealth.

The Queen must be informed and consulted on every aspect of national life to the widest possible extent. She is also free to put forward her own views in private for the consideration of her ministers, but the final decision always rests with Parliament. That eminent

Above left *The Queen, with Prince Charles and Princess Anne, leave Buckingham Palace in the Irish State Coach for the State Opening of Parliament in November 1973.* **Above** *The pageantry of the State Opening itself in June 1970 begins with the entry of Princess Margaret and Lord Snowdon, with Princess Alexandra, into the Parliament building.* **Left and opposite page** *The Queen's procession, which includes Prince Philip, the Prince of Wales and Princess Anne, preceded by the Macebearers, the Herald and the Lord Chancellor, as it moves towards the House of Lords.*

Victorian, Walter Bagehot, described the sovereign as one who had "the right to be consulted, the right to encourage and the right to warn".

She does not merely rubber-stamp a document. She likes to be well briefed about current events, and although she has no power to alter the decisions of her various parliaments, she insists on knowing exactly to what she is putting her signature. Current parliamentary activities in Britain are discussed at the regular weekly meeting with the Prime Minister.

Her Majesty's advice and reaction to parliamentary affairs is frequently sought because of her vast political knowledge. Up to the time of the Silver Jubilee celebrations she had been served by seven prime ministers: five

The Queen and Prince Philip drive to the Opening of Parliament on 24th November 1976 in the Irish State Coach **left. Below** *The colourful and ornate thrones set against a background of ancient heraldic devices in the House of Lords. The impressive, traditional scene* **opposite** *as the Queen, Prince Philip and Princess Anne face the assembly.*

Conservatives and two Socialists. Her involvement in State affairs has been so rich and varied that Prince Charles has paid tribute to his mother as a repository of vast constitutional and political knowledge.

If she has no official engagements at mid-day the Queen helps herself to a light meal, served buffet style. Hopefully she would have her husband or one of her children with her to share a relaxing lunch.

As part of the recent efforts by most of the royals to understand at first hand what is happening beyond the palace gates, the Queen now holds monthly lunches for about 12 people. Her guest list is deliberately wide, ranging from pop singers and comedians to ambassadors and visiting statesmen. They have proved to be highly successful, with both Sovereign and subjects getting to know each other better in a semi-formal atmosphere. One lucky guest recalls: "She goes out of her way to make you feel at ease, and by the time you've reached the second course you

ing statesmen, guests at Buckingham Palace, staff and those fortunate enough to be in a line-up for a smile and handshake, conversation can go so far …then a degree of aloofness may be necessary. I doubt that any group of people in the world can use the affirmative "Yes" so effectively as they drawl it out and turn away from someone being either excruciatingly boorish or far too forward. "Yeees" and a quick move in another direction can be taken as a definite royal cut!

Prince Charles once employed a more exhausting response to a group of

The time-honoured ceremony of the State Opening of Parliament by the Queen. On this occasion, in November 1976, Princess Anne **above** *attended.* **Centre left** *The Queen and Prince Philip enter the Chamber of the House of Lords.* **Top left** *The Lord Chancellor, Lord Gardiner, delivers the Queen's Speech to her on bended knee.* **Opposite page** *The Queen and Prince Philip during the reading of the Queen's Speech by Her Majesty.* **Bottom left** *They leave the Chamber at the end of the ceremony.*

tend to forget that you are in the palace and begin to let your hair down …not too far down though."

One can never really let one's hair down in the presence of the Queen. No matter how friendly she may appear to be due to her natural politeness and genuine interest in people, she may never forget who she is and what she represents. Over-familiarity is, therefore, stylishly put down. The Royal Family generally counts among its intimates three types of people – relations, overseas regal families, and long-standing friends. With these an informal pattern of banter is permitted. With others, however, politicians, visit-

local politicians who were trying to give the impression that THEY had a special relationship with HIM at an agricultural show in Australia. Super-fit, commando-trained Charles shortened his stay with them by dashing round the

Though she takes her duties seriously, the Queen takes the opportunity to relax even on formal occasions. **Opposite page** *This charming picture was taken in Belgrade during her State Visit to Yugoslavia in October 1972.* **Top** *Bright and smiling at the National Theatre which she had just opened in October 1976.* **Above** *The Queen enjoying a conversation with the stars of the film "Death on the Nile" when she attended the première at the Shaftesbury Cinema in October 1978.* **Above right** *The Queen arrives at Sadler's Wells Theatre for a ballet performance in February 1976.*

grounds at a breakneck pace, leaving a trail of perspiring politicos behind him.

When someone is introduced to the Queen they are briefed beforehand to call her "Ma'am". Etiquette is such that one never takes her hand unless it is offered and then the grip must not be too strong – neither must it be too weak. She has a distaste for "wet-fish" handshakes.

If the guest or nervous participant in a formal line-up has reached the stage of conversation then it too must be properly orchestrated. No one talks to the Queen…she always begins a discussion. People meeting her are warned beforehand that they must not let a brief chat develop into a monologue. This is because her time is usually short so she values a few words with everyone rather than being engaged in chit-chat with just one forceful acquaintance.

When she does stop to have a dis-

times, due to the forceful characters of both Prince Philip and Prince Charles. They have minds of their own – convictions regarding social and national responsibility, and they occasionally push through their own views...prepared to stand by what they say. Because of this, Philip more than

cussion with someone the person is often astonished at how much she knows about him or his interests. This is because she is very well served by her staff, who give her a detailed briefing on whom she is likely to meet. All the members of the family carrying out public duties receive this service, which, thanks to their training and excellent memories, creates exactly the right impression.

Speeches for the Queen and Prince

The Queen's visit to Windsor and Maidenhead in October 1974 was undertaken in heavy rain, but these pictures show that neither her enthusiasm nor that of the large crowds could be diminished by the weather. Holding her own sensible, if unglamorous, umbrella, she carried out the entire programme as originally arranged, after her arrival by river **photographed left,** *in order not to disappoint the people of the borough.*

Philip are generally researched and written by their staffs, after which they give final approval, and perhaps make a few alterations. Princess Anne also has her speeches written for her, but Prince Charles always writes his own. In either case, whether it be one of the senior members of "the firm" or the junior directors, great care is taken to avoid controversy: a policy that might result in a speech without much sparkle, but at least it avoids political fireworks.

This can prove an impossible task at

Evenings at home when there is no need to entertain or prepare for the next day, are often spent watching television. The Queen and all her family like comedy shows and pick up as many of the current TV catch-phrases as any other households. Prince Charles and Prince Andrew have a taste for zany idioms and tend to use them more than the other royals when they are with their friends.

Amid all the demands on her time as Sovereign, Elizabeth has always managed to fulfil what to her is still the most important role in her life – being a

wife and mother. She has helped her children through all the usual pains of youth and those moments of bewilderment with life. Her encouragement is always there whenever one of them thinks the going is getting too tough. Princess Anne, now a mother herself and setting up her new home and way of life with her husband, Mark, and children, can still turn to her parents for help and advice.

Elizabeth remembered the warm, loving atmosphere of her own childhood so she arranged that there would be no barriers of governesses and nannies between herself and her own children. Nursery staff were employed – but mother and father were the people the children usually saw first thing in the

Charles has found himself in hot water, but he has declared that he honestly felt that what was stated needed to be made clear, no matter how unpopular it might be with some sections of the community.

On the lighter side of speech-making, copies of an address – prepared on special large-charactered typewriters – usually include in brackets the note "pause for laughter". The widely-spaced sheets are read on the eve of delivery – in Charles' case with a glass of milk in his hand as a nightcap.

morning and last thing at night.

As toddlers the children would snuggle alongside their mother to look at a picture book, or to listen to a story. They were all capable of pranks and mischief, however. Charles used to race round the corridors of Buckingham Palace with his friends, play risky games of hide and seek on the roof of Windsor Castle, or slip a piece of ice down the collar of a footman. When they deserved it, they would get a good spanking, particularly if they were rude to servants. The Queen and Prince Philip viewed such things very seriously because their victims could never answer back.

To teach them the value of money, pocket money has been given in small amounts. Although Prince Andrew is now entitled to an income of more than £17,000 a year, the Queen insisted that

Holiday times in the 1960's for the growing Royal Family. **Above right** *The Queen with 2-year-old Prince Andrew arriving at Liverpool Street Station in February 1962, after their holiday at Sandringham.* **Centre right** *The Queen Mother, and her three youngest grandchildren, on board the Royal train in April 1970.* **Bottom right** *The Queen, with Princess Margaret and her two children, leaving Liverpool Street Station by car in 1971 after spending the New Year at Sandringham.* **Above** *The Queen, with her corgis, leaving the station in February 1965.*

the 18-year-old should not be handed this amount. It is being kept in trust for him and he is given a small allowance each week.

At home Elizabeth and Philip are ordinary parents to their children – a mother and father they can turn to for advice and help. When any of the Royal Family refers to the Queen in public, however, it is always on a very formal basis. She is never called "my mother" in a speech...always "the Queen," although Prince Philip is frequently called "my father".

Charles has said of his father's influence on his education: "His attitude was very simple. He told me what were the pros and cons. Of all the possibilities and attractions he told me what he thought best. Because I had come to see how wise he was, by the time I had to be educated I had perfect confidence in my father's judgement.

Above Lady Sarah Armstrong-Jones and Prince Edward look all set for a good time as they leave for Sandringham in December 1968: Viscount Linley seems to have his doubts. **Left** The Queen with 5-month-old Prince Edward leaving Kings Cross for her summer holiday at Balmoral in August 1964.

When children are young you have to decide for them. How can they decide for themselves?"

It was his father's influence, above all others, that persuaded Charles to choose a career in the Royal Navy. Philip always felt that Charles should have a service career and the best training, as far as Prince Philip was concerned, was in his own beloved navy. The reason? "It has several advantages as a training ground" explained Philip. "You have to develop a professional ability. Aboard ship you learn to live with people, and this is the most important thing."

The closeness of this remarkable family unit has given the royal children the confidence to venture into the world.

The Queen takes a special interest in the youngest of the family, 14-year-old Edward, who was the last to leave home and is now having to cope with the tough life of Gordonstoun. In between dealing with that huge daily official mail bag, she sends him letters regularly, passing on family gossip and words of encouragement. To help him through his schooldays she is trying to keep him out of the limelight – letting him cope with the business of growing up without the problems of publicity.

Throughout the childhood of all her offspring there were always requests for the young princess and princes to appear in public. The Queen resisted them all, no matter how worthy the

The photographs on these two pages show the Queen, Prince Philip, their four children and grandson Master Peter Phillips leaving Balmoral Castle for a walk in the grounds during the summer of 1979, and were released to commemorate the Queen's 32nd wedding anniversary on 20th November that year. Balmoral has been in continual use as a quiet summer retreat for the Royal Family since it was rebuilt by Prince Albert in the 1840's, and the Court moves there for the duration of most of August and September each year.

cause asking for their presence. She remembered how, as a young princess, she was suddenly thrust into the public arena. She insisted that her youngsters should have a normal childhood, as far as this was possible. To her, they were above everything else, children; so the Queen protected them and carefully nurtured them to the stage when they could be made aware of their Stately duties.

All the youngsters, however, had to suffer an odd aspect of upbringing, unique to royalty. As part of their training for a ceremonial life, they were taught to stand motionless for long periods to accustom them to the discomforts ahead. (The late Duke of Windsor, when commenting on coping with the problem of endless standing in public, once said that the best advice his father had ever given him about public appearances was always to take the weight off his feet whenever he

could and to go to the toilet whenever possible!)

Making friends outside their own close circle is difficult for the royal children. They are very wary of becoming too close to people or making easy friendships because they suspect – correctly in some instances – that many are interested purely for social advantages or to gossip about them afterwards. As a result it is a privilege indeed to be counted as one of the palace "in people". This means that you have been vetted and found truly trustworthy as well as an amusing and interesting companion.

The Royal Family have become reluctant to express any controversial

One of the most delightfully informal occasions when the Royal Family is out in force is the annual three day event at Badminton, home of the Duke of Beaufort, whose wife is a cousin of the Queen. These pages show the family together in April 1973: **left** *studies in concentration as, on top of a farm-cart, the Queen and Prince Philip watch the events with the Queen Mother, Princess Margaret, Lord Snowdon, Prince Andrew, Prince Edward, Viscount Linley and Lady Sarah Armstrong-Jones. They are accompanied by the Duke of Beaufort (wearing glasses).* **Above** *The Queen with Prince Andrew on the final day, when the veterinary inspection is held.*

views in public because, apart from sometimes causing too much of a stir, once recorded their remarks take on a permanency that can become embarrassing for the future. They avoid taking a stand on an issue. Views are often put forward as rhetorical questions rather than statements. The simplest remark can sometimes cause offence, as Prince Charles once discovered during a tree-planting ceremony in Wales when he said: "Thank

goodness it's an oak and not one of those ghastly spruces." There were immediate letters of protest from hundreds of forestry workers who had devoted their lives to planting "ghastly spruces".

Most of the members of the family appear to be established in people's minds as "horsey-types" – perhaps because the one hobby that they are most frequently seen participating in is either at a race track or in, or around a

Top Princess Anne waits for her horse to be saddled up before she competes in the event. **Above** Anxious moments for the Queen, Princess Margaret and the Queen Mother. **Above left** With the Queen and her mother are Prince Edward and Viscount Linley. **Left** The Duke of Beaufort shows off his hunting hounds to the Queen and the royal children.

show ring or polo field. They are interested in horses, but not to the exclusion of other hobbies and interests. Every one of them has a liking for photography for example – both still and movie. The Queen and Prince Philip often keep a cine film record of their tours abroad, and there is an amusing collection of still photographs showing Press photographers in their off-guarded moments – one way, I suppose,

Left *The Queen, Queen Mother and Prince Andrew with the Duke of Beaufort watching events at Badminton in April 1972.* **Below** *Prince Philip and Princess Anne enjoy a clear vantage point on the same day, during which Lieutenant Mark Phillips competed.* **Below left** *The Queen's camera is at the ready, whilst Prince Edward and Lady Sarah Armstrong-Jones watch intently as the trials get underway in 1973.*

Acting is an interest of both the Queen and Prince Charles. She used to perform in pantomimes at Windsor as a child – once playing Prince Charming to Princess Margaret's Cinderella – while Charles has acted in public on a few occasions when he took part in student revues during his days at Cambridge University. In one of them he sat on stage as a target for custard pies, and in another sketch he walked on under an umbrella with the remark: "I lead a very sheltered life you know!"

Acting has now, however, to be limited to family charades. On one occasion the Queen led the rest of the family to the opening of a cottage Lord Snowdon had just bought. The Queen Mother cut a ribbon across the door in her well-established "official opening" manner, while the rest of the family played the parts of the applauding public.

Prince Philip, Prince Charles and the Queen Mother all enjoy fishing. They cast for salmon and trout, usually when they are on holiday at Balmoral. Charles is considered such an expert on fly fishing that he has been able to write knowledgeably about it.

Most of the family have tried their hands at painting, but Charles, Andrew and their father have proved to be the most adept in this field, Philip being particularly sensitive with oils.

in which the family can get their own back on the media.

They are great home-movie buffs, constantly taking cine shots of each other, like any other family. A get-together at Buckingham Palace often includes a film show, with the typically silly scenes that parents and children find privately amusing the world over. When they gather to see the latest production, though, they do not have to squeeze into the front room where "dad" has hung the screen from a wall. On the first floor of Buckingham Palace is a large private cinema, the decor of which is unlike any other. The walls have red cloth paper and dotted about are polished cabinets containing col-

lections of fine porcelain. The seats are painted gold.

In the "interval" between changing films the audience can pull back one of the plush curtains, open a french window and step onto a balcony giving them a view of the gardens. It is slightly different, is it not, from the average neighbourhood theatre? Charles likes making pictures which are slightly zany in their humour. Whilst on a training exercise in Canada with his Royal Navy helicopter squadron, he produced, directed and edited a movie in which he played "Bluebottle," the mentally sub-normal midget of Goon Show fame, who was being bossed around by all the other officers in his group.

With a rugged, outdoor father to show the way it is not surprising that all the boys, and Anne, are keen on sport. Charles, as we know, is a skilled polo player, but lately he has taken up the craze of cross-country team eventing. This is a hairy, weekend pastime in which groups of four riders charge across a local hunt course in competition with other teams. It has tremendous neck-breaking possibilities, a perfect challenge for Charles, who frequently falls off, brushes himself down, remounts and gallops off again.

Although he goes cross-country team eventing with hunts, he does not share Princess Anne's consuming interest in fox hunting. Charles has turned out now and again, though, resplendent in topper, cravat and blue riding coat with gold lapels, a riding habit that would make Beau Brummel envious.

Andrew shows all the signs of taking after his older brother as a daredevil. He is keen on football, rugby and ice-hockey, and has the same desire to fly. He won his glider pilot's wings while serving with Gordonstoun's Air Training Corps and he is about to begin

Above *The Prince of Wales with his grandmother the Queen Mother, watch anxiously at Badminton in 1972.* **Top** *The Queen and Prince Philip at Badminton in Silver Jubilee year.* **Above, far right** *The Queen Mother shields the wind from her face, but Lady Sarah braves the weather, in 1977.* **Right** *Only just separated from the crowd; the Queen, Queen Mother and Princess Margaret share a few rugs as they watch the proceedings.*

Overleaf *The Queen with the Prince of Wales and the Duke of Gloucester driving down the course at Ascot in June 1980.*

skill as an expert on pedigrees that over the last 25 years she is estimated to have won more than a million pounds in prize money.

Exactly when Philip first met the Queen varies from biographer to biographer, friend to friend. They certainly started to fall in love with each other at their meetings during the war, when the young Princess noticed him as a possible suitor, but there were earlier meetings which were of no romantic significance at the time.

According to Miss Marion Crawford – the famous "Crawfie" – who was governess to Princess Elizabeth and Princess Margaret from 1932 to 1949, they met at the beginning of 1939. At this time Elizabeth and Margaret went with their father to visit Dartmouth Royal Naval College. 13-year-old Elizabeth, at the age when she was beginning to take an interest in boys, was impressed by the tennis prowess of the blonde nephew of Earl Mountbatten. Philip was 18 at the time and had just begun his training at Dartmouth. To him the two Princesses were just little girls who had to be entertained and he is said not to have made much of a fuss over them.

As we know, King George VI was not keen, at first, on his "Lilibet" being involved so early in life with Philip, when she was still only in her late teens, but he clearly changed his attitude after their wedding when he wrote to Eliza-

beth: "I can see that you are sublimely happy with Philip."

Marrying Princess Elizabeth brought Philip a stable family life for the first time. Until then he had been virtually a nomad, from a royal line exiled from its throne in Greece, a child living with relatives throughout Europe after the break-up of his parents' marriage, and a solitary naval officer who had never really known a permanent home.

His mother, Princess Alice of Batten-

The photographs on these two pages were taken at Royal Ascot in June 1980. Driving down the course at the beginning of the afternoon were **opposite page, top: left to right,** *the Queen with Grand Duke Jean of Luxembourg, the Queen Mother with Grand Duchess Josephine Charlotte, and Princess Anne riding with Princess Margaret. In the Queen's carriage, too, were* **opposite page, left** *Queen Margrethe of Denmark and Prince Philip.* **Right** *The Royal guests make their way from their carriages to the Royal Box, whilst* **top right** *security officials make thorough searches at the entrance gates.*

The Derby is the most prestigious Classic event in the British horse-racing calendar, and the Queen attends Epsom annually for the occasion. On 4th June 1980, for instance, she arrived by car **left** for the afternoon's programme, and, as usual, stood at the side of the course **lower right,** with the Queen Mother to inspect the runners. Prince and Princess Michael of Kent **right** and Princess Alexandra also attended. The Queen, who freely admits her ambition to breed a horse to win the Derby, has entered many of her own horses for the race since she came to the throne.

burg, was a sister of Earl Mountbatten and a member of the British Royal Family. A brave woman, she stayed in Athens during the German occupation helping Jewish refugees escape from the Gestapo. In 1949 she founded a reclusive order of nuns, the Christian Sisterhood of Martha and Mary, then led a humble existence with them until her death in 1969.

Philip is a man of great integrity – someone who has been used to standing alone and fighting for himself – without expecting favouritism of any sort. One aspect of this side of his character emerged during the early days of his marriage.

Princess Elizabeth had joined him in Malta to share, as near as possible, the ways of a naval officer's wife. It was during the days when the Pritish Mediterranean Fleet still filled Valetta harbour, and Philip was one of hundreds of young officers belonging to a force that continued to prove that Britannia ruled the waves. He might be the husband of a future queen, but he

was also a navy man devoted to his career. The possibility of standing on the left-hand side of a sovereign seemed remote.

Like all budding Nelsons or Drakes

The depth of the Queen's interest in horse-racing, and particularly in the Derby, is evident in these photographs which show her in animated conversation with other members of the royal party. **Below** *She gestures expressively in conversation with Princess Michael, and* **centre right** *with Queen Elizabeth the Queen Mother.* **Bottom left** *Prince and Princess Michael in the paddock and* **bottom right** *with the Queen and Queen Mother in the royal stand as the racing gets under way.*

he had occasionally to take examinations in his chosen profession to further his chances of promotion. While Elizabeth was in Malta with him he failed a course in anti-submarine warfare by a narrow margin. It was suggested that because the marks were so marginal he should be allowed through. When Philip heard about this suggestion he refused such an easy passage and insisted on taking the examination again. He did, and passed with flying colours!

Philip achieved his ambition of being given a ship of his own in 1950, when he was 30 years old. His days as skipper of the frigate *H.M.S. Magpie* were short lived, however, because the illness of George VI was becoming painfully evident. The Queen-to-be and her husband had to start preparing for the duties that were inevitably so near.

After less than a year with his own ship, Lieutenant-Commander Philip Mountbatten left the sea in June 1951 to

Right *The Queen and Queen Mother at Epsom in June 1980 for the Derby: at the side of the course they inspect the runners as they ride past before the start of the race.* **Below** *On this occasion, as the Queen was making her way to the course from the Royal Stand, she was approached by a Bunny Girl who presented her with a single flower.*

industry and exports and he introduced the Duke of Edinburgh Award Scheme to encourage young people to excel in endeavours ranging from mountain climbing to playing music and writing poetry. Above all, he became a drum beater for Britain and the Commonwealth, willing to fly anywhere to give a speech on behalf of the people and the group of nations he had fought for and adopted as his own.

Nothing seems too much trouble for a cause he might throw his weight and energy behind. When he was touring the United States, raising money for the Variety Club of Great Britain, a pushy local businessman in Miami offered to hand over a cheque for 100,000 dollars if "the dook" would jump into his swimming pool. Philip stripped off, dived in, and collected the money.

One of the first ways in which Philip impressed the public was with his geniality. The Queen had been reluctant, at first, to go around with what is now a familiar, happy face, because she thought her office was such that she should try to maintain dignity and solemnity. Philip always had a ready laugh, a quick joke, and a generally pleasant demeanour as he went about his public business. How could anyone fail to like a man with such an obvious sense of well-being?

Over the past 20 years he has become a royal personage entirely of

join his wife and family in Britain and to take part in State duties. He was given what the navy called "extended leave" – a military status he still lives under today, though now he is an Admiral of the Fleet.

After the coronation he could have stayed at home and lived off his wife's prestige and income, but instead he set out from the beginning to do something useful for the community. He became involved with promoting British

Racing at Royal Ascot **top** *brings out the best in horsemanship and fashion.* **Above** *Two smartly dressed Royal ladies, Princess Margaret and the Duchess of Kent, riding together down the Ascot course in June 1972.* **Right** *In June 1980, the Queen makes her way from the Royal Box to the paddock, accompanied by Prince Philip, Princess Margaret and the Queen Mother: in the background are the Duke and Duchess of Gloucester.*

Yet it is always noticeable that he seems, clearly, to be a strength to the Queen. If she has forgotten to follow the programme exactly and there might be some confusion, the Prince has an unobtrusive way of reminding her about some oversight.

As they drive through the crowds it is usually Prince Philip who suggests that they might sit on the boot of an open car so that she can be seen to better advantage.

Together they make a well-matched, loving team.

his own making, more than someone in the shadow of the Crown; a man of importance in his own right. Yet he never forgets in public that it is the Queen, above all, who matters. He goes out of his way when they are together to draw attention to her.

A strong-willed husband and father he may be at Buckingham Palace, but in public he goes to great lengths to make it clear to those watching that he is the consort – and nothing more – to the Queen while on official duties.

The great affection they have for each other is clear in public. When the Queen is obviously enjoying herself she always glances across to her husband to signal her pleasure. Somehow, he always manages to have turned his head in her direction at the very same moment.

Prince Philip has a charming manner with his wife. It is a delightful mixture of obeisance to her as the monarch, combined with that of a fond husband. He stays a step or two behind her as they walk along, allowing her to set the pace. He never attempts to upstage her; a difficult task for any husband, and, one imagines, an onerous role for someone so forceful in his ways.

On the morning of one of the four days of Ascot, the Royal Family use the course for their own private race. The pictures on this page were taken in 1972, and show Prince Charles **top left,** *Princess Margaret* **centre left,** *the Duchess of Kent* **left,** *and Princess Anne* **above** *enjoying the freedom of the track. Amongst those accompanying the Queen on that day was the Master of the Queen's Horse, the Duke of Beaufort* **top picture.**

Prince Philip is five years older than his wife. They are third cousins and great-great grandchildren of Queen Victoria. They met again when, through his links with his uncle, Earl Mountbatten, he used to visit Windsor Castle during the Second World War as a young naval officer. Elizabeth was only 16 at the time, and developed a typical teenage crush on the dashing young sailor.

Philip was educated in Britain and eventually followed the footsteps of Earl Mountbatten and joined the Royal Navy. After graduating from Dartmouth Naval College, just before the outbreak of the war, he went to sea as a second lieutenant. Two years later he faced his first blooding in action on board a battleship against the Italian fleet off Cape Matapan. As a regard for his courageous and cool behaviour under fire he was mentioned in des-

patches. He was serving on the battleship *H.M.S. Valiant* at the time and right in the midst of fierce shell fire was manning a searchlight. His Captain said of him: "Thanks to his alertness and appreciation of the situation we were able to sink in five minutes two eight-inch gun Italian cruisers."

Much to the distress of the young Princess Elizabeth he was not a popular choice with her parents. At first King George and Queen Elizabeth thought their elder daughter should meet other young men before deciding

*Royal Ascot's traditional mixture of the stately and the outrageous: the customary carriage-ride of the Royal Family and their guests – Princess Margaret with Princess Alexandra **centre left** in 1970, and the Prince of Wales and Queen Mother with the Grand Duchess of Luxembourg and Prince Hendrik of Denmark in 1980 – contrasts quaintly with the eccentricity of the latest fashions, personified by Mrs Gertrude Shilling **top right**.*

on a husband.

Philip's nationality, too, was a problem; he was a Greek national although he was trying to become a naturalised Briton. In addition his four sisters had all married into German aristocracy – unions that did not go down well in Britain at that time.

It was not until two years after the war was over that he was able to gain naturalisation papers and become a British subject – Philip Mountbatten. A few days after hearing this news the King told an ecstatic Elizabeth that she could marry her sailor. The wedding brought the first post-war cheer to a glum world in 1947.

Their first child was born a year after their marriage, on a gloomy Sunday evening at the end of November 1948. Instead of pacing up and down a hospital corridor for hours in the classic manner of an expectant father, Prince Philip sweated away a few hours with some hectic games of squash.

Above left *Princess Margaret, with her two children, greets her nephew Prince Andrew in December 1967 as they all meet at Liverpool Street Station to board the Royal train for their New Year holiday at Sandringham.* **Far left, and left** *The Queen with Prince Andrew and Prince Edward leaving King's Cross for Balmoral in August 1966.* **Above** *Back to work as the Queen, followed by Prince Andrew and Prince Philip arrive in London from Sandringham in January 1965.*

Princess Elizabeth celebrated her thirteenth birthday at Windsor in April 1939. Naturally earnest and conscientious, she lacked the strain of devilment which characterised her younger sister. She had inherited much of her adored father's personality and modelled herself on him. Serious, shy, immature, inexperienced, and perhaps a little young for her age, she began her holidays the following summer with a family cruise along the South coast of Britain on the royal yacht *Victoria and Albert*.

On 22 July, the Royal Family sailed up the River Dart to visit the Royal Naval College, set on a hill above the Devonshire town of Dartmouth. For the Princesses it was an exciting break from the secluded and familiar routine of schoolroom life at Buckingham Palace or the Royal Lodge, Windsor. With the royal visitors on board the yacht was Lord Louis Mountbatten. A naval man himself, he had telephoned his old friend, the college commander, to suggest that his nephew, Prince Philip of Greece, who was a naval cadet

there, would be a good choice to act as royal escort. As a prince in his own right, he was used to mixing with royalty and wouldn't be overawed.

Princess Elizabeth was at a rather awkward, in-between age and still very much a schoolgirl. Prince Philip was a tall, slim, self-confident 18. The gap was wide, not just in age but in experi-

Far left *The Queen helps Prince Andrew onto the Royal train at King's Cross in August 1964.* **Above** *Accompanied this time by his elder brother and sister, Prince Andrew arrives back at Liverpool Street in January 1964.* **Left** *The Queen shepherds the royal children onto the train in August 1966.*

ence of the world, yet this was the meeting that would change both their lives. (They may, in fact, have met before as Prince Philip had attended the marriage of his cousin Princess Marina to the Duke of Kent in 1934 and had been a family guest at the coronation of King George VI in 1937. Apparently, the young people had made no great impression on each other on either of these occasions.)

The scene was set for this momen-

Overleaf *The shining magnificence of the Household Cavalry as it leaves Buckingham Palace for the Trooping the Colour ceremony at Horse Guards Parade.*

tous meeting when the *Victoria and Albert* arrived at Dartmouth. But, as a foretaste of the difficulties the future would bring them, an unexpected problem almost caused the visit to be cancelled. That evening the college authorities contacted the royal party to inform them that there was an outbreak of both chickenpox and mumps at the college. Elizabeth and Margaret, eagerly anticipating the next day's excitements, were crestfallen at the thought of being left on board the yacht. Rather than disappoint them, their parents decided that they would be allowed to go.

Next day, in blue dresses with matching coats, the Princesses accompanied their parents ashore. The two girls were dispatched to amuse themselves at the house of the college commander, Admiral Sir Frederick Dalrymple-Hamilton, and it was here that Philip met them. The weather was changeable and while it was raining the

The Royal Family on parade for the Silver Jubilee Trooping the Colour ceremony in June 1977 **opposite page.** The Queen is generally escorted by the Duke of Edinburgh **left,** the Prince of Wales **far left** and the Duke of Kent. Until his death in August 1979, Earl Mountbatten of Burma also took part in the parade; he is seen on the right of the photograph **above,** with Prince Philip, Prince Charles and the Duke of Kent.

Princesses played with a clockwork railway in the nursery. Later they played croquet in the garden and certainly Philip had joined them by then.

The tall, blonde, blue-eyed Prince, looking exceedingly smart in his cadet uniform, must have made a striking impression on the two young schoolgirls. Princess Elizabeth, according to Crawfie, especially admired the way he could jump. He didn't seem to pay any special attention to her and, in fact,

spent a lot of time teasing her sister. He spent the rest of the day escorting them round the college and grounds and generally entertaining them. In the evening he and other cadets went aboard the royal yacht to attend a dinner given by the King. The Princesses were not present. Keeping to their normal routine, they had gone to bed, but the next day they again went ashore and met Philip, who continued his escort duties.

When the time came for the *Victoria*

and *Albert* to raise anchor, a flotilla of small boats from the college gathered speed; one by one the boats fell back, until just one remained. Philip continued to row after the yacht until the King became anxious for his safety. The signal to turn back was flying from the mast but Philip would not see it. At last the King called for a megaphone and finally Philip obeyed the order to return, shouted perhaps by the King or else by Lord Louis Mountbatten. Motionless, Princess Elizabeth followed the boat's progress through her father's binoculars until it was out of sight.

George and Elizabeth were worried by their daughter's strong feelings for Philip. In March 1944, the King wrote, "We both think she is too young for that

ended the Princess was 20, independent and self-willed. She placed a photograph of Prince Philip in a prominent place on the mantelpiece in her sitting room. The King started giving private dances at Buckingham Palace and invited suitable companions for the two Princesses.

Philip was invited to spend a holiday at Balmoral in August 1946, and this seems to have been the turning point. The King and Queen had to acknowledge that their daughter was truly in love. Even though the couple had parental consent at this point, there were serious problems to be sorted out centering on Philip's Greek nationality.

He could not marry the Princess

The Queen at the Trooping ceremony in June 1975 **above left. Opposite page, lower** *Another view of the Queen at the head of her troops on the same day, and* **bottom left** *the Prince of Wales and Duke of Edinburgh following Her Majesty on their white mounts.* **Below** *A picture taken in June 1972, with the Queen wearing a black armband in mourning for the Duke of Windsor who had died the previous week.* **Below left** *A mounted detachment of the Household Brigade about to ride past the Queen at the main gate of the Palace in June 1978.* **Opposite page, above** *An impressive view down the Mall in 1978.*

now as she has never met any young men of her own age."

They liked Philip and felt that he had all the attributes to make him a suitable consort for a future Queen, but no one knew better than they the exceptional demands that marriage to a monarch entailed. They had been blessed with a specially happy marriage and they wanted the same for their daughter.

By the time the Second World War

without adopting British nationality, but the political situation in Greece was exceptionally difficult. Earlier, there had been doubts as to whether the Greek monarchy would be restored.

The British Government decided to postpone Philip's naturalisation until after the Greek general election and plebiscite on the monarchy, planned for March 1946, in case it should be interpreted as an official indication of their political stance.

The plebiscite resulted in a majority in favour of the monarchy but this still didn't help Philip. The British Government now felt that it would be undiplomatic for a member of the Greek Royal Family to renounce his nationality so close to the restoration.

There was nothing the young couple could do but wait. The King and Queen

Above, and above left *The Queen taking the salute and watching the ranks of the Household Brigades ride past the Gates of Buckingham Palace on her official birthday.* **Left** *The music during the Trooping is provided by several different battalions, but the most magnificent spectacle is provided by these massed bands: the priceless solid silver drums were a gift from King William IV.* **Below left** *The Queen and Prince Philip return to the Palace after the Trooping.* **Below** *A view of the Victoria Memorial (incorporating the figures of Truth, Motherhood and Justice) from inside the Palace gates as the Queen takes the salute.*

Above *The full brilliance of scarlet and white stands out to make Trooping the Colour a spectacular and memorable ceremony.* **Right** *Even on dull days, these long red cloaks of the cavalry add an impressive splash of colour.*

felt anyway that the couple still needed time to be sure of their feelings.

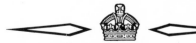

Although Philip's nationality was Greek, he is, in fact, a member of the royal house of Denmark. Prince William of Denmark had been invited to take the Greek throne in 1836 and had then taken the name of King George I of Greece. Prince Philip, his direct

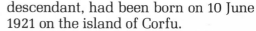

descendant, had been born on 10 June 1921 on the island of Corfu.

The Greek throne proved to be very unstable. George I, Philip's grandfather, was assassinated in 1913; Constantine I, Philip's uncle, deposed in 1917 and later restored to the throne, abdicated in 1922; and George II, Philip's cousin, abdicated in 1923, was restored to the throne in 1935, expelled in 1941 and restored again after the plebiscite in 1946.

During one of the earlier periods of unrest, the baby Prince Philip had left Greece in an improvised cot made of orange crates on a British light cruiser, in 1922. His father, Prince Andrew, had been rescued from threat of execution in Athens by the direct intervention of

The military highlight of the year is the ceremony of Trooping the Colour which takes place on the second Saturday in June. Its origins lie in the mid-eighteenth century, when troops billeted in various parts of a town were more easily able to rejoin their regiment if its colours were prominently displayed at the rallying point. Today the ceremony is one of pure pageantry, to compliment Her Majesty on her official birthday. The pictures on this page show why the parade has its distinctive reputation for colour and precision, and illustrate aspects of the hour-long ceremony surrounding the Troop itself **top:** *mounted militia* **above right** *and massed bands* **right** *make their own impressive contributions.*

King George V.

Prince Philip was the youngest child of Prince Andrew and Princess Alice of Battenberg. His four sisters were considerably older than he and while he was still quite young, his parents drifted apart. Prince Andrew moved to Monte Carlo, leaving his wife with sole responsibility for their young son.

Princess Alice was the youngest daughter of Prince Louis of Battenberg, the sister of Lord Louis Mountbatten, and a great-granddaughter of Queen Victoria. She turned to her brothers for help and the elder, George, made himself responsible for his nephew's education and care until his death in 1938.

He sent Philip to preparatory school

Prince Philip arrived, Kurt Hahn had been imprisoned because of his opposition to Nazism. He was eventually released and he moved his school to Gordonstoun in Morayshire, Scotland.

Prince Philip became a pupil at the new school, demonstrating fine qualities of leadership and responding well to challenge.

After the death of his Uncle George, Philip came under the wing of his uncle, Lord Louis Mountbatten. When Philip's naturalisation finally came through, he adopted the name Mountbatten as a tribute to the man he admired so much.

But although Philip now had a suitably British royal name, he had to wait for the final approval of his devotion to Elizabeth.

Above *Her Majesty is followed by Prince Philip as she enters Horse Guards Parade and rides past lines of soldiers to the far side of the parade ground. There she will take the salute as the Brigade of Guards* **top** *and the Household Regiments march past. At the end of the ceremony, she leaves the parade ground preceded by a detachment of mounted guards and leads the remainder of her troops back to Buckingham Palace.*

at Cheam in England and then to Salem School in Bavaria, Germany. Kurt Hahn, former adviser to Prince Max of Bavaria, had founded the school in 1920 as an experiment to combine the best of British and German teaching methods and character building.

By 1933, the school was world famous and the fact that Prince Philip's second sister Theodora, was married to the Margrave of Baden, made it a particularly good choice. By the time

It came, at last, on 9 July 1947. The Palace announced:

"It is with great pleasure that the King and Queen announce the betrothal of their dearly beloved daughter the Princess Elizabeth to Lieutenant Philip Mountbatten RN, son of the late Prince Andrew of Greece and Princess Andrew (Princess Alice of Battenberg) to which union the King has gladly given his consent."

When the engagement was announced between the then Princess Elizabeth and Lieutenant Philip Mountbatten, King George VI said: "I wonder if he knows what he's taking on.

"One day Lilibet will be Queen and he will be Consort. And that's much harder than being a King."

He did add, however: "He's the man for the job all right."

But there have surely been times since when Philip, looking back, has acknowledged with a rueful grin that father-in-law was right – being Consort is much harder than being King.

He is as much a workaholic as ever, and hardly less active in his moments of leisure, even if, these days he tends to tire more easily. But although he may sometimes flop out exhausted at the end of a long and tiring day, he does not really know how to relax. He continues to tilt at life as though determined not to waste a single minute of it, and contrives to make a lot of minutes do double duty. He listens to the radio news while shaving and devours the contents of the day's newspapers along with his breakfast. Keen to get on with the affairs of the day, Philip is not a man to linger over meals.

"It would suit him down to the ground if he could simply swallow a

Bright sunshine and blue skies attended the 1971 ceremony of Trooping the Colour. **Top** *The view from the roof of Buckingham Palace as detachments of the Household move from the Palace.* **Opposite page** *The return to the Palace: the Queen's Escort followed by foot soldiers in the Mall after the Trooping.* **Right** *The Queen riding sidé saddle on her mare Burmese, is followed by Prince Philip as she approaches the parade ground in 1973.* **Above** *The Queen caught off-guard as she exchanges a joke with Prince Philip on the same day.*

couple of protein pills and carry on working", says an ex-palace servant.

Breakfast is often the last his wife sees of him until the evening. If he is off on his travels – and he is arguably the most travelled man in the world, averaging 75,000 miles a year – it may be the last she will see of him for days.

Charles, lunching with his mother at the palace on one occasion, asked if Papa would be joining them for lunch.

"Lunch", sighed the Queen, "if he takes on much more he soon won't be here for breakfast!"

"I am quite used to an 18-hour day," he said once. But after the age of 50, 18-hour days take their toll, and there are times, on a royal tour or at the end of a day of non-stop engagements, when it shows.

His aides sometimes worry that he tries to do too much. If his work pace can hardly be said to have slackened much it is slightly less frenetic than in his younger days.

Then, with requests to go here, there and everywhere, streaming in at the rate of 300 a month, he wanted to take on everything. It was clearly impossible, even though he did once travel 1,500 miles to squeeze in 30 different engagements and make 15 speeches in the course of a single week.

Today, more sensibly, he limits himself to some 250-300 engagements a year, perhaps 80 of them involving speeches. Add on functions and travels he undertakes with the Queen, and it still amounts to a substantial work-

A mixture of moods on the balcony of Buckingham Palace after the annual Trooping the Colour ceremony. **Above and right** *Hearty laughter after the Silver Jubilee Trooping in 1977: with the Queen and Prince Philip are Marina Ogilvy, Princess Anne, Princess Alice of Athlone, Captain Mark Phillips, Angus Ogilvy and Princess Margaret.* **Top right** *A hint of uncertainty in 1974 from the Queen Mother, Lady Sarah Armstrong-Jones and Viscount Linley, Princess Anne, Prince Edward, Prince Charles and Princess Margaret.* **Centre right** *The Duke and Duchess of Gloucester with their two children, Alexander, Earl of Ulster, and Lady Davina Windsor, join the Queen Mother and Princess Margaret in 1978.*

load. Philip has shaped the part of Consort in his own image – non-stop, hard-working, outspoken, both prodder and booster of national morale, pricker of pomposity, patron of science, industry, technology. He used to be hot on education, too, but has tended to steer clear since it became so much a political football.

Like every other Royal, he is sup-

Left *As the Queen re-enters the forecourt of the Palace, guests on the balcony, including members of the Royal Family of Thailand and the family of the late Lord Mountbatten, watch the proceedings in 1980.* **Above** *The Queen and Prince Philip among a balcony of Royals* **below** *in 1977, including Lord Mountbatten (third from left) and Colonel Sir Henry Abel Smith (second from right) the son-in-law of Princess Alice of Athlone (standing between the Queen and Prince Philip).*
Overleaf *The Queen and Prince Philip on the Palàce balcony after the Trooping the Colour ceremony in 1974.*

stant disposal, horses and carriages at the ready for the new sport of carriage driving which he has taken up since synovitis of the wrist brought polo-playing days to an end, an extensive wardrobe of suits and uniforms and a brace of valets to take care of them for him. So it can't be all bad, as Philip himself realises.

One of his guests on a royal occasion was Donald MacJannet, the American

Lord Mountbatten **above,** *at his home, Broadlands near Romsey, Hampshire, and* **left** *standing in front of the impressive Georgian mansion.* **Right** *Two views showing only some of the hundreds of floral tributes which covered the lawns of Romsey Abbey where Lord Mountbatten was buried on 5th September 1979.* **Opposite page** *Members of his family stand sorrowfully in Westminster Abbey as his coffin is lifted to begin its long journey to the Hampshire countryside.*

posed to stay out of the political arena. Theoretically, he is barred from speaking on what he has called "matters loosely-termed political".

Philip does not suffer fools gladly, hates wasted time or arrangements which are less than perfect and can be short and sharp with those who ask what he considers to be stupid questions.

He can be impatient with too much protocol or anything he regards as

humbug. Excessive security used to irritate him, too, but these days, even if he still does not like it, he appreciates how necessary it really is.

The faults of "impatience and intolerance," which his Gordonstoun headmaster Kurt Hahn noted in schooldays, are still there, though better controlled, perhaps. There is also a stubborn streak.

Elizabeth has the same stubborn streak – perhaps they both inherit it from Albert or Victoria – which occasionally leads to a clash of wills.

His years as Consort have not been without their rewards. Early naval pay of around £11 a week has become a State allowance of £135,000 a year. Of course it is not all pocket money by any means but he isn't short of cash.

He has cars and aircraft at his con-

principal of the kindergarten in Paris which was the first school Philip attended.

In those days he went to school in clothes which were sometimes patched, had to stay behind on one occasion because it was raining and he did not own a raincoat, and had to save for ages in order to buy his first bicycle.

Meeting his old headmaster again all those years later, immaculately-garbed as befitted his role of Consort, he said to MacJannet: "Look at me now!"

After the death of King George VI, and Elizabeth's succession to the Throne, Philip's role, as he quickly discovered, was to change drastically.

For five years he had been the master in his own home, the strong and forceful husband. Now his nebulous role of Consort was underlined by what happened the morning following their return from Africa, where they had heard of the King's death.

They were together, as they had so often been on public occasions, as they walked through from their old home, Clarence House, to St James's Palace

where Elizabeth was to make her Declaration of Accession.

But once there, tradition required that he leave her to stand alone while he, as a Privy Councillor, took his place among all the other members of the Accession Council.

It was further emphasised by what happened at the State Opening of Parliament later that year.

The Queen's parents had always sat

side by side on two thrones for this top ceremonial occasion. But following the death of the King, one of those thrones was whipped speedily away and Philip, that first year, found himself relegated to a chair of State one step down from the throne occupied by his wife.

"The part the Duke of Edinburgh will play will be that of a husband supporting his wife," explained the Lord Chancellor's office. Later, the second throne was to be restored.

So perhaps the new Queen had echoed her great-great-grandmother's words: "It is a strange omission in the Constitution that while the wife of a King has the highest rank and dignity in the Realm assigned to her by law, the husband of a Queen regnant is entirely ignored."

Not so much ignored as humiliated at times. Philip must have been horrified

Left, *the Queen and Prince Philip leave the precincts of the Abbey with other Royal guests including, on the far right, ex-King Constantine of Greece.*

The Queen and Prince Philip always maintained a close affection for the late Earl Mountbatten and his family. Less than two months after the Earl's assassination at the end of August 1979, his 32-year-old grandson, Lord Romsey, was married to Miss Penelope Eastwood at Romsey Abbey. The wedding took place on 20th October, and many members of the Royal Family were among the guests: the Queen and Prince Philip **opposite page** leaving the Abbey after the service; the Duke and Duchess of Gloucester **top left;** the Duke and Duchess of Kent **top right;** the Prince of Wales **right,** with the Queen; and Prince and Princess Michael of Kent **far right.**

to learn that not only was he classed as holding an "office of profit under the Crown" but that that office of profit was "husband of the Queen".

Philip found also that it was not only in size that Buckingham Palace differed from Clarence House, but in atmosphere. At Clarence House things had been relatively informal, with members of their small staff free simply to tap on a door and walk in.

At Buckingham Palace, as was quickly made clear, that would no longer be tolerated. It may seem odd that a royal page, inherited, like the Queen's Private Secretary, from her father, should set the standard, but that is what happened. Clarence House aides who moved over with them found that they had to contact the page first – "You must be properly announced" – if they wanted to see the Queen.

Equerry Michael Parker was perhaps a rare exception. He would still stroll casually into Philip's study after simply tapping on the door.

But then Parker was an old and trusted friend, sharing a relationship which went back nearly a decade to their wartime naval days together.

But even Parker's breezy outlook and sense of fun could not always dispel the sense of gloom which descended upon Philip during that early phase of his wife's monarchy. There were too many other things which irritated and frustrated him.

The most frustrating part of it all was this nebulous quality of his new role as Consort. No one seemed to know what he was supposed to do, only what he was not to do and hardly anyone seemed to care.

There were compensations, of course. Parliament increased his State allowance to £40,000 a year.

A royal warrant issued by the Queen decreed that he should "henceforth upon all occasions and in all meetings except where otherwise provided by Acts of Parliament, have, hold and enjoy Place, Pre-eminence and Precedence next to Her Majesty". First Gentleman of the Realm.

He was named as Regent (in place of Princess Margaret) with responsibility for overseeing his son in the event that Charles should succeed to the Throne while still a minor.

It is only rarely that the Queen and Prince Philip make use of Balmoral Castle other then for their summer holiday, but in January 1977 it was the scene of a camera call **above and opposite page, left** *for photographs to be published on the 25th annniversary of the Queen's accession to the Throne.* **Left** *The Queen at her desk at Balmoral in the summer of 1972.*

With Elizabeth's accession, the relationship between she and Philip, as wife and husband, underwent a slight and subtle change. Previously Philip saw to the running of things in their married life and Elizabeth had been content that he should do so.

New to the manifold duties of monarchy, despite her apprenticeship as Princess, she devoted the major part of her time and energy towards mastering the job. If she needed advice, and guidance, she turned not to Philip, but to the top-level royal aides who had served her father before her, as, indeed she was almost bound to do.

If and when personal life clashed

Right *Three photographs taken in the summer of 1972 at Balmoral and released at the time of the Silver Wedding celebrations in November of that year. In the centre picture, they are seen walking in the grounds of the Castle with their two younger sons, Prince Andrew and Prince Edward.*

with the requirements of monarchy, then monarchy, she felt, came first. Philip could not be expected to see it altogether the same way. If his wife suddenly had too much to do, then he had too little that was important and meaningful to a man of his temperament.

In the 25 years since those early, frustrating days, Philip has without doubt shaped his indefinable role as Consort in his own image.

On a personal level, despite the

anomaly of being married to a wife who does not bear his name, and fathering children to whom his name is only a second-string, his marriage has been a happy one.

Today, as always in their moments together, they find plenty to talk about, their conversation broken at times by Elizabeth's throaty laughter (so seldom heard in public) and Philip's responding guffaw.

Despite being a Royal, Philip's early life was cut off from riches and palatial comfort.

Like his own son, Andrew, he was an afterthought baby, conceived while his parents were exiled in Switzerland, born – on the Ionian island of Corfu – seven years after the youngest of his four sisters.

A Prince of Greece without a drop of Greek blood in his veins.

Two ancient bloodlines meet and mingle in him. On his father's side he comes from the Danish royal house of Schleswig-Holstein-Sonderburg-Glücksburg which, in the days when monarchs ruled as well as reigned, supplied not only Denmark with its kings, but exported them also to Greece, Sweden, Norway and Russia.

On his mother's side he is descended

In May 1979, Prince Charles became the fourth member of the Royal Family to compete at the Royal Windsor Horse Show, when, in the uniform of his Welsh Regiment, he took part in an obstacle course **above, and top.** *As usual, Prince Philip entered the Four-in-Hand Driving heats, and the photographs on the right show him at various stages of the course.*

from the Mountbattens, who were Battenbergs until they changed the family name at the same time as King George V was changing his, and can trace their lineage back through some 44 generations to approximately AD 600.

He also has some English blood from Queen Victoria and a dash of the Russian Romanov.

George I of Greece married the teenage Grand Duchess Olga, of

Prince Philip taking his team of horses through the ford at Windsor in 1974 **above** *and enjoying a quick drink after the run* **far left. Above left** *The Queen takes one of her corgis in hand during the 1974 Show, and* **left** *she inspects part of a mounted display at the Show in May 1978.*

Russia, fathering two daughters and five sons, one of whom was Prince Andrew, Philip's father. Andrew married Alice, the daughter of Princess Victoria of Hesse and her cousin Prince Louis of Battenberg.

Andrew's brother, Constantine, took over the throne on the assassination of their father. Unfortunately for him, Constantine was married to a sister of the German Emperor, a fact which did not go down too well with Britain and

*Members of the Royal Family at the Royal Windsor Horse Show in May 1980. On this, as on many occasions, Prince Philip competed in the Four-in-Hand Driving Championships, and finished second at the conclusion of the weekend event. The pictures on this page show him taking part in that competition. The Duke was also a spectator at some of the other events, as was Prince Andrew with **bottom centre** Princess Alexandra and **bottom right** the Queen. With them **top left and right** was Mr Angus Ogilvy, the husband of Princess Alexandra.*

France as the First World War ran its bloody course.

They intervened to depose him and install his second son, Alexander, in his place.

The rest of the family, including Andrew, Alice and their four daughters, were sent into exile in Switzerland where they lived on borrowed money, attended by servants who loyally went without pay.

In 1920, Alexander, a king who was virtually a prisoner in his own palace, was bitten by a pet monkey. Blood poisoning set in and he died in agony.

To the fury of Britain and France, a plebiscite in Greece favoured recalling the exiled Constantine as king. So back

they all trekked, including Andrew and Alice, now pregnant again. Philip was born on 10 June, 1921 on Corfu in a Royal villa with the suburban name of "Mon Repos".

A local doctor delivered him on a dining-room table. The new Prince of Greece was soon doomed to exile, however.

A revolutionary junta in Athens stripped Andrew of his nationality and kicked him out. He went into exile on board the British cruiser *Calypso* with Philip sleeping in a padded cot made from an old orange box by the ship's carpenters.

Philip's father drifted into a life of easy pleasure, as far as funds would permit, first in Paris and later on the French Riviera. So a broken home was added to all the other uncertainties of Philip's young life.

Paris in the early 1920s was a Bohemian city of exiles. The poorer ones scratched a living as best they could, working as seamstresses, laundresses, as drivers, or in restaurants.

The Greek Royals were not quite re-

duced to that, though another of Andrew's brothers, Prince Nicholas, augmented what little money trickled through to him from Greece by giving painting lessons while his daughter, Princess Marina, later to marry the Duke of Kent, quickly became adept at making her own clothes.

In the public mind, it is the late Earl Mountbatten who is most closely identified with Philip's youthful upbringing.

Though an almost father-son relationship was eventually to develop between "Uncle Dickie" and his

Above *The Queen is warmly greeted by the Lord Mayor of London on her arrival at Guildhall for a luncheon following the Silver Wedding service at Westminster Abbey.* **Right** *The Queen Mother, Prince Charles, Princess Anne, Princess Margaret and Lord Snowdon in the foyer of the Guildhall on that occasion.* **Above right** *The Queen Mother, with Pricess Margaret and Lord Snowdon in Westminster Abbey, preceded by the Duchess of Gloucester and Lady Sarah Armstrong-Jones.* **Far right** *The Royal Family during the service.* **Opposite page** *The Queen looks around the Abbey before the service begins. Behind her are the Duke and Duchess of Gloucester, the Duke and Duchess of Kent, Princess Alice of Athlone and Princess Alexandra.*

nephew, it was the elder of the two Mountbatten brothers, George, successor to his father as Marquis of Milford Haven, who was responsible for his sister Alice's young son first coming to live in Britain.

His own son, David, was already a boarder at what is now known as Cheam School and he generously offered to pay for his sister's son to go there too.

Schooldays at Cheam marked the beginning of a close friendship with the slightly older David which was to continue into young adulthood.

It was close enough for Philip to have David as his best man when he married,

but cooled following his cousin's revelation that after a stag party the night before the wedding Philip might have had something of a slight hangover on his wedding morning.

Holidays were spent with relatives in various parts of Europe. Soon there was no longer a home in Paris to visit.

Within the short space of two years his sisters were all married to German princelings. Sophie, the youngest, became the bride of Prince Christopher of Hesse, later to be killed while flying with the Luftwaffe in the Second World War.

Even more than most bridegrooms, Philip found himself forced to take a

back seat in the arrangements for his own wedding. When the bride is a future Queen, even the bride's mother does not have all that much of a say. The wedding becomes a national event and other forces move in and take over.

The hardest blow of all for him to bear in the preparations for the wedding was the fact that his sisters' names were not included on the invitation list. Invitations could go to his mother and other relatives, even to old friends like Helene Cordet and her mother, but not to his sisters.

By marrying Germans they had become German nationals and the memory of the Second World War was still too fresh in British minds in 1947 for anyone German, however closely re-

lated, to be invited.

The best Philip could do was to arrange for an extra set of wedding photographs to be printed for his sisters. His cousin, Princess Marina, obligingly flew out to Germany with them shortly after the wedding.

It was unthinkable to King George VI that his elder daughter, the future Queen, should emerge from the Abbey as Princess Mrs Lieutenant Mountbatten.

So, with only 24 hours to go, he elevated his future son-in-law to the triple title of Duke of Edinburgh, Earl of Merioneth and Baron Greenwich. "It is a great deal to give a man all at once," the King noted, "but I know Philip understands his responsibilities on his

In May 1969, the Queen and other members of the Royal Family attended a naval review to commemorate the 20th anniversary of the establishment of NATO. They watched from the Royal Yacht Britannia **above** *and the Queen, equipped with binoculars,* **top picture** *took a lively interest in the proceedings.* **Above left** *Accompanied by Prince Philip, she waves as a warship passes by.* **Right** *Princess Anne and her great-uncle, Lord Mountbatten, also attended the review.*

marriage to Lilibet".

The King did not, however, give back to Philip the title of Prince, which he had relinquished in order to become a

naturalised British citizen.

This was not a deliberate omission on George VI's part but due to his misunderstanding of the situation. The

King thought that, by giving Philip the style of His Royal Highness, he was automatically making him a prince.

In fact, he was not, and it was not until several years after succeeding to the Throne that Elizabeth put right what her father had inadvertently omitted.

After the wedding on 20 November 1947, they went off on honeymoon to Romsey. Despite his new suits, shirts and shoes, Philip took along only two suitcases, one large, one small. Brides are different, of course, and it took fifteen cases to hold everything Elizabeth took on honeymoon with her.

She also took along her pet corgi, Susan.

The outbreak of the Second World War brought Philip a foretaste of what was to lie ahead of him in the immediate postwar years, when red tape of various sorts delayed both his naturalisation and betrothal.

After the Battle of Matapan Philip was promoted to sub-lieutenant. He visited Royal Lodge, Windsor, to see the King and Queen. They invited him to stay for tea for which Margaret and Elizabeth joined them.

There was also an invitation to Coppins, the country home of the Kents. His cousin, Princess Marina, whose husband was to be killed soon after in a wartime air crash, invited him to a dance to celebrate her wedding anniversary.

Perhaps she was trying her hand at a spot of matchmaking by inviting Elizabeth, now in her mid-teens also. The two of them danced together for the first time.

As a sub-lieutenant, Philip was posted to *H.M.S. Wallace*, a destroyer engaged on convoy duty in the Channel and the North Sea. Nine months later he was promoted to lieutenant and appointed second-in-command.

Second-in-command of another destroyer in the same squadron, *H.M.S. Lauderdale*, was a breezy young Australian, Michael Parker. He and Philip turned out to be two of a kind, hardworking and conscientious on duty, high-spirited and skylarking when not.

It became something of a point of honour between them as to which ran the tightest ship. Shipboard rivalry developed into a close and rollicking

Above *The Queen, Prince Philip, Princess Anne and Earl Mountbatten on the aft deck of the Royal Yacht. For Lord Mountbatten, whose own naval career spanned over forty years, this occasion was of great interest, and* **left** *Princess Anne seemed to enjoy it too.*

friendship, later to result in Philip, feeling the need for moral support in his new and much more public role of royal son-in-law, seeking Parker's support.

Among Philip's Christmas cards that year was one from Elizabeth, enclosing a photograph of herself. He decided to send her one in return. But the only photo to hand was one in the rank of sub-lieutenant which had been taken

Whether or not Princess Marina had been matchmaking when she invited Elizabeth and Philip to that anniversary dance at Coppins, others were now quite convinced that the two of them should marry.

Philip was almost 25 when he returned to Britain at the end of the war.

He bought an MG sports car to get around. His destination was sometimes Buckingham Palace, but more often the Royal Lodge at Windsor, where the King liked to relax at weekends.

Of course Philip did not go primarily to see the King, but his elder daughter. His courtship of her adhered to the accepted pattern of a quieter, less permissive age.

They walked the corgis together and went riding in Windsor Great Park. They played croquet on the lawn and sometimes if the weather was warm enough, swam in the blue-tiled pool. They were seldom alone. Usually Elizabeth's parents were around. Or servants.

Opposite page The huge Silver Jubilee procession making its slow progress from Buckingham Palace towards Admiralty Arch on 7th June 1977. **Below** The Queen's magnificent State Coach, used for the first time since her Coronation in 1953, passes along the sanded streets toward the City of London. **Left** The Queen, Prince Philip and the Prince of Wales after their entry into St Paul's Cathedral for the Jubilee service.

prior to his latest promotion.

So he sent that and for some time it occupied pride of place on her mantelpiece until it was replaced by a photograph showing a bearded and less recognisable Philip. Today both photographs, bearded and clean-shaven, are among the collection of family photos which clutter the Queen's desk.

He spent part of one leave with the Royal Family at Windsor. Always a good talker, he amused the King and Queen with his jaunty tales of shipboard life. Both enjoyed his sense of humour.

With H.M.S. Wallace back in Britain for a refit after the Sicily landing, he was again invited to Windsor around Christmas.

Even if they went out for a walk they would find a giggling, teenage chatterbox named Margaret tagging along. To avoid gossip, and speculative newspaper headlines, public outings had to be circumspect.

One of the tasks Prince Philip set himself after the coronation was to try to bring the monarchy well into the twentieth century.

It did not take him long to cut through the maze of mostly Victorian-inspired tradition and ritual which enmeshed the Royal Family when the Queen came to the throne in 1952. And now the Duke of Edinburgh can look back with the knowledge that he has done much to update and change the face of the Crown.

The Queen decreed that instead of referring publicly to herself and her husband as Queen Victoria had done with her "We Victoria..." she would always say "My husband and I".

But quite early in the Queen's reign there were rumours that Prince Philip had fallen foul of the "old guard" in Buckingham Palace. Senior courtiers who had served the previous monarch were said to be setting out to force him to stop his meddling.

It was suggested that they regarded him as a young upstart who was seeking to change the way that tradition had long dictated should be observed at the palace and other royal homes.

One of the problems was that certain officials felt they should only deal with the monarch and when Prince Philip tried to take some of the administrative load from his wife's shoulders he was deemed to have offended against protocol and to be endeavouring to usurp the powers of the monarch.

In matters of State the Queen was virtually out on her own. There was hardly anything at all with which the Queen's husband was permitted to help. In domestic matters such as the running of Buckingham Palace, because she was Queen as well as monarch, again everyone went to her. Prince Philip's actual comment on this apparent impasse was: "The fact that they report to the Queen is important to them and it's frightfully difficult to persuade them not to go to the Queen but to come to me."

But, over the years, and by persistence he did succeed in persuading some

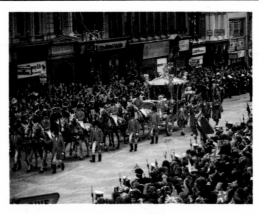

Above *The Queen's coach in procession up Ludgate Hill towards St Paul's Cathedral on Jubilee Day, 7th June 1977.* **Opposite** *The Queen, Prince Philip and Prince Charles are greeted at the West door of St Paul's by the Dean of St Paul's and his assisting clergy.* **Below** *The Queen and Prince Philip, accompanied by the Lord Mayor and Lady Mayoress of London, leaving the precincts of St Paul's churchyard to begin their long walk past cheering crowds towards the Guildhall.*

of them to take some of their queries and requests to him. He certainly did succeed in wholly taking over the management of the royal estates. Meanwhile he made it very apparent indeed that he believed the continuance of any system, however "royal" it might be, beyond its practical usefulness, was quite ridiculous and should be stopped.

Quite fearlessly he nudged the monarchy towards a flexibility which has

fitted it to carry on strongly into the twenty-first century.

He once said on American television: "Most of the monarchies in Europe were really destroyed by their greatest and most ardent supporters. It was the most reactionary people who tried to hold on to something without letting it develop or change."

Today, 34 years after their marriage, the Queen and her husband can look not only on an exceedingly happy family life, but also on the changing image of the monarchy, enabling it to both satisfy the die-hard traditionalist and accompany Great Britain smoothly and naturally into the greater European community.

To suggest that a monarch is an anachronism is frequently challenged by Prince Philip's public assertions that there can be no better head and figurehead of state than a monarch.

"A monarchy is the best form of Presidency", is how Lord George Brown, former Deputy Leader of the Labour Party, has termed it. We all of us need at the end of the day some totem pole around which we can gather.

"I would rather have as a sybmol a Monarch whom we do not elect than a President whom we do. Ours is the best system. The Prime Minister can get into trouble. The Monarch is always there no matter who is Prime Minister, no matter what the trouble.

"Presidents... are simply politicians or generals shot into the job.... It is my view that he (Prince Philip) and his wife do it because they think Britain needs them. For myself I have no doubt Britain does need them.... It is better to have a Royal Family who will operate and co-operate with the elected party than have a President who has to be elected himself and therefore does not have to co-operate."

The new-look monarchy has of course required considerable give-and-take by both the Queen and Prince Philip in their three decades of married life.

It called for special skills and not only from Prince Philip. His habit of breezing head first into any company, and taking over, wasn't at first easy to take to and although the Queen, even now, retains something of her natural reserve, his open-handedness has rub-

bed off on her.

Prince Philip has never made any bones about the fact that he finds his wife's favourite pastime, horse racing, nothing more than a bore. He not only avoids accompanying her to race meetings whenever he can but even at Royal Ascot, traditionally the most glittering week of the so-called "Sport of Kings", where he has to put in an appearance, however brief, he has been known to carry a transistor radio in his top hat so that he could listen to a cricket test match while compelled by loyalty and protocol to face towards the horses.

The Queen, meanwhile, who dislikes sailing in small boats, is rarely present to watch her husband competing in the yacht race at Cowes Regatta.

On the other hand, the Queen has of late put in an appearance at the Sandringham "bachelor" weekend shooting parties originally introduced by the ebullient King Edward VII and taken up by Prince Philip with gusto. Although the Queen does not join the men with a gun, she does walk up to 10 miles a day over the estates, a pack of dogs at her heels, making occasional diversions to see "how the men are getting on".

Only for a few weeks after she became monarch did the Queen retain the surname of Mountbatten with which she had been wed. In April, 1952, it was ordained by an Order in Council that she, her children and descendants,

*All smiles **opposite page, top** as the Royal Family acknowledges the deafening cheers of an estimated million people who surged in front of the Palace gates and round the Victoria Memorial **opposite page, bottom** to acclaim their Sovereign of 25 years. The Queen and Prince Philip are joined by their four children, their son-in-law Captain Mark Phillips, and their uncle, Earl Mountbatten of Burma. **Right** The vast crowd fills the Mall as it makes its way from the Palace after the Queen's final appearance on the balcony.*

Overleaf *A section of the huge crowds which thronged round the Victoria Memorial to catch a glimpse of the Queen on the balcony of Buckingham Palace after her Silver Jubilee service on 7th June 1977.*

Opposite page *Two sections of the enormous crowd around the Victoria Memorial waiting for the Queen's Silver Jubilee procession in June 1977. Many had taken up their places days in advance to be sure of a good view, and most had a flag to wave or a patriotic message to send.* **Top left** *The Queen at the commissioning of HMS Invincible at Portsmouth in July 1980.* **Top right** *Princess Anne at a naval ceremony in 1971.* **Above** *The Queen at the launching of the RNLI lifeboat "Silver Jubilee" at Henley in July 1972.* **Below right** *The Queen and Duke of Edinburgh attending a ceremony at the Tower of London in December 1978.* **Above right** *During the filming of the television series "Royal Heritage", the Queen and her niece, Lady Sarah Armstrong-Jones read the title deeds of The Little Cottage in the grounds of Royal Lodge Windsor, which was a gift from the people of Wales to the Queen and Princess Margaret in 1936.*

except for females who married, should be known as Windsor.

The King himself, not long before he died, had decided upon this with Winston Churchill. Although Prince Philip made no particular fight for his wife to retain his surname, by the time their third child, Prince Andrew, was born eight years later he had persuaded her to make a compromise.

It was announced that "certain des-

cendants" of the Queen, in particular the grandchildren of her younger sons, would be known as "Mountbatten-Windsor". After a Declaration in Council had made this official in February 1960, the palace explained that the Queen had "for some time wanted her husband's name to enjoy perpetuation".

One of the first steps the Queen took after noticing what seemed a public "demotion" of her husband on her accession to the throne, was to find official appointments for him to which some of his boundless energies could be directed.

The very first was that of Ranger of Windsor Great Park, which meant he was nominally in charge of the vast

royal estates within the bounds of the castle's Home Park and the wide range of farmlands and forest beyond.

It had been the custom for the professional Deputy Ranger, an estate manager, to administer all this valuable territory, and report periodically upon his stewardship to the monarch.

But things soon changed when Philip became Ranger – all manner of practices and procedures unaltered for generations were now drastically swept by a new royal broom, and many were swept right away. One of the very first demands Prince Philip made on the royal estates was that they were to become self-sufficient and were no longer

to be regarded as mere sporting estates.

This was not to say that the traditional pheasant and partridge shoots at Windsor and Sandringham, and the grouse shoots and salmon fishing at Balmoral, were to be abandoned as great annual events. But it did mean that each guest was only allowed so many of his (or her) personal bag, and that the rest were sold to the big London hotels at the highest possible price.

Similarly, fruit growing at Sandringham was commercialised to such an extent, that today the Queen cannot help herself to whatever she wants from the estates' orchards of Cox's Pippins, for they have to be bought from the contractor who rents these orchards from the Crown.

And at Windsor, where greenhouses were once given over to the growing of orchids and other exotic flowers for the royal tables, today Philip the Ranger ensures that regular crops of mushrooms, vegetables, chrysanthemums and Christmas trees are sent to Covent Garden market to increase the Crown revenues.

In the manner in which he has revolutionised the royal estates, Prince Philip persuaded the Queen to take the monarchy much closer to her subjects. No longer was the crowned head to be seen only from a respectful distance by applauding crowds along the routes of State Drives.

Today the Queen goes on "walkabouts" among her subjects, chatting to

Following the State Visit to Britain of the Emperor of Japan in October 1971, the Queen and Prince Philip paid a return visit in May 1975, as part of a wider tour of the Far East. **Centre picture** *The Queen and Prince Philip with the Emperor and Empress Nagako during the welcoming ceremony at the Imperial Palace in Tokyo.* **Top left** *The Royal visitors look slightly bemused as they take tea, Japanese fashion, under a huge parasol, at Katsuba Villa, Kyoto.* **Top right** *During the visit, the Queen went to the Commonwealth War Cemetery at Hodogaya, near Yokohama, where she laid this wreath.* **Bottom picture** *The Queen and Duke watching pearl divers on Mikimato Island.*

people at random instead of adhering to the age-old procedure of only speaking to carefully-chosen people correctly introduced by members of her court.

This was Prince Philip's idea, fought for in the face of much opposition but finally achieved.

Just how far the Queen has developed as a "Queen of the people for the people", under the persuasion and encouragement of her thrustful husband, can be judged from two of her experiences in recent years.

In the sixties, when Queen Elizabeth II drove beside Queen Frederika of Greece to a London theatre, she found herself amid a storm of booing and shouted vilifications from a Communist-led demonstration against the Greek régime.

Never in her life had the British Queen had anything so hateful happen to her, or appear at least to be in part directed against her. And that night, after she had left the theatre early, royal servants noticed that she was in tears when she returned to the palace.

Only once before within the memory of the palace staff had it been known

State Visitors to Japan do not stay at the Emperor's Palace, but at the Akasaka Palace, a modern and specially constructed guest-house in Tokyo. **Below** *On the day of their arrival, the Queen and Prince Philip admire the spacious gardens and rock-pools.* **Above** *One of the Emperor's family, Princess Mikase, shows Prince Philip around the interior of the building, which contained beautifully arranged flower and shrub displays.*

for the Queen to lapse from the calm and unemotional bearing traditionally expected of her – that being when, on

the advice of her ministers, she had to refuse an agonised father's ultimate appeal to the Crown that the death sentence passed on his son for the murder of a policeman, should be commuted. The afternoon before her decision was publicly announced the Queen paced the palace gardens alone, in anguish.

But how the Queen has toughened with the closer-proximity policy encouraged by her husband was clearly demonstrated at Stirling, in Scotland, recently when a mob of drunken students shouted obscenities and made vulgar gestures at her. They jostled so close that police had to form a protective ring close around her. Never for a moment did the Queen flinch. She met it with smiles and afterwards declared she had "quite enjoyed" herself.

Prince Philip initiated the new "meet-the-people" procedures to the Royal Family, and tried it all out personally long before he urged his wife and elder son and daughter to follow suit. Both Prince Charles and Princess Anne were shy about it in the beginning but soon developed the knack, particularly among young people.

The Queen, meanwhile, demonstrated so much personal magnetism and warmth that to countless people to whom the monarchy had become an outdated institution, the Crown was suddenly held in respect, admiration and affection.

Because the Queen must be seen to be completely non-political Elizabeth, inevitably, is prevented from any open association with many facets of the

nation's life. But Prince Philip is not restricted in such a way and whenever he has felt strongly that it was for the good of Britain that he should do or say a certain thing, he has done it or said it – despite ensuing controversy.

After nearly 30 years of being "uncrowned" consort, Prince Philip's views on the monarchy have considerable relevance. In a television interview he said he could detect a "very considerable" change in the public attitude to the Royal Family.

"In 1953 we were a great deal younger", he said. "A young Queen and a young family were infinitely more newsworthy and amusing. Now we are getting into middle age. I daresay when we are a bit more ancient there might be a bit more reverence again.

"But now we are in the least interesting period of a glamorous existence.

State occasions for the Queen. **Opposite page** *Entertaining the Amir of Bahrein on the Royal Yacht Britannia during her State Visit there in February 1979: with them is the Crown Prince, one of the Amir's grandsons.* **Above left** *The Queen and Prince Philip with President Scheel and his wife during their second visit to West Germany in 1978.* **Above** *A happy evening for the Queen, Prince Philip and Princess Anne whilst on their State Visit to Yugoslavia in October 1972.* **Left** *President Giscard d'Estaing of France admire the splendour of Buckingham Palace when he and his wife visited the Queen in 1977.*

ately responds to with that beautiful, ready smile that brightens up the dullest day. She has always been the favourite among Press photographers because she invariably takes the trouble to pause well within lens range and turns in their direction. In a presentation line-up she usually pauses to talk to someone about four persons from the end – a handy distance for the cameramen.

Left *A glowing portrait of the Queen Mother, taken by Norman Parkinson, in the grounds of Royal Lodge Windsor, for her 80th birthday in August 1980.* **Top** *Ten years earlier, the Queen Mother, with her Lady-in-Waiting, drives through London after attending an official engagement.* **Above centre** *She acknowledges the cheers of the crowds as she leaves Westminster Abbey after a service there in the early 1960's.* **Above, and far right** *More recently, these colourful pictures were taken during her visit to the Chelsea Flower Show in 1976.*

People have got accustomed to us and take us much more naturally. There used to be much more interest but now they take it as a matter of course...."

Without doubt one of the most popular royal personalities is the Queen Mother, the world's favourite grandmother. She is now in her eighties, but is still very active and carries out her share of public duties. Wherever she goes she is greeted with warmth and affection, something she immedi-

The Queen Mother has had to suffer much in her life, yet she remains cheerful. She was barely a queen before she and her husband had to cope with wartime leadership. They refused to leave London during the Blitz, insisting on sharing all the dangers of their subjects. She then had only a few years in which to enjoy a peaceful reign before George VI became ill. The older generation of staff at Buckingham Palace still remember how much of a comfort she was to her husband, keeping his spirits high despite his great pain.

Recently she had the sadness of seeing her younger daughter's marriage break up. During this time she was not only a motherly solace to Princess Margaret, but also a loving "granny" to her children.

She never expected to be a queen, but proved to be one of the finest Consorts a British king could ever have had.

The Queen Mother was born Elizabeth Bowes-Lyon, the fourth daughter of Lord and Lady Glamis of Glamis Castle in Angus, Scotland – which was the setting Shakespeare chose for Macbeth's murder of King Duncan.

By the time she made her début at court at the age of 19, she was already beginning to turn the heads of London society as a beautiful, long-dark-haired girl with fiery blue eyes.

Drawing room gossip of the time praised her as being irresistible to men, but the gamine young Bowes-Lyon soon took a liking to King George V's second son, the Duke of York. After spending

These pictures show how regal the Queen Mother looks in formal evening dress. **Right** She arrives at the Japanese Embassy for a reception in 1971. **Far right** A cheerful smile from the Queen Mother as she attends a performance of "Mayerling" at the Royal Opera House, Covent Garden in February 1978. **Above** She attends a dinner given by Mrs Thatcher at No 10 Downing Street in November 1980. **Above right** Resplendent in tiara and jewels, the Queen Mother meets actors and actresses after the Royal Film Performance in March 1981. **Opposite page** One of several official photographs of the Queen Mother, taken by Norman Parkinson to commemorate her 80th birthday in August 1980.

one of several weekends at Glamis Castle with her, the 25-year-old Duke told his mother: "The more I see Elizabeth the more I like her." He fell madly in love with her but it needed three years of wooing before Elizabeth agreed to marry him. She was wary of marrying a king's son because of the enormous responsibilities it could bring – fears that were to prove justified.

The first few years of kingship were far from easy, as George was ill-prepared for the enormous task that

It was the turn, on 17th November 1980, of the Queen Mother to attend the annual Royal Variety Performance at the London Palladium **above** *arriving with Lord Delfont. After the show, during which the entire company of stars sang "Happy Birthday to You" in honour of her 80th birthday, the Queen Mother went backstage to meet the performers. These included* **opposite page, top** *Larry Hagman and his mother Mary Martin, and* **opposite page, below** *Bruce Forsyth, Cleo Laine and Sammy Davis Junior. Prince Charles, who accompanied his grandmother to the performance, is seen* **left** *in animated conversation with the singer Grace Kennedy.*

had suddenly been thrust upon him. He had a lot to cope with and Elizabeth was a marvellous helpmeet always available to cheer him up.

It was a period too, when, because of the abdication crisis, the future of the monarchy was in doubt. The new Queen helped to restore affection towards the throne by making an attempt to go out and meet the people, setting the style that is now almost commonplace with the Royal Family.

When her elder daughter was suddenly brought to the throne while she was so young, it was her mother, always in the background, who gave her encouragement and wise counsel and did what grannies do all over the world – looked after the children.

Left The Queen Mother leaving St Paul's Cathedral London after attending a service there in 1977. On 1st August 1979, the Queen Mother became the first woman to be installed as Lord Warden of the Cinque Ports, in succession to Sir Robert Menzies, former Prime Minister of Australia. The installation ceremony took place at Dover, and despite poor weather, thousands of people turned out to watch the spectacle as the Queen Mother left Dover Castle in procession **far left,** inspected guards of honour drawn from the Army **top** and Navy **above,** and received flowers from the local children during her walkabout.

Today they are still very close. When Charles wants to relax he frequently joins the Queen Mother at one of her Scottish retreats to go fishing with her. At this stage of her life the "Queen Mum" is a very happy and contented woman. She has seen her daughter become one of the most admired monarchs in history, she is surrounded by loving grandchildren and continues to

Left and below left *The Queen Mother, with the Lady Mayor of Dover, meets local dignitaries outside the huge marquee in which the installation ceremony took place.* **Below** *The Queen Mother receiving the keys of Dover Castle as a symbol of her authority as Lord Warden of the Cinque Ports.*

be close to the hearts of millions of people throughout the world.

She is a remarkable woman, who has probably the unique record of having been the daughter-in-law of one king, the sister-in-law of another, the wife of another, the mother of a queen and is now happily seeing the maturing of a grandson who will be a future king.

At an age when some women are sitting in armchairs doing their knitting, the Queen Mother is remarkably active, walking over the heather-covered moors of her beloved Scotland, standing up to her waist in fast-flowing water casting for salmon, or carrying out a hectic round of official duties. "I love meeting people," she frequently tells those who ask how she manages to keep up such a dashing pace. "Most people are really very nice, you know."

She became a queen by an odd quirk of history – the abdication of the Duke of Windsor as Edward VIII. If one believes in fortune tellers, however, she knew her fate from the age of seven,

The greatest joy of the Queen Mother's later years has been her six grandchildren, and now her great-grandchildren, son and daughter of Anne and Mark. She has always had a soft spot, however, for Charles, more than for any of the others. Apart from being her first grandchild, he also reminds her of her late husband with

his gentle, kindly ways.

Charles spent many years of his early childhood with his grandmother during the time that the Queen and Prince Philip were on tours abroad. As he grew into his teens it was often the Queen Mother he would turn to for help in sorting out the confusion of growing up.

when a gipsy woman held her palm and told her that she would be a queen one day.

(The "Queen Mum" had her future foretold when she visited a gipsy tent, which was one of the side-shows at a garden party at Glamis Castle. She was 10 years old at the time.

She dashed giggling from the tent to her governess and said, "The gipsy was silly. She read my palm and said that one day I'll be a queen. Who wants to be a queen?")

Elizabeth Angela Marguerite Bowes-Lyon – the Lady Elizabeth Glamis – was the third daughter of the Earl and

The ancient ceremony surrounding the Garter service, with its traditional splendour. Pictures on this page show various parts of the procession from Windsor Castle to St George's Chapel, in which guards, the brightly-tabarded heralds, members of the Order, and Yeoman of the Guard take part. **Below** *A view of the procession from the Castle towards the lower part of the grounds.*

Countess of Strathmore and Kinghome. She was born on a Saturday, in the summer of 1900, at the family's country house, St Paul's Walden Bury, a brick, Queen Anne house near Stevenage in Hertfordshire.

Her father had a Scottish ancestry dating back to Robert the Bruce, King of

Scotland, while her mother, Nina Cecilia, was of English stock. She was the daughter of the Reverend Charles William Cavendish-Bentinck, a cousin of the Duke of Portland.

Among her ancestors was one wretched Lady Glamis who was burnt alive as a witch in Edinburgh in 1540.

The Bowes-Lyon name comes from the eighteenth century, when a rich County Durham industrialist, George Bowes, agreed to get the Strathmore

Top *The full magnificence of the ceremonial and the many hundreds of people who fill the Castle grounds to watch it.* **Above left** *The Queen Mother's part of the procession, in June 1976.* **Above right** *A frock-coated band leads members of the Household Brigade towards St George's Chapel.*

family out of debt. The ninth earl wished to marry Bowes' daughter Eleanor. The dowry that went with her was his entire fortune and all his estates in the North and Hertfordshire.

In exchange for the wealth and hand in marriage of such a valuable daughter the Strathmore family name

of Lyon had to be changed to Bowes. After the old boy died the name quickly became Bowes-Lyon.

The Queen Mother's father was a quiet, kindly, religious man. As Lord Lieutenant of Forfar, he lived the classic role of an Anglo-Scottish gentleman of his day, being mainly concerned with shooting, cricket and forestry.

His wife had the greatest influence on their youngest daughter. The Countess of Strathmore was a straight-laced lady interested in embroidery and music. She was so accomplished musically that she could attend a concert, return home, go straight to the piano, and play the pieces from memory. She is said to have been a lively woman with a great sense of humour... qualities which her daughter inherited in abundance.

Much of her daughter's childhood was spent at Glamis, the old Scottish castle dating back to the fourteenth century. It was here that the teenage Elizabeth discovered interests which have lasted throughout her life. She learnt to play both cricket and tennis, developed into an accomplished gardener and became skilful at fly fishing.

She also saw the horrors of war at Glamis during 1914-1918 when the castle was turned into a convalescent home for wounded soldiers.

She was too young to be a nurse so she helped as best she could by serving meals to the wounded, writing their letters, playing cards with them, or just cheering them up as a fun-loving pretty girl. An art she still retains.

These bitter days gave her an understanding of the world of ordinary folk, people she would normally have never met as a daughter of the upper class at that time.

She became aware of how the war brought, for a brief period, a sense of common feeling to a class-ridden nation. Four of her brothers were wounded – one of them fatally.

The memories of that time remained with her always – hence what many today call her "common touch" – though the world she belonged to soon returned to its exclusive pleasures and aristocratic goings-on after the Armistice of 1918.

The Strathmores, with a fortune worth nearly a million pounds – the equivalent today of £20,000,000 – resumed their conventional parental role of launching their daughter into Society.

She must have been a knockout on the London and Scottish social scenes in the days when "coming out" had a much happier and feminine ring to it. Contemporary pictures show her as an impish-eyed, petite (5 ft 2 ins) beauty,

The Garter ceremony brings a lavish splash of colour and pageantry, no matter what the weather. Although the 1970 ceremony below centre was attended by favourable weather, the following year's proceedings took place in heavy rain. This meant that the Queen and Prince Philip had to be driven from St George's Chapel to Windsor Castle in a closed car right instead of an open carriage. Below, left and right The Queen, fully robed, prepares to join the pageantry surrounding the installation ceremony.

trim of waist and with gentle mouth and soft jaw line.

Her blue eyes were described as brilliant and she was said to have a lovely skin and complexion. Her peaches-and-cream look has been the envy of many women throughout her life.

She had the reputation of being full of high spirits, one of the best ballroom dancers of the early 1920s and generally thought great fun to be with. She was once praised as "a sweet-faced, pretty and gentle-natured girl".

Her entry into the heart of royal circles came about through being on various committees of the Girl Guides. Princess Mary (later Lady Harewood) was also a keen guide, and befriended the Scottish lass.

The King and Queen were anxiously looking around for suitable brides for their sons, particularly David. The delightful friend of daughter Mary, Lady Elizabeth Bowes-Lyon, fitted the bill perfectly.

A year after she was first introduced to the Royal Family, Queen Mary, who was staying near Glamis, drove over to the young Elizabeth's Scottish home. Rumours began to fly that a suitable girl had been found to steady the gad-about

Prince of Wales.

But it was not David who became deeply interested in her – it was Albert, a less dashing creature than his brother.

His health was not good. He suffered from a stammer which occasionally caused bouts of anger and made him shy socially. Yet he was good looking, a fine tennis player, rode well and could be kind and considerate.

Overshadowed by his popular elder brother, Bertie became involved, through his friendship with the Bowes-Lyon brothers, with the delightful Lady Elizabeth Bowes-Lyon. Her kindness

and patience helped him overcome his initial nervousness and uncertainty.

A few months after Bertie spent a weekend at Glamis Castle, Queen Mary confided to a friend that her son "is very much attracted to Lady Elizabeth Bowes-Lyon. He's always talking about her."

Although she was blissfully happy in his company, the thought of moving from a quiet country life into the public glare and an unceasing round of royal duties was something that needed thinking about.

Bertie is said to have proposed three times before being accepted. The King

In June 1972, the weather was again good enough for a full procession on foot from the Castle to the Chapel for the afternoon service. **Above left** The Queen Mother's escort on this occasion was Emperor Haile Selassie of Ethiopia: the Queen and Prince Philip follow further back in the procession. **Left** Amongst the members of the Order attending that year were Lord Butler and Lord Longford – here seen heading the procession. **Above** The Sovereign of the Order and her consort: The Queen and Prince Philip in the Chapel cloister.

seemed not entirely sure of his son's chances of winning Lady Elizabeth. He told him: "You'll be a lucky fellow if she accepts you."

Both he and the Queen were quite sure, however, that Elizabeth was the woman who could make their son happy. She was a commoner, but, as the heir, David, was thought certain to marry a suitable person and produce an heir of his own, they thought this would not be a problem.

In fact elder brother David gave her a hint of what was to happen during the abdication 13 years later, when she expressed her doubts about marrying Albert George.

The future Duke of Windsor told Elizabeth: "You had better take him and go on in the end to Buck House."

It was only much later, after George VI's death, that her true feelings about the marriage became clear. She agreed to marry him, but only out of a sense of duty. "I fell in love with him afterwards," she revealed to a friend a few years ago.

The 22-year-old Lady Elizabeth Bowes-Lyon accepted the marriage

Every year, the Queen, as Sovereign of the Most Noble Order of the Garter, holds an installation service at St George's Chapel, Windsor, attended by all members of the Order. One of the most traditional and spectacular ceremonies in the official calendar, it attracts many thousands of people to the grounds of Windsor Castle. **Top**

The Queen and Prince Philip leave St George's Chapel after the service and stand at the foot of the steps which are lined by other members of the Order. Among the other royal members on this occasion were **above left** *the Queen Mother and Grand Duke Jean of Luxembourg, and* **right** *the Prince of Wales.*

The Queen and Prince Philip **above left** and Queen Elizabeth the Queen Mother **left** being driven back to Windsor Castle at the end of the installation service. **Top right** Prince Charles and **above** the Queen leaving St George's Chapel; built by King Edward IV in the late-fifteenth century.

proposal – eventually – of His Royal Highness Prince Albert George one January day as they strolled in the woods at her Hertfordshire home.

Bertie then sent a telegram to Sandringham with the pre-arranged signal: "All right. Bertie."

A date was fixed for the wedding at Westminster Abbey – 26 April 1923.

It was to be the first time in 500 years that a prince of the Royal House had been married there. The last was King Richard II in 1382.

It was so rare, however, for the son of the King of England to marry a commoner – albeit such a well-connected one – that there was a dispute among the royal advisers and church leaders about the rank and status of the future Duchess of York.

Some voices were raised against allowing the marriage at all, but these were eventually silenced because of a number of sound reasons. One was that the British had just come through a bitter war with a nation led by a cousin of the Royal Family, Kaiser Bill of Germany. There was considerable opposition, therefore, towards further links with foreign royalty.

A home-grown bride was a popular choice.

Dignity all but abandoned in strong winds at Windsor, after the Garter installation service at St George's Chapel on 16th June 1980. **Top right, and above** *The Queen and Prince Philip are taken by surprise, as further up the steps, the Prince of Wales, Queen Margrethe of Denmark, Queen Elizabeth the Queen Mother and Grand Duke Jean of Luxembourg attempt to cope with the weather.* **Right** *Prince Charles and Queen Margrethe prepare to enter their car for the drive back to Windsor Castle.*

Elizabeth's friend, Princess Mary, married the Earl of Harewood – still classed as a commoner despite his grand title and estates in Yorkshire. This helped to break the ground for another person of less-than-regal blue blood to be welcomed into the fold.

But, above all, it was argued that the heir to the throne, David, Prince of Wales, would surely soon mend his dashing ways and settle down and raise a family with some suitable princess. The offspring of the new Duke and Duchess of York would not be in line for the throne anyway . . . would they?

Their wedding provided one of the first signs of national cheer in a country just beginning to face the aftermath of the First World War.

The streets were packed with happy crowds as the bride, wearing a dress of simple mediaeval style with a square neckline made of fine chiffon, drove by. Queen Mary had loaned her a train of old Flander's lace, which had underneath it a longer train of Nottingham lace.

There was massive unemployment, with thousands out of work in the lace trade and this gesture was made in the hope that it might boost their business.

Another indication of the Establish-

Top left and far right *The Prince of Wales and Queen Margrethe before and after the ceremony. Queen Margrethe is third cousin to our own Queen, and acceded to the Danish throne on the death of her father, King Frederick IX, in January 1972.* **Top right** *The Queen Mother is escorted by Grand Duke Jean of Luxembourg: he is distantly related to the Queen through his ancestors in the House of Orange, and through his wife, Grand Duchess Josephine-Charlotte, whose great-great-Grandfather, King Leopold I of the Belgians, was Queen Victoria's uncle.* **Above** *An amusing bonus for the photographer as the wind plays havoc with the plumes of the Guard of Honour.*

ment's awareness of the harsh world of the working classes was the guest list for the wedding. Among the three-thousand seated in Westminster Abbey were 30 apprentices from factories throughout Britain who had been invited, and provided with new suits, by the Duke of York who was president of the well-meaning Industrial Welfare Society . . . an earlier version of the Duke of Edinburgh's Award Scheme.

The couple's honeymoon was hardly a romantic affair. Much of it was spent at Glamis, in biting winds, rain and snow. Elizabeth ended up confined to bed with whooping cough.

They soon returned south to their first home, White Lodge in Richmond Royal Park, which was given to them by the royal parents.

Elizabeth's new father-in-law quickly showed his affection towards the young bride. King George wrote to his son a few weeks after the marriage: "The better I know and the more I see of your dear little wife, the more charming I think she is, and everyone feels in love

Scenes from the Garter ceremony of June 1978. **Above** *The Queen and Duke emerge from St George's Chapel Windsor at the conclusion of the Garter service, and drive away by carriage* **above left** *towards the Castle.* **Left** *Prince Charles with the Queen Mother following in the carriage procession.* **Below left** *A detachment of the Yeomen of the Guard entering the Chapel before the service.* **Below** *Some of the members of the Order, including Lord Longford and Sir Harold Wilson, approaching the Chapel.*

with her here."

The new Duchess's own family were not, as one might expect, overflowing with pride that she had hooked one of the best catches of her generation. A relative summed up their attitude when he merely said: "Thank God she has married a good man."

Settling down in her new home was not the easiest of tasks for the new bride, though. She was bothered in the first few months of married life by what can only be called "mother-in-law trouble".

White Lodge had been one of Queen Mary's favourite royal homes and, while the newly weds were on honeymoon, she set about furnishing it for them . . . in her own very stuffy Victorian taste. Little regard was given to what the bride wanted in her home, and very little space was allowed for her own favourite family treasures.

All the wives of Mary's sons had to learn to bow to her wishes, but, as she saw how happy Bertie became with his bride, the formidable old Queen

Above Lord Butler of Saffron Walden *was among the Members of the Order attending in 1978.* **Above right** *The Queen and Duke of Edinburgh at the foot of the steps of the Chapel; further up are the Queen Mother, Prince Charles and Earl Mountbatten of Burma.* **Right** *A smiling Queen Mother leaves after the installation service.*

mellowed over the years and developed a close, kindly relationship with Elizabeth.

Her relations with the King, on the other hand, were always very happy. By nature a gruff man, given occasionally to harsh words, George V was absolutely charmed into submission by the young bride he called Lilibet.

She was to write after his death: "Unlike his own children I was never afraid of him. In all his 12 years of having me as a daughter-in-law he never spoke one unkind or abrupt word to me and was always ready to listen and give advice on one's own silly little affairs. When he was in the mood he

could be deliciously funny too."

She was warmly accepted into the family but Elizabeth still had to endure the strict formality of George and Mary's court. In sharp contrast to the very easy-going life among her own folk, she had to get used to a strict and proper régime.

Going to the palaces of her in-laws, even for a close family gathering, was always a matter of great formality, with everyone dressed correctly for whatever time of day it might be. A small lunch or supper was, inevitably a very stiff affair.

Elizabeth slowly managed to change much of this. She began by persuading the King and Queen to let her play the piano at after-dinner gatherings. She would start with a few classic pieces,

Opposite page *The Queen smiling in pouring rain as she arrives for an official function during one of her annual visits to Scotland. She wears a colourful tartan sash over her evening gown.* **This page** *Wearing the Garter Star at the Commonwealth Prime Ministers' Conference at Lusaka in 1979, the Queen chats with President Nyerere of Tanzania* **above, right,** *and with Mrs Thatcher* **right. Below** *The official photograph shows the Queen and Prince Philip with the entire gathering of Commonwealth Prime Ministers.*

then sing popular ballads – getting the others to join in!

She also changed the Duke of York. Her gaiety and abundant self-confidence began to rub off on Bertie. The socially shy and highly-strung young man, ashamed of his stammer, was transformed in a few years to an outgoing, self-confident public figure, backed by a wife who encouraged him to have faith in himself.

The Duchess of York also became a public figure in her own right and the world came to know, for the first time, the warmth of that famous smile. As she went about visiting hospitals, attending meetings to raise money for the poor or taking part in ceremonial duties, she always appeared then – as now – to be thoroughly enjoying herself. *The Times* once commented: "She lays a foundation stone as if she has just discovered a new and delightful way of spending an afternoon."

She liked meeting people, and seemed always interested in their business, no matter how humble. Many of those who today talk about "that lovely lady" are thinking about the young Duchess of York and her wanderings through the country in the Depression years. She had a gift of seeming to smile at every individual in a group or crowd and the smile seemed to be a personal recognition.

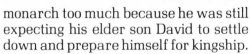

The 1981 Epsom Derby. A military band **opposite page, below** *greets the Queen's motorcade* **top.** *Prince Philip arrives separately* **right and opposite page, above.** *Other pictures show the Queen, Prince Philip and the Queen Mother, with Prince and Princess Michael of Kent, Princess Alexandra and Angus Ogilvy, and the Duchess of Gloucester, studying the runners.* **Centre** *The winner, Shergar.*

Three years after their wedding, the Yorks had their first child, a daughter called Elizabeth Alexandra Mary. The fact that she was a girl disappointed King George, who had hoped for his grandchild to be a boy.

A girl, then, became third in line to the throne, but this did not bother the monarch too much because he was still expecting his elder son David to settle down and prepare himself for kingship.

What happened in the years that followed were to thrust Elizabeth and her family from the quiet backwater they had planned for themselves to the very forefront of history . . . and the gay Scottish lass was on her way to becoming "Queen Mum" to the world.

Throughout her life she has set an elegant style in her dress, especially with her celebrated pearls and hats, yet some of her favourite moments are when she can wear casual, old clothes. Birkhall, Sandringham and Royal Lodge, Windsor, are places where she

More scenes from the 1981 Derby. **Bottom** The arrival of the Queen and her mother. **Below centre** The Queen makes her way to the Royal Stand and **below** royal scrutiny as the runners canter before the Queen and Queen Mother. **Left** A quartet of royal ladies: the Duchess of Gloucester, the Queen, Princess Alexandra and the Queen Mother. **Opposite page** A nail-biting time (above) as the runners round Tattenham Corner (below). **Below left** Applause for the winner from Prince Michael, his wife and his brother-in-law, Angus Ogilvy.

can get away from the formality of other royal homes and go walking or fishing in baggy, comfortable clothes and rubber boots.

While her elder daughter is deeply involved in flat racing, the Queen Mother is interested in the more dramatic sport of steeplechasing. She bought her first horse in 1949 and since then has put into training a string of successful jumpers which, over the years, have brought her more than 300 wins. In only her second season she had a great success with a powerful brown horse, Manicou, which won the race named after her husband, the King George the VI Stakes, at Kempton Park. Manicou was put to stud and has sired a generation of successful jumpers.

During the early days the Queen, the then Princess Elizabeth, and her mother jointly owned a chaser. The daughter gave up her interest in jumpers though, after their horse broke

a leg and had to be destroyed. The Queen is remembered as being heart-broken and she has never been fond of steeplechasing since.

With her busy, official life continuing without any signs of retirement, and her active social activities, the Royal Family is justifiably proud of the lady affectionately known as the "Queen Mum". An American Army sergeant once referred to her as "a swell gal". One of her entourage put it another way when he said recently: "No one comes any better."

She has a particular characteristic, seen also in Princess Margaret. Her hands are very small and delicate with, even today, milky, smooth skin. It is a pity she always wears gloves in public because only her close friends and family are able to see those elegant hands.

She shares with Prince Charles a preference for doing things at her own pace. She does not like to be rushed and has a forgivable habit of arriving late for appointments. Her reason for being delayed is very often that she has met some people whom she has found interesting – so has thrown a busy schedule to the wind just to talk to them.

The Castle of Mey, with its wild seas and generally foul weather, is a perfect private retreat. She spends most of the time alone there, although it is now a tradition when the Royal Family sails around Scotland in August on board the royal yacht *Britannia* that they go ashore for a few days with Grandma. It has taken many years for her to get the castle back into shape. She now recalls her feelings when she first saw the crumbling structure when she was out

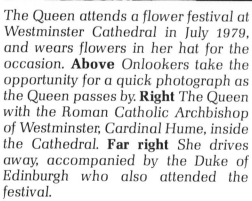

native air. So have you both been fitted for your place in the people's life and your separate lives are now, till death, made one.

"You cannot resolve that your wedded life will be happy, but you can and will resolve that it shall be noble . . . the warm and generous heart of this people takes you today into itself. Will you not, in response, take that heart, with all its joys and sorrows, into your own?"

When the present Queen married Prince Philip, King George VI paid one

of the finest ever compliments to his consort.

The King wrote to Princess Elizabeth: "I have watched you grow up all these years with pride under the skilful direction of Mummy, who as you know is the most marvellous person in the world in my eyes . . ."

Bringing up two daughters, having to support a less-than-confident husband and carrying out arduous public duties cannot have been an easy task.

Yet, as we now all know, Elizabeth proved how justified was the King's high praise of her.

Princess Elizabeth was born on 21 April 1926, at the Duchess of York's parents' home in Bruton Street, Mayfair. By all accounts it was not an easy birth.

The baby was christened Elizabeth Alexandra Mary by the Archbishop of York in the private chapel at Buckingham Palace.

The ecstatic father wrote to Queen Mary: "You don't know what a tremendous joy it is to Elizabeth and me to have our own little girl."

The Queen attends a flower festival at Westminster Cathedral in July 1979, and wears flowers in her hat for the occasion. **Above** *Onlookers take the opportunity for a quick photograph as the Queen passes by.* **Right** *The Queen with the Roman Catholic Archbishop of Westminster, Cardinal Hume, inside the Cathedral.* **Far right** *She drives away, accompanied by the Duke of Edinburgh who also attended the festival.*

driving in the area: "I felt a great wish to preserve, if I could, this ancient dwelling."

Perhaps the Archbishop of York, the Most Reverend Cosmo Lang, foresaw the hard years ahead in his wedding address: "You, dear bride, in your Scottish home, have grown up from childhood among country folk and friendship with them has been your

For most couples the following few months would be an idyllic period of settling down together as a family with their first child. Not for the Yorks, however. The baby had hardly been taken home, when the Duke and Duchess were told that they were going to Australia and New Zealand on an official tour.

The tour was to be their first major public duty together in the Empire – but they had to abandon their first child in London for six months in the hands of Nanny Clara Knight.

The nurse had been in charge of the young Elizabeth from birth, but the first-time mother had the natural

worries of any woman over leaving her child behind.

When she and Bertie were leaving home to board the battleship *Renown* for their journey across the globe, the young mum went back twice to kiss her baby after she had placed Elizabeth in the nurse's arms in the hallway. On the way to the railway station from Bruton Street the chauffeur had to circle Grosvenor Gardens twice so that Elizabeth could recover her composure before facing the crowds.

Throughout the tour cables were sent each week to the anxious parents giving news of their daughter. A photographer took pictures of the child so that they would miss as little as possible of their daughter's progress.

These little touches helped, but how many mothers could endure the first few months of their child's life in this way?

The tour was, nevertheless, a roaring success, much of it due to Elizabeth. Bertie had to make several speeches,

Top picture More flowers for the Queen during her three-day State Visit to Denmark as the guest of Queen Margrethe II and Prince Hendrik in May 1979. **Above right** The Queen admits that she is "not particularly renowned for my green fingers" but she pays an annual visit to the Chelsea Flower Show, held in the grounds of the Royal Hospital: she is seen here in April 1980. **Above** The Queen talks with photographic staff during her tour of Fleet Street newspaper offices in March 1976. **Right** The Queen meeting foreign students when she visited Overseas House in London in December 1980.

but, with his stammer, every one was a terrible ordeal.

Before leaving England, he had taken lessons from a speech therapist which helped to improve his delivery in private – but public speaking held other terrors. Elizabeth would each evening help him rehearse a speech for the next day . . . then sit on the platform or stage looking straight ahead pretending not to notice as he struggled to get his words out.

This strong, silent support in public and her painstaking help in private eventually brought its rewards with almost-perfect diction in the end . . . but this took many years to achieve.

When they returned from their first overseas tour – and everywhere they went she was a sensation – Elizabeth was reunited with a daughter who had grown to twice the size while she was away.

The royal pair, united as a proper family at last, then spent three blissful years together in their new home at 145 Piccadilly.

These were the days of the flappers . . . the Roaring Twenties . . . the Charleston and daring new American cocktails. Their new home was bang in the middle of the startling new wave of nightlife and they joined in briefly with the rest of the "darlings" of their generation.

They often dined out in public and went to the neighbourhood nightclubs,

though Elizabeth with her love of dancing, had more enthusiasm for this way of life than Bertie.

The twenties were also the days when the workers of Britain were beginning to protest against their pitiable working conditions and appalling slum housing.

Bertie and Elizabeth, showing a care for the underdog that she still has today, hoped they could use their influence to improve the lot of the bulk of the population. She was frequently hostess to both trade union leaders as well as bosses at number 145 when they came to discuss how the sad state of the nation away from the nightclubs could be improved.

Elizabeth did not merely hand around cups of tea and cream cakes, she also accompanied the Duke on tours of depressed areas.

Her interest in the pathetic conditions of the slum-dwellers was not limited just to smiling at them through the windows of a passing limousine. She would talk of what she had witnessed and try to put pressure on the politicians and leading industrialists who also called at her salon.

She and Bertie sought to find a more useful, positive role for royalty. The Duke paid tribute to her help in a speech once at Glasgow: "No-one knows better than I do how great is the

When the old social ritual of the presentation of debutantes to the Queen was abolished in 1957, it was replaced by a series of summer garden parties at Buckingham Palace and Holyroodhouse. **Above left and left** *The Queen talks with groups of guests in the grounds of Buckingham Palace in July 1979.* **Above** *A contingent from the Far East at one of the parties in 1969.* **Opposite page, above** *A small section of the many hundreds of guests taking tea during a garden party in the late 1960's.* **Opposite page, below** *The view from the top of Buckingham Palace shows the enormous size of the parties, as the lines form ready for the Queen to appear: another picture from 1979.*

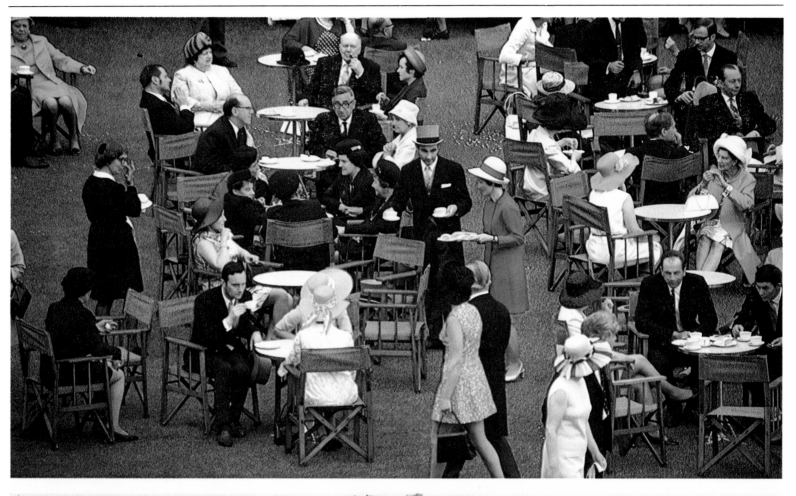

In May 1976 the Queen presented new colours to the 1st and 2nd Battalions of the Coldstream Guards in the grounds of Windsor Castle. **Left** The Queen inspected her soldiers as they stood in precise ranks **below left. Below** The presentation of the new colours to the standard-bearer and **bottom** a quick chat with officers before the ceremony. **Bottom left** After the presentation, the new colour was borne before the Queen as the Guard marched past.

help which she has given me in my public duties."

Flappers and social work apart, the Yorks were still a family as well as public do-gooders. Four years after the birth of Princess Elizabeth, their second child came along.

In view of what happened in a stormy later life that is now so well publicised, it might seem almost appropriate that Princess Margaret Rose was born on a day of thunder and lightning.

The Duchess gave birth to Margaret at Glamis Castle on 21 August 1930. She was the first member of the Royal Family to be born in Scotland for more than 300 years.

While the weary mother wanted to

recuperate in peace, the local pipe band celebrated the event noisily by marching about the neighbourhood with a small army of villagers, rounding off the day with a bonfire on a nearby hill. Fortunately the Queen Mother likes the sound of pipes.

A name that first came to mind for the new arrival was Ann. There would have been quite a mediaeval ring to "Anne of York", but King George V was against it.

The Duke was completely captivated by his new daughter. From birth she was a beautiful child, with dark blue eyes that always seemed to sparkle.

The two sisters were also a great joy to their grandfather. While the Yorks were living in Piccadilly, the Duchess would occasionally hold the eldest child at an upstairs window so she could wave good morning to her grandfather standing at a window half a mile away across Green Park in Buckingham Palace.

The West End address was useful for being near the rest of the family and their society friends, but the excitement of the nightclub life began to wear off. Elizabeth and Bertie wanted a

In Scotland, the Queen is Sovereign of the Order of the Thistle and she attends an annual service at St Giles' Cathedral in Edinburgh, as she does at Windsor for the Order of the Garter. **Above** *The Queen, followed by Prince Philip, leaves the Cathedral, past ranks of heralds, after a service in May 1969.* **Left** *The Queen in the full robes of the Order.*

better-ordered and tranquil life in surroundings suitable for bringing up children.

Life for the two girls was becoming too public. If Elizabeth wanted to go for a walk or play among flowers, trees and ducks like any other child, she had to do so under the gaze of the staring crowds in Hyde Park or Battersea Park.

The two Princesses became such public property that passengers would travel on the top deck of buses just to look down into the back garden of 145.

By this stage the royal parents realised they must find somewhere more private outside London.

They chose as a country retreat the Royal Lodge in Windsor Great Park, a

house once occupied by the Prince Regent.

It was in a bad state of repair, and the gardens needed attention, but the Yorks grabbed the chance of taking over the lodge like any other young couple who wanted to create their own "home".

The building and grounds not only became a weekend retreat, but also their favourite house, as Elizabeth jumped into the task of being a country-wife and home-maker; choosing furniture, picking curtains, stocking the kitchens, ordering a coat of fresh paint here and new wallpaper there.

It might have been a bit too chintzy for modern tastes, but she turned a neglected, old dwelling into a snug hide-away of domestic bliss. Making the place habitable took them more than a year.

Here the York children grew up in a family environment that our present Queen remembers well and has tried to create for her own children.

Princess Elizabeth, who called herself Lilibet because it was easier to pronounce, was given her first pony there.

As Margaret grew up she followed her mother's lead in learning to play the piano. She is still an accomplished musician and she and the Queen Mother play duets together.

The entire family had to "muck-in" and sort out the garden, which was a disordered mess of weeds and thorn bushes. Elizabeth and Margaret were given their own special part of the garden to work on, though neither of them developed the same enthusiasm for horticulture that the Queen Mother shows even today.

Windsor was where one of the Royal

Royal inspection time. **Opposite page** *The Queen inspecting a detachment of the Yeomen of the Guard in 1979.* **Far left** *The Queen chats to an old soldier during the Founders Day Parade at the Royal Hospital, Chelsea in June 1975.* **Left** *Princess Anne meets the Army on manoeuvres, during a visit to one of her regiments in West Germany.* **Below** *Princess Margaret, seemingly out of context in evening dress, inspecting a guard of honour during a two day visit to army units in West Germany in May 1980.* **Bottom picture** *Bearskins off, and three cheers for the Queen after the presentation of colours in 1977.*

173

Family's "doggie" lineage began. Those famous corgis entered the scene. The first of the long line was introduced – Rozavel Golden Eagle, known to the family as "Dookie". The Duchess had grown up with dogs around her and she thought her children should have their company too.

Elizabeth and Bertie lived like any other family at Windsor. There was laughter and fun away from servants, mother could cook, in her own kitchen, simple meals that did not have the usual formality of banquets.

Bath-time was just as in any other household, with giggling youngsters flinging soapsuds into the eyes of mum and dad. There was a nursery where Elizabeth would read the girls bed-time stories, and later, when they were old enough, she taught them to read.

The Royal Lodge was a place for happy childhood. When the Queen Mother stays there these days, it brings back her fondest memories.

While the education of the two girls was taken care of by their famous governess "Crawfie", the Duchess had to take on the role of preparing the children for their royal futures.

This involved schooling them in how to greet various persons "of rank" whom they would meet in the course of

their lives. Elizabeth would enter the room where the girls were playing and announce herself as perhaps a visiting king, prime minister or bishop to test them on the correct responses.

As the girls grew up Elizabeth had to cope with the usual chores of every mother. Helping them with their homework . . . making sure they behaved properly outside the home . . . choosing clothes and taking them to parties . . . and the early confusion of being teenagers.

All these maternal duties were more difficult because the family was so much in the public eye.

Then there were the feelings of both joy and anxiety when her daughters fell in love.

Princess Elizabeth's romance with Philip was so delightfully uncomplica-

Above *The large and impressive military display which greeted the arrival of President Saragat of Italy at Windsor Castle for a four-day State Visit in April 1969. These lines of soldiers and the mounted guards behind them are drawn from the Household Brigades, and their colour is lowered as the Royal procession passes by.* **Left** *Another visitor to Britain – this time in May 1967 – was the late King Faisal of Saudi-Arabia: he drives with the Queen through Hyde Park in London to watch a ceremonial display by the Hussars* **opposite page.**

ted that it seems almost out of a fairy tale, while Princess Margaret's turbulent relationships have always needed the help of a devoted, understanding and forgiving mother.

The year 1936 was a year of destiny that changed the future of Britain and that of Elizabeth Bowes-Lyon.

On the death of George V, the Prince of Wales came to the Throne as Edward VIII – only to give it up in less than a year to go into voluntary exile and

marry the American divorcee Mrs Wallis Simpson.

He had begun his reign seemingly full of promise but 325 days later he proved a failure as a monarch.

By the time the King decided he preferred his divorcee to the throne, the Duchess of York had been one of the royals for 13 years. Yet she dreaded the moment when kingship was thrust on her husband's unwilling shoulders.

George V had always regarded Bertie as a second fiddle, denying him access to State papers, considering them to be none of his business. It had never been expected that he would be a king, so he was never provided with the special education and grooming for monarchy.

The womanising and night-clubbing of her husband's elder brother were of a world the Duchess had little liking for.

Although his world was not their world, Uncle David was a welcome visitor who amused the two Princesses with his natural frivolity. He was always such fun and he enjoyed being

voiced abroad, Elizabeth and Bertie could see trouble brewing from the very start of Edward's relationship with the divorcee from Baltimore. They feared the final outcome because there could be no suggestion of a king marrying a divorced woman and remaining king.

It was a hurtful time, in which Elizabeth feared Bertie and herself could come out the losers. By all accounts she did not approve of Mrs Simpson and even today the whole business is something she will not discuss, even with her most intimate friends.

in a family atmosphere that he, by the age of 42, had never managed to create for himself.

Trouble came to a head when King George V died at Sandringham in January 1936, with the Duchess of York among those taking part in the harrowing vigil around the death bed.

Although the British public did not know of the rumours that were being

When her husband had to shoulder unexpected kingship, she had to lay aside the private life they both valued so much. She has always felt that Bertie's life was probably shortened as a result of being burdened with the responsibilities laid upon him by the Abdication.

The Duke and Duchess of York, and the rest of the family meanwhile,

developed that very British trait of behaving in an impeccably polite but frosty manner when Edward brought "that woman" into their company.

In her memoirs, the Duchess of Windsor recalls an occasion when she and Edward got a cold reception when they called on the Yorks to show them a new American station-wagon. "It was a pleasant hour, but I left with a distinct impression that while the Duke of York was sold on the American station-wagon, the Duchess was not sold on David's other interest."

The Royal Family hoped the Mrs Simpson affair was an infatuation that would pass, just as his other women in the past had faded.

Then the King was dead – and it was long live King Edward VIII, even though he wanted to marry a divorced commoner, and a foreigner to boot.

The events of the next two years were to shake the monarchy, some still say irreparably, and the lives of Elizabeth, her husband and their children, were never to be the same again.

Now that brother David was King, though uncrowned, everyone hoped he would see sense and drop the American woman. Optimistically, Prime Minister Stanley Baldwin said at the time of the accession: ". . . he has the secret of youth in the prime of age; he has a wider and more intimate knowledge of all classes of his subjects, not only at home, but throughout the Dominions and India, than any of his predecessors . . . we look forward with confidence and assurance to the new reign."

The Queen holds regular inspections of her personal bodyguards at ceremonies at Buckingham Palace and Windsor. The most widely known of her bodyguards are the Yeomen of the Guard, or Beefeaters, who took part in an inspection ceremony in July 1974. **Top left** *The Queen with officers on the terrace of Buckingham Palace before inspection.* **Opposite page, top** *A proud and smiling Queen walks down the lines of Yeomen.* **Opposite page, lower** *After the inspection, a salute of three cheers for Her Majesty.* **Left** *The Queen poses against a background of scarlet, gold and white in this official photograph of the occasion.*

crisis . . . enter into a morganatic marriage, whereby she would be his wife, but not his Queen, and their children would have no position in the line of succession . . . or he could renounce her.

Edward VIII struggled in a battle for several months with his ministers and his own sense of duty to both the woman he loved and his country.

The agonies of waiting by the Duke

He underestimated the influence of Mrs Wallis Simpson. The late King had had no illusions, for he is reputed to have told Baldwin: "After I am gone, the boy will ruin himself in 12 months." And to have told a close family friend: "I pray to God that my eldest son will never marry and have children, and that nothing will come between Bertie and Lilibet and the Throne."

Soon after he became King, Edward began to lose interest in the job, especially when he realised that it was the Government that ruled the country, and not him. His advice was by no means always welcomed or taken.

He did not bother to keep up with Cabinet papers and made few public appearances. His entire life was centred around Wallis Simpson.

Wallis was granted her second divorce – from Ernest Simpson – discreetly, at Ipswich, on 27 October 1936. But when the public got to know of it the storm broke. While Elizabeth and Bertie waited anxiously the King had to make one of three choices.

Defy his ministers, marry the woman he loved and bring about a monumental

The Duke and Duchess of Windsor on their way to attend the unveiling of a memorial plaque to the Duke's mother, the late Queen Mary, in June 1967 – in the centenary year of her birth – at Marlborough House **above left. Above** *The Windsors leaving Claridge's for the ceremony.*

and Duchess of York did not go unnoticed by the love-torn King. Edward, by then the Duke of Windsor, acknowledged their bewilderment in his memoirs.

"Bertie had most at stake: it was he who would have to wear the Crown if I left, and his genuine concern for me was mixed up with the dread of having to assume the responsibilities of kingship."

But Edward wanted to have his monarchial cake and still eat it, keeping the Throne and Mrs Simpson. "I cannot with full heart carry out my duties in the loneliness that surrounds me," he said.

Eventually he made his monumental decision. He told Prime Minister Baldwin: "I want you to be the first to know I have made my mind up and

December 1936: "I never wanted this to happen. I'm quite unprepared for it.

"I've never even seen a State paper. I'm only a naval officer, it's the only thing I know about."

Those close to the King believed he could not have done the job without the support of Elizabeth. He acknowledged this himself in his first New Year's message to the Empire and the Commonwealth when he said he shouldered his new responsibilities "with all the more confidence in the knowledge that the Queen and my mother Queen Mary are at my side".

He also paid full tribute to Elizabeth in another broadcast: "With my wife and helpmeet by my side, I take up the heavy task which lies before me."

The abdication had not helped the future of the monarchy. Millions of subjects across the globe needed reassurances that the institution would

The Duke died on 28th May 1972, only a month before his 78th birthday. His body was flown from his Paris home to Gloucestershire for a temporary lying-in-state **opposite page, top right** before it was transferred to Windsor **opposite page, lower right** for a public lying-in-state **above.** The funeral took place on 5th June, and was attended by many members of the Royal Family, including the Queen, Prince Philip and the Queen Mother seen, **upper right,** with the Duchess of Windsor, and Princess Margaret and Lord Snowdon **lower right. Left** The Duchess says farewell to the Dean of Windsor as she leaves for Paris after the funeral.

nothing will alter it. I mean to abdicate and marry Mrs Simpson."

During the final hours of decision-making Elizabeth was in bed with influenza. When news came that she was to be Queen she said to her children's governess, Marion Crawford: "I am afraid there are going to be great changes in our life, Crawfie . . . we must take what is coming to us, and make the best of it."

According to the late Lord Louis Mountbatten, a frightened George VI told him on the first night of his reign in

survive untarnished. They doubted its value.

If ever a lack-lustre, shy and nervous princeling turned reluctant king needed the help of a strong woman it was now.

His speech impediment, delicate health and general lack of confidence were liabilities that did little to encourage his new subjects. Many

The Queen and other members of the Royal Family at the annual Remembrance Day service at the Cenotaph in Whitehall, in November 1979. **Top right** *The Queen places her wreath at the foot of the Cenotaph, followed by Prince Philip* **right** *and Prince Charles* **lower right.** *From the Home Office balcony, the ceremony is watched by (left to right)* **above** *King Olav V of Norway, Princess Michael of Kent, Princess Alice of Gloucester, Captain Mark Phillips and Princess Anne, and the Queen Mother.*

thought that he would be just a rubber-stamp king.

Elizabeth knew that it was vital that she should back her husband solidly to restore confidence in a shaken monarchy and nation.

She was firmly convinced that she could do the job; she felt the British people would be behind her, and so she set out to sustain the new King through thick and thin.

Elizabeth had always seemed to be taking the lead, knowing instinctively how to approach strangers and put them at their ease. But a change became noticeable. The King finally found confidence in himself and was able to give support to his wife.

No-one was happier than Elizabeth to see how things were developing. She was so proud of her husband, and the way he had measured up to his responsibilities.

Above *A full view of the wreath-laying in November 1972.* **Above right** *The Queen laying her wreath on that occasion and* **opposite page** *standing back at her place, with the Duke of Kent and Prince Philip behind her.* **Right** *Prince Charles laying his wreath during the 1976 service.*

She accompanied him on public engagements and official tours. Her support became legendary.

It is a tribute to her courage that she changed from an unambitious duchess to a determined wife of the reigning monarch in a matter of days.

By the time they went on their first State visit to Paris early in 1938, Elizabeth was firmly in control in her role. So much so, that the French were completely won over.

As the early years of kingship progressed, George became more sure of himself. He found, with some surprise, that interest and affection were directed towards him as well as towards the Queen.

Britain there was another, more serious crisis.

Elizabeth was barely a queen before she and the man she had transformed from George the Meek into a confident, but still self-effacing leader, needed all the strength they could muster. They had to cope with wartime leadership.

As horrific as it was, and as great as the suffering of the British people was during the Second World War, it resulted not only in victory, but also gave a tremendous boost to the reputation of the monarchy.

After the Windsor debacle, royalty needed help, and it was during those six dark years from 1939 to 1945 that the people's loyalty to the Crown was re-established.

Most of the credit for this has been given by historians to Queen Elizabeth, the Queen Mother. Deservedly so.

By the time war broke out most parents with money or influence were sending their children out of the cities or even out of the country altogether – to America, Canada and Australia.

The Princesses, Elizabeth, now aged 13, and Margaret, aged nine, were already at Balmoral, so it was decided to leave them there for the time being. King George and Queen Elizabeth decided to set an example to the rest of Britain, however, by staying at home.

A basement room in Buckingham Palace was converted into an air-raid shelter, although the style was slightly different from most back-garden dug-outs.

It was furnished with regency chairs and a settee, and the reading matter – replaced regularly by servants – was mainly hunting, shooting and fishing or society magazines, such as *Country Life* and *Sphere*.

It would be hard to find in British history a consort who equalled the achievements of Elizabeth in being a "helpmeet" or who achieved such popular esteem and private worth.

But she still had her doubts. Elizabeth once asked Ramsay MacDonald, the Scots politician, a few months after she became Queen: "Am I doing all right?"

The joint reign began among chaos, but just as they were beginning to establish themselves in the soul of

It is now an annual event for the Queen Mother to plant a wooden cross in the Royal British Legion's Field of Remembrance at Westminster Abbey two or three days before Remembrance Sunday. In these photographs she talks with the Pensioners of the Royal Hospital, Chelsea and walks beside the long lines of wooden crosses on the lawns of the Abbey before planting her own cross **left** *in front of the Legion's wreath of poppies.*

This essentially simple act of remembrance is no mere formal ceremony for the Queen Mother, who has known and suffered the loss of close relatives in the conflicts thus commemorated. Of her six brothers, one was wounded, another taken prisoner, and a third killed during the First World War; one of her nephews and her brother-in-law Prince George, Duke of Kent, were killed in action in World War II.

spected the damage later with her husband and Winston Churchill, was one which endeared her forever to those Londoners who were in danger nightly. "I'm glad we've been bombed," she said, "It makes me feel I can look the East End in the face."

Bombs fell six times on royal homes during the war, including 145 Picca-

Before the expected bombardment of Britain began the royal couple toured the country, calling at army camps, munitions factories and the back streets of small towns. The Queen's cheerfulness and that ever-present smile worked wonders on the morale of other women who were worried about the fate of their own children and menfolk.

When German bombers began their devastating shelling, Elizabeth visited the cities most heavily bombed: Coventry and Plymouth, and frequently the East End of London.

George and Elizabeth slept at Windsor during the raids, but were always back at Buckingham Palace by daylight. Their London home was bombed twice... once on the night of 10 September 1940 and again three days later during a daring daylight raid.

They had a narrow escape during the second attack when two bombs exploded in the palace quadrangle below the windows of a room they were both occupying at the time.

The Queen's reaction, when she in-

dilly. It was completely destroyed.

The more the bombing in the East End, the more frequent did the Queen's visits become to the homeless, wounded and bereaved.

As one cockney bomb victim put it; "She came with courage in her eyes and when she left she left some of it with you. Suddenly you felt like carrying on when you hadn't before."

Churchill, never at a loss for the right words, was more colourful; "Many an aching heart found some solace in her gracious smile."

armies in North Africa there was a blackout on his movements and, as she told Queen Mary later, "I imagined every sort of horror and walked up and down my room staring at the telephone."

Elizabeth also insisted on sharing, where possible, the deprivation of the rest of Britain. She bought no further clothes other than the normal ration allowance, making do with what she had collected before the war . . . still mainly Hartnell, though frequently patched up, for six years.

Heating in the palaces was cut down to the minimum. Extra warm woollies had to do, while a tiny electric fire would heat bedrooms. To save fuel again there was a line painted nine inches above the plug-holes in baths to mark the emergency hot water limit.

Meals were stipulated by Elizabeth

4th August 1980 – and London celebrates the 80th birthday of Queen Elizabeth the Queen Mother. A band marched past Clarence House that morning, playing "Happy Birthday to You" **right** *while an unprecedented number of well-wishers showed their affection for their Queen Mother with banners, balloons applause and song.* **Below right** *Brownies look over a monster birthday card which they had prepared in honour of the event.* **Above** *The Queen and Princess Margaret help the Queen Mother as she receives gifts from her admirers.*

And that was in the days when victory seemed unlikely and there was not much to smile about.

Elizabeth also shared with the people on the other side of the palace gates the suffering of losing someone in the war. Tragedy came to the family in 1942, when Bertie's youngest brother, the 39-year-old Duke of Kent was killed in an air crash when the present Prince Michael of Kent was only seven weeks old.

The Queen Mother immediately took on the task of bringing solace to his widow and the rest of her in-laws, especially the stricken Dowager Queen Mary.

She shared the same worries as others, too. When the King flew to his

to be the same as everyone else was getting on ration. The mainly meatless sausages and powdered eggs were still served on gold and silver dishes, though. Certain standards had obviously to be maintained.

When food rationing ended, Elizabeth recalled proudly; "Even our bread was the same kind of war bread every other family had to eat. Except for game that occasionally appeared, nothing was served that was not served in any ordinary war canteen."

Right *The Queen Mother emerging from the drive of Clarence House to acknowledge the greetings of the waiting crowd. Behind her are the Queen and Princess Margaret, and four of the Queen Mother's six grandchildren: Lady Sarah Armstrong-Jones, Viscount Linley, Prince Edward and the Prince of Wales.* **Below** *The Queen Mother, clearly delighted by the crowd's congratulations, takes up the rhythm of their birthday choruses.* **Below right** *The Queen Mother holding one of the many sprays of flowers and birthday cards offered to her.* **Below, far right** *She waves from the balcony of Clarence House to the crowds below.*

When war broke out, there was very little respect for the monarchy. King George VI had been on the Throne for less than three years and was an unproved leader, with a reputation for weakness.

Thanks to the supportive efforts of Elizabeth – both publicly and behind-the-scenes – George emerged at the end of the world's greatest conflict as a man of great strength, both spiritually and physically, who helped to inspire the country through so many perilous years, indeed, the whole Royal Family emerged with its reputation revitalised: to become the institution that is so respected and loved today.

Churchill was able to write to George after victory was won; "This war has drawn the Throne and the people more closely together than was ever before recorded, and Your Majesties are more beloved by all classes and conditions than any of the princes of the past."

Looking over the King's shoulder when he read that letter was Elizabeth ... smiling, of course.

Although there was happiness, especially with the marriage of a daughter and future queen to the man she loved, the last few years of Elizabeth's life with her husband were clouded by his ill-health.

He had to have an operation, lumbar sumpathectomy, to relieve thrombosis in his leg. Then, in 1951, cancer was diagnosed and a lung was removed. He had always been a heavy smoker – in private – and his recovery amazed the nation.

Throughout her married life the Queen Mother had to take some hard knocks, but this was the hardest blow of all. For three years she knew her husband, who by this time she loved so

dearly, was slowly dying.

She smiled in public, as did all the family, and those in the know gave the impression that nothing was wrong. George VI was alive . . . long live the King.

How many women could keep so public a family together . . . give great comfort to a doomed husband . . . and still keep smiling when she showed her face? Superhuman behaviour that is usually required only of our monarchy.

Opposite page *The Queen Mother hands over some of the scores of presents she received on her birthday to the Queen and Princess Margaret. The Queen Mother was greeted in style by the Society of Toastmasters who toasted her health in vintage champagne* **top. Above** *Prince Charles and Prince Edward exchange comments as Princess Margaret watches the Queen Mother's reception. The Queen Mother accepted all gifts offered to her:* **right** *she takes a small parcel from a young boy.*

After the removal of his left lung, George VI never recovered his strength. Elizabeth gave him love, confidence and strength but these were not enough.

During the worst part of his illness, Princess Elizabeth was pregnant, expecting Prince Charles. The Queen Mother insisted that her daughter should not know the real state of her father's health, lest it should affect the birth of the baby.

But as a new life entered the world, the baby's grandfather was lying sick under the same roof in Buckingham Palace.

At the beginning of 1952, the King went to London Airport to see Elizabeth and Philip fly out to Africa on a royal tour.

Their last view of King George was of a very sick man as he waved them on their way. They had got as far as Kenya when George died in his sleep at Sand-

made me by your wonderful tributes to my dear husband, a great and noble King.

"No man had a deeper sense than he of duty and of service, and no man was more full of compassion for his fellow men.

"He loved you all, every one of you, most truly. That, you know, was what he always tried to tell you in his yearly message at Christmas; that was the pledge he took at the sacred moment of his Coronation 15 years ago.

"Now I am left alone, to do what I can to honour that pledge without him."

Elizabeth, Queen Mother, refused to allow sorrow to overcome her. Within a day of her husband's death she was

The official celebrations of the Queen Mother's eightieth birthday in London on 15th July 1980. **Opposite page** *The main body of the procession in the Mall on its way to St Paul's Cathedral.* **Top left** *The Queen Mother with the Prince of Wales in the procession. Among the many members of the Royal Family who attended were Princess Anne and Lady Sarah Armstrong-Jones* **left,** *and the Gloucester family, including the Duke and his son Alexander, Earl of Ulster* **above** *and his wife, the Duchess, and mother Princess Alice* **bottom left.**

ringham on February 6. He had lived 56 years.

The next time she saw her daughter, the Queen Mother had to bow to the new Sovereign. Although desolate with grief, she kept her feelings hidden as preparations were made for the funeral.

Protocol demanded that she send a message to the millions around the world who shared her sadness:

"Your concern for me has upheld me in my sorrow and how proud you have

playing with her first two grandchildren, Charles and Anne.

"I have got to start sometime and it is better now than later," she said.

She decided to find a new role for herself; not seeking to emulate the desolated Queen Victoria as a permanent widow in black.

She was soon out and about again, making the rounds of garden parties, military reviews, ceremonials and the rest. But, after being a consort for so long, she went to great lengths not to overshadow her daughter, who at so

young an age had had to take on so much responsibility.

In whatever she did, the Queen Mother made it clear that she was now "Number Two" . . . Britain had a new Elizabethan Age.

The colourful spectacle of the thanksgiving service for the Queen Mother's eightieth birthday at St Paul's Cathedral. **Left** *The Queen Mother accompanied by the Queen, and followed by Prince Philip, and his sons, proceed to their places.* **Below left** *Other members of the family, including Princess Alexandra, Prince and Princess Michael, the Duke and Duchess of Kent, the family of Princess Alice, Duchess of Gloucester, Princess Margaret, Princess Anne and Captain Phillips, make their way up the nave of the Cathedral.* **Below right** *Members of the Royal Family await the arrival of the Queen Mother.* **Below** *The scene as the Queen Mother is joined by the Queen and Prince Philip, and the service begins.*

There are many sides to the Queen Mother . . . and they are all good.

During her public and private life in Scotland she leaves a trail of fond memories and anecdotes.

Her boundless energy, sense of humour, courage and thoughtfulness see to that.

The Queen Mother's courage is spot-

lighted in a wartime story never told before.

During a tour of Kingseat Hospital, near Aberdeen – turned over to the Navy and its dreadful casualties from the convoys to Russia – the official party passed a closed door.

As if she had sixth sense, the Queen

Left and below *The scene at St Paul's Cathedral at the end of the service of thanksgiving for the Queen Mother's eightieth birthday: she chats with the Lord Mayor of London as she awaits the arrival of the carriage, whilst her children and grandchildren and other members of the Royal Family stand behind.*

Below left *The Queen Mother and Prince of Wales and* **below** *Princess Margaret, Lady Sarah Armstrong-Jones and Princess Anne in the procession.* **Opposite, below** *The Queen and Prince Philip with Prince Andrew and Prince Edward leaving Buckingham Palace.* **Opposite, above** *The procession returns to the Palace after the service.*

asked what was behind that door and was told it was a very badly-injured and burned Navy officer.

She was told: "It might distress you to go in. He is so bad he is in a room by himself."

The Queen replied: "But that is the very reason why I should go in."

She spent some time in the room alone with the officer, talking and comforting him.

The Queen Mother still shows her special brand of courage when she dons waders and walks into deep pools on the River Dee to fish for salmon.

"She is quite fearless. I have seen her waist-deep in fast-flowing parts of the Dee," said one local angler.

Her sense of humour bubbles to the top when times are hard.

For instance, as she struggled to land a salmon on the Dee a few years ago, a coachload of tourists spotted her and converged on the opposite bank.

The protective gillie tried to shield her from the unexpected guests and catch the salmon's tail at the same time as she brought it in.

But the double act was too much and the fish slipped from him and got away.

The colourful pageantry of the Queen Mother's eightieth birthday celebrations in London on 15th July 1980. **Left and opposite page, bottom** The Queen Mother, accompanied by Prince Charles, leaves Buckingham Palace at the beginning of the drive to St Paul's Cathedral. **Far left** The Duke and Duchess of Kent waving to the crowds. **Below** The Queen, Prince Philip, Prince Andrew and Prince Edward. **Lower right** Prince and Princess Michael of Kent share a carriage with Princess Alexandra of Kent, her husband Angus Ogilvy, and their daughter Marina. **Opposite page, top** The Queen Mother's carriage returns from Admiralty Arch up the Mall towards Buckingham Palace.

Despite it all the Queen Mother returned the smiles and waves of the tourists and accepted the loss more graciously than any other angler might have done.

Her ancestral home is Glamis Castle, still in the hands of the Strathmore family.

She has strong links with Glamis and her love of the area is reflected on annual visits to Lord Roberts' workshop in Dundee where disabled ex-Servicemen are employed.

The same pride is shown by the people of Mey in Caithness, where the Queen Mother added the Castle of Mey to her Deeside home of Birkhall as a Scottish residence, after she was widowed.

It is largely due to her presence that the local branch of the British Legion built a club and hall for the community.

Each year in August, at the Legion's Sports Day, the Queen Mum arrives to walk round informally, speaking to locals and tourists.

To the locals one of her good deeds

Formal and informal groups after the Queen Mother's eightieth birthday celebrations in July 1980. **Opposite page** *The Queen Mother with her two daughters, her son-in-law and her grandchildren (and ultimately a publicity-seeking corgi) at Buckingham Palace after the service at St Paul's. A smaller group, with the Queen Mother and her grandchildren, was also photographed* **far right. Above** *The Royal Family on the balcony of the Palace as the Queen Mother acknowledges the acclamations of the crowd below.* **Right** *Prince Charles accompanied his grandmother on both journeys to and from the Cathedral that day.*

was to take over the castle and turn their Caithness backwater into a tourists boom area over the years.

Pressmen who have covered royal events in Scotland have many stories to tell of the Royal Lady they think is "fabulous". To them the word radiant should have been created specially for her.

While waiting with pressmen one day at Glen Muick, as a Highland regiment appeared from a Cairngorm march, she told them: "Isn't it a beautiful view," and then handed one of the

photographers part of her packed lunch – a banana!

She has a great love of Scottish music and dancing, and it was she who organised Scottish Country Dance lessons for her children and grandchildren at Balmoral.

Perhaps the feelings of Scotland for a most gracious Lady are best shown in the reasons why Aberdeen conferred the Freedom of the City on her in 1959. They were: "Manifold Services to the Commonwealth and Empire; fortitude in times of peril; the charm and grace of her personality."

As she sits in the apartments of her London home, Clarence House, in The Mall, she usually refers to her kinfolk at Buckingham Palace as "those along the road".

It is among "those" and their off-spring that the Queen Mother gets her greatest pleasure these days. She is, after all, not only a grandma but, thanks to Princess Anne, a great-grandmother.

With the children of other royals also clamouring for her jolly company as well, she is also a very busy grand-parent, and grand-auntie.

Of more than a score of children, teenagers and mature young people who lay claim to her time, no-one is closer to her than Prince Charles.

He once wrote about the Queen Mother: "I admit that I am hopelessly biased and completely partisan. Ever since I can remember, my grandmother has been the most wonderful example of fun, laughter, warmth, infinite

security and above all else, exquisite taste in so many things.

"For me she has always been one of those extraordinarily rare people whose touch can turn everything to gold... Her greatest gift is to enhance life for others through her effervescent enthusiasm for life."

How many grandmas can sip their cocoa in the evenings with that sort of tribute ringing in their ears?

The Queen Mum began to enjoy grandparentage before she was widowed. Because of George's illness Elizabeth and Philip had to take on many royal duties, and this left Charles and Anne in the hands of their grandma.

When they were not on parade as royals, Philip still served abroad in the Royal Navy and Elizabeth would join

The photographs on this page were taken during the visit by the Queen Mother to the City Temple in London for a thanksgiving service to commemorate the 80th anniversary of the National Free Church Women's Council. She met Catherine Bramwell-Booth, the Church Army Commissioner, and her sister. This occasion was in April 1980, only a few months before the Queen Mother's own 80th birthday.

on this occasion with his grandfather, shortly before King George's death, is now one of the Queen Mother's most treasured mementoes.

Remembering how she had missed the early months of her own daughter's development whilst abroad, the Queen Mother spent every spare minute with her two grandchildren when their mother and father were away.

She bought Charles a miniature set of gardening tools, though they failed to arouse any permanent interest in becoming a royal son of the soil.

She set Princess Anne well on the road to her most famous – some think only – pursuit, riding, when she bought for her granddaughter's fourth birthday her first saddle.

Although today brother and sister

Above left *The Queen Mother with her two daughters at Windsor in June 1980: an official portrait by Norman Parkinson to commemorate her 80th birthday in August of that year.* **Far left** *The Queen Mother visiting the Ex-Servicemen's Mental Welfare Society Convalescence Home at Leatherhead in April 1980.* **Left** *Leaving St Paul's Cathedral in 1977.* **Above** *The scene at Clarence House on 4th August 1978, with the Queen Mother waving to the crowds who had come to wish her well on her birthday.*

him as a sailor's wife.

As a result, much of the early lives of Charles and Anne were spent in their grandmother's company. They are still incredibly close to her and seek her advice on any major decisions.

Her first grandchild came on the scene at 9.14 on the evening of 14 November 1948. Queen Elizabeth was the first to congratulate her daughter, after Prince Philip, and to thank her for giving her a grandson.

Princess Elizabeth said to a friend a few days later: "I still find it hard to believe I have a baby of my own!"

Another year and nine months passed and the Queen Mother was a grandma again with the birth of Princess Anne on 15 August 1950.

In October 1951, Princess Elizabeth and Prince Philip represented the King on a tour of America and Canada – so Charles had to spend his third birthday with his grandparents. A picture taken

understand and appreciate one another much more than they used to, their differences in temperament were clearly marked during their long stays with grandma.

The Queen Mother found Charles the more sensitive of the two – much more ready than his sister to run to granny when he fell over and grazed a knee, or ask for her support when he and Anne quarrelled.

Anne was a bossy little creature so

*Prince Charles is known to have a close affinity with his ancestors in his love of Balmoral Castle, and it was here that he chose to pose for official pictures to celebrate his thirtieth birthday on 14th November 1978. In some, he wears a Hunting Stewart kilt and sporran which belonged to his grandfather, King George VI. **Above and right** The Prince with his golden Labrador, Harvey.*

grandma had to take great care to make sure Charles grew out of his shyness and gained self-confidence.

As the time came round to choose a school for Charles, both the Queen Mother and the Queen were against the rigours of Gordonstoun.

Prince Philip strongly favoured sending his son to this spartan life in the north of Scotland. When Prince Charles expressed doubts about the school, his father pointed out: "It's near Balmoral. And your grandmother goes up there to fish. You can go and see her."

During his early days at Gordonstoun Charles was particularly grateful for the nearness of the Queen Mother. She very soon realised how lonely and homesick he was. On visits to her at Birkhall, on the Balmoral estate, the Queen Mother offered sympathy, gave her grandson the sort of food he liked

and cheered him up.

They have always had a relationship that seems more intimate than those of the others. When he was at school in Australia, and feeling a little lonely, the Queen Mother joined Charles to cheer him up, and they went fishing together for a few days in the Snowy Mountains above Melbourne.

Whenever Charles wants to escape from the formalities of his own hectic life he often joins her at one of her two homes in Scotland. At Balmoral they often go off casting for salmon together in the wild waters of the river Dee.

Charles reminds her of her late husband. She sees something of the late King's sensitivity to other people's thoughts and feelings in him.

Whenever he is travelling the world, he sends a steady stream of letters to "grannie", sharing his experiences with her.

She loves to hear all his news, to see how he's looking and make sure he's not

overdoing things – whether it be with friends or his daredevil adventures.

She has said: "He is a very gentle boy, with a very kind heart, which I think is the essence of everything."

They make one another laugh and find it the easiest thing in the world to talk to each other non-stop.

Although not as close, Princess Anne still stays in regular contact with her grandmother. After telling her mother, Anne 'phoned the Queen Mother to let her know that she was expecting her first baby.

Great-grandma was delighted when Master Peter Phillips was born on 15 November 1977. The Queen Mother said: "This is one of the happiest days of my life."

Master Phillips was the first grandchild of a ruling sovereign for five centuries to be born a commoner, yet he is fifth in line to the throne.

No-one is ever likely to replace Prince Charles in the Queen Mother's affections, but she always seems equally proud in the company of her next eldest grandson Andrew. She has seen him grow up from a mischievous toddler to a roving-eyed young man. She spots a touch of the Duke of Windsor in him.

The quiet Prince Edward, less flamboyant than his older brothers, impresses his grandma by being the "brains" of the family.

Where the gentle touch and kindness of a grandma has been most valuable, however, has been with Princess Margaret's children, Viscount Linley and Lady Sarah Armstrong-Jones.

After spending almost 60 years shaking hands with thousands, making speeches, laying foundation stones, launching ships, inspecting troops, attending banquets and touring the

The christening of Master Peter Phillips at Buckingham Palace on 22nd December 1977. **Above** *The Queen admires her first grandchild who had been born the previous month.* **Below** *Mother and child with senior members of the family, including the Queen Mother, Earl Mountbatten and Princess Alice, Countess of Athlone, then in her 95th year. The group below includes Prince Andrew, Princess Margaret and her son Viscount Linley, and the parents and sisters of Captain Phillips.*

world you would think she has had enough.

Not a bit of it. According to one of her staff: "We have a terrible job keeping her down. She always wants to be off and about doing things.

"There always seems to be yet another foundation stone to lay... a town she wants to visit again... or a banquet she fancies taking on because she enjoyed herself so much the last time.

"And, of course, she is so popular with all generations throughout the world that we have to turn down hundreds of invitations every year. It's

a pity, but she would push herself to exhaustion if we didn't do this.

"How she keeps up the pace is amazing, but I suppose she comes from an era when everyone expected to work hard. The way she puts every ounce of herself into whatever she's doing must shame many of the younger generation today."

One of her ladies-in-waiting is also reported to have said recently: "She is younger than any of us. We can't keep up with her."

As she whizzes about at a breathless rate she never appears to be bored, rarely shows she is irritable, even with the most annoying of hangers-on, and that glorious smile is always there.

splendidly-dressed officers in their scarlet trying not to look too perturbed because the day was proving a "wash-out" so she said to one of them: "I hope your colours don't run."

On another occasion recently, when she was launching a ship, the "Queen Mum" had to sit in a wheel-chair because she had sprained an ankle. The usually fussy group of big-wigs around her cared little that the thousands of shipyard workers and their families could not see her in the chair.

The Queen Mother was having none of this. She ignored the advice not to "stretch herself" and limped to the bow of the ship and placed herself in a spot where everyone could see her.

"It doesn't hurt too much and I'm still not so old that I can't walk, gentlemen," she said.

She is eager to tackle anything that's different. In all her years of sitting in innumerable grandstands around the

The photographs on the left show Master Peter Phillips dressed in the robe of Honiton lace used for Royal christenings since 1840, though not feeling totally at peace with the world! Captain Phillips looks on indulgently. **Below** *Three generations of the Royal Family as the Queen joins Princess Anne and her son.*

For a woman who has met so many in a lifetime of service, you would think that there is nothing new of interest in whatever she is doing or in those she meets.

Yet she still brings a warmth, approachability and sense of freshness to her royal duties which delights the crowds that clamour to see her.

As years have gone by and she has developed that image of a cuddly lady in pearls, she seems to succeed even further in turning a starchy ceremony into a relaxed get-together.

When, in March 1980, for example, she was presenting shamrock to the Irish Guards, of which she is colonel-in-chief, it poured with rain throughout the day.

She could see the humour in all the

Official pictures released to celebrate the thirtieth birthday of Princess Anne on 15th August 1980. **Above** *A delightful study of the Princess with her son, Peter, aged 2½, in the grounds of their home at Gatcombe Park in Gloucestershire.* **Right** *The Phillips trio; Captain Phillips joins his wife and son in the play area at their home.*

world you would think she must have seen every sport and activity possible, from tossing the caber to sheep-shearing.

But she heard this year that she had been invited to watch the Rugby League Cup Final at Wembley. "I like the look of that – I've never tried that before," she told her staff. So she went to see her first RL game and thoroughly enjoyed herself.

Children adore meeting her – that granny image again – and she always

makes a point of seeking them out. She invariably chooses the right words to say to nervous and curious kids.

One little lad asked her if it was true that her daughter was Queen and she replied in a matter-of-fact way; "Yes, isn't it exciting?"

She is associated with more than 300 organisations from the Aberdeen Angus Cattle Society, via the Royal School of Needlework and the Bar Musical Society to the small group of neighbours in Scotland, the Birkhall Women's Institute.

One of her favourite interests was until recently London University. She had been Chancellor since 1955, and over the years had kept more than 200 engagements with them. She liked mingling with the students because it kept her in touch with the attitudes of youth.

She was very proud of "her" centre of learning. In a speech she once referred to it, with a hint of a smile, when she said that "the Commonwealth is a loose association of states held together by the University of London."

Generations of students, many of them full of left-wing republican ideas, took her to their hearts. They were always inviting her along to the union and they made her a life member.

At their dances she gamely took the floor with escorts who were more used to disco hip-swinging than formal waltzes. She once reassured a stumbling president of the union, who was having great difficulty putting his feet in the right place: "Don't worry, you haven't knocked my tiara off yet."

There is a charming story of how she arrived once to find a demonstration organised by the London School of Economics taking place. The police tried to guide her away from it (she always has only one detective with her) but she insisted on going up to the leader who was holding a big placard.

"Good Lord, that's the man I was dancing with last night," she said. Sheepishly the leader laid down his placard. And everyone, of course, smiled. Especially the Queen Mum.

Her enthusiasm for gardening led her to accept the patronage of the London Gardens Society. This takes her away from the vast, carefully-laid-out acres of palaces and castles to simple, back-street homes within the capital.

The talk is usually about bedding-roses and fertiliser as she shares a cuppa and chat with fellow green-fingers. One nervous gardener trying to be on his best behaviour was astonished once when the Queen Mother told him in a matter-of-fact way "I always find horse manure seems best for roses – don't you?"

With such a well-known horsey family about her, the royal roses should be blooming.

On one of her gardening walks a woman of about her own age wished her a "happy birthday" when it was still a few weeks away. The Queen Mother asked her how she knew the birthday was due and the woman explained they both shared the same date, 4 August.

The royal visitor just nodded and

More official portraits of Princess Anne and her son. **Above left** *Mother and child in the Spring of 1978; a photograph released on Princess Anne's 28th birthday later that year.* **Above** *A formal study by Lord Snowdon, also published for the first time on Princess Anne's 28th birthday.* **Left** *A thirtieth birthday formal portrait of the Princess, taken this time by her cousin Patrick Lichfield at Gatcombe.*

said no more, but among the post at that suburban address a month later there was a greetings card from Clarence House.

Away from the public eye she likes to spend her days quietly with a few close friends and her grandchildren. She is very informal in private. She once told a companion to turn down the sound on television when the National Anthem was being played. "When you're not present, it's like hearing the Lord's Prayer while playing Canasta."

Depending on the time of year, she lives in the Royal Lodge at Windsor, Clarence House in London, where she does most of her entertaining, or at one of three homes in Scotland.

Summer usually finds her at Birkhall, the mansion on the Dee, and

auctions. One of her most recent acquisitions is a rug woven behind bars by an admiring prisoner who based the pattern on the colours of her coat-of-arms – gold, blue and green.

She uses Mey when she really wants to get away from everything... ceremony, noise and bustle, and even family.

She puts on old clothes and wellies for walks around the moors or along the shoreline, singing to the seals – though she rarely forgets to fling the odd string of her famous pearls around her neck, no matter how scruffy she's looking.

She says of Mey, after all these years of building up her own special hide-away; "It is a delight to me now."

She is a fanatic about health through exercise – and her longevity must be

not far from the rest of the family at Balmoral, or at either Glamis Castle or the Castle of Mey.

Mey, a lonely gale-swept place in Caithness in the far north of Scotland, has been one of her greatest extravagances.

When George VI died she inherited capital and private estates worth several million pounds. She used much of these funds to buy what was a grim, tumbledown house with wind howling through the chill corridors which were Macbeth-like in their gloom and foreboding.

Over the years she has installed central heating, and furnishes the castle with pieces of furniture from

Prince Michael of Kent married Baroness Marie-Christine von Reibnitz in 1978. Their son, Lord Frederick Windsor, was born on 6th April 1979, and the photographs above and opposite show him and his parents outside St James's Palace where he was christened on 11th July. The Queen attended the ceremony **centre left. Left** *The Queen with Prince and Princess Michael and their infant son.* **Top left** *The entire group of Royal guests which included Princess Olga of Yugoslavia and ex-King Constantine of the Hellenes.*

due to the fact that everyday come rain or storm, she goes out.

In Scotland she walks for mile upon mile without showing any signs of tiredness.

She has had two serious operations in the past, for stomach problems, but now she just has nothing more serious than the occasional cold. She would never use a minor ailment as an excuse to put off a public engagement.

Her sense of duty means ignoring ill-health, pushing oneself to the limits, never complaining.

Above right The Queen, with Prince Philip and Princess Anne, arrives at Claridge's for a State banquet given by the Grand Duke and Duchess of Luxembourg, during their visit to Britain in June 1972. **Above** Another visit to Claridge's for the Queen when President Gowon of Nigeria, as guest of Her Majesty, gave a banquet for her in June 1973. **Far right** The Queen with some of the Commonwealth Prime Ministers, including James Callaghan, Archbishop Makarios and Dr Hastings Banda, during the Commonwealth Conference in July 1977 in London. **Opposite page, above** The Queen with President and Mme Pompidou at the Versailles Theatre during their State Visit to France in May 1972. In October of the same year, the Queen and Duke of Edinburgh, this time accompanied by Princess Anne, paid a State Visit to Yugoslavia, and are seen **opposite page, below** with President Tito and Mme Broz before attending a banquet in their honour.

As she has got older, members of her staff – who have stayed with her for years – try to persuade Elizabeth to give up this or that activity.

Her answer is often: "But what am I going to do with my time? I still have duties to perform, you know."

Like all good grandmothers she has kept up with the times, and seldom chided the young.

She has been firm, without instilling fear – although those who may, unwittingly, have caused her temporary displeasure have been quietly made aware of it.

thing her French hosts during visits to the Loire and Cognac recently had not realised), and she never eats chocolate – though she loves puddings.

Does she mind sometimes being called "the pearly Queen" by the Press, I asked one of her staff. "No, she loved the idea. And, of course, she's met the real 'pearlies' personally. They got on marvellously."

She watches television – but not programmes like *Panorama*. She prefers old comedies, and "Dad's Army" was her favourite.

She retires each night at about 11.

When she's "out and about" on her travels she tries to make sure that expenditure on her behalf is kept to a minimum.

For example, she worries about going too often to the Cinque Ports (of which she is Lord Warden) in case the cost of entertaining proves heavy on the rates.

She frequently advises town clerks to cut down their suggested six-course

---

Princess Anne takes the stage after a dancing display at the Lyceum Ballroom in London **above left** *to present the annual Carl Alan Awards* **below** *in January 1975.* **Left** *Princess Anne as a member of the Order of Lady Ratlings at their annual luncheon in London in July 1975.*

Every day, for years, she has received on average five invitations, most involving travel and speeches.

Whenever possible, she flies by helicopter: "It's so much more convenient for everyone, no traffic hold-ups or people waiting in the rain," she has said, adding: "I like it, too."

She rises early in her apartment at Clarence House and reads all the papers except "the smuttier ones".

After breakfast – she eats well, but not a lot and has never been on a diet – she goes through the appointments and mail with her private secretary, Sir Martin Gilliat.

She selects the lunch menu, and then goes for her walk; much easier when she's in Scotland at her favourite home the Castle of Mey, near John O' Groats.

But there have been times when, incognito, she has popped down from Clarence House to Fortnum and Mason's in Piccadilly.

Among those who come to lunch are High Commissioners, Ambassadors and the increasingly small number of her contemporaries.

Before lunch, perhaps a gin and tonic or gin and Dubonnet. Never, despite her Scottish heritage, whisky.

She never touches smoked salmon, preferring only the fresh variety; hates caviare and pâté de foie gras (some-

his divorce. She has never discussed her views of them outside the immediate Royal Family, but is thought to be well-disposed towards both.

She has made it clear, however, that she disapproves of divorce. Nonetheless she has kept a close relationship with Princess Margaret, and has been quick to defend her in the face of public criticism. And when the Queen Mother

Princess Anne meets Chelsea Pensioners on her arrival **below left** *at Kensington and Chelsea Town Hall for a charity ball in February 1979, and is subsequently introduced to the borough's Pearlies* **left. Below** *The Princess stops to speak with some of the performers at the Royal Tournament at Earl's Court in July 1977.*

chooses to stand alongside someone, it is remarkable how quickly criticisms melt away.

At weekends she usually joins the Royal Family at Windsor. She likes to be with her grandchildren and great-grandchildren but sometimes the Queen comes over for Sunday afternoon tea. There is a deep affection between them.

She has been a widow since 1952, and despite rumours to the contrary – usually originating from America and France – there has never been another man in her life.

She has buried herself in work. For example, she recently spent three days

menus to three at the most.

She is credited with having done much to "democratise" the Royal Family; to have taken the first steps. But she has always felt that Lord Mountbatten – she was greatly distressed by his murder – deserved most of the credit.

Events of the past do not seem to trouble her unduly. She apparently prefers to forgive and forget. She

disliked the Duchess of Windsor, for example, and did not watch any of the television series about the Abdication.

But on a visit to France she proposed to call on the Duchess at her home outside Paris. Unfortunately the Duchess was too ill to see her.

She has met Group Captain Peter Townsend since the days of his doomed romance with Princess Margaret, and she has also seen Lord Snowdon since

As Colonel-in-Chief of the newly formed Royal Regiment of Wales, Prince Charles presented the regiment with its first colours in June 1969, a month before his Investiture, in the grounds of Cardiff Castle. This simple but impressive ceremony included the reading of the Queen's Commission **right,** *the parade of the Colours* **below** *and an inspection of the Regiment* **bottom.**

in rainy Kent and Sussex, and then came back to attend a school speech day. She has also taken a keen interest in the running of her small farms.

At Mey she has an Aberdeen Angus herd marshalled by a magnificent bull called Cannonball, and she has a small farm of Cheviot sheep.

Then there are her horses, all jumpers, down at Lambourn in the Fulke Walwyn stable. She loves horse-racing. Her reaction when Devon Loch slipped up on the point of winning the Grand National?

"She felt very badly about it – not for her own sake, but for everyone else connected with it," recalls a racing friend.

At Christmas she sends cards to all her present and former staff. She remembers their birthdays. And she personally inspects the presents that arrive for her.

Elizabeth, the Queen Mother, is a living history of the twentieth century – a unique witness of events that make our times

When she was born Queen Victoria was still alive and Britain's last great colonial war was being fought against the Boers in South Africa.

She now flies about the world in jets and helicopters – she once clocked 30,000 miles in a year – yet the Wright Brothers were still experimenting in their bicycle shed at the time of her birth. The did not make their first powered flight until three years after she was born.

Six years were to pass before Emmeline Pankhurst began her suffragette movement, and another 28 years before women got the vote.

She has seen wars, disasters and revolutions ... lands discovered, conquered and lost ... dictators, kings and presidents come and go ... the map of the world altered many times ... industrial depressions as well as great days of glory for Britain ... and her world change from a well-ordered class-conscious society to the anything-goes eighties.

The rules that governed her day were laid down in the Victorian era.

The Prince is also a Colonel in the Welsh Guards, and on St David's Day 1975 he participated in the annual ceremony of the distribution of leeks **above** at Caterham Barracks in Surrey. Wearing frock coat uniform **top left,** the Prince had a leek pinned to his cap **left and above right.**

No-one called on anyone without first sending round a card. The upper-class father paid £1,000 for the hire of a London house for "the season" – the equivalent of £20,000 today. Another £50 – around £1,000 in 1980 – would go on each of his womenfolk's clothing.

The debutante, and even her less financially-favoured sisters, were strictly monitored to ensure their virtue. They went up the aisles whiter and purer than a Barbara Cartland heroine in that pre-permissive era.

A "swinger" in those days was said to be "headstrong" and watched by mamas, aunts and chaperones to prevent any hanky-panky among the aspidistra plants.

When the Queen Mother was a young girl there were very properly-managed balls at which a young man begged to be included on a girl's dance card.

The social calendar dictated that the London summer season of debutante balls and fashionable dinners was to be followed by migration to Scotland or Yorkshire for grouse shooting in August. The hunting shires were the venues in November and winter, and early spring would be spent in the South of France until the new season began in April.

Whether sunning at Cannes or

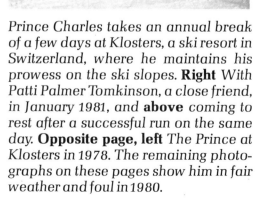

Prince Charles takes an annual break of a few days at Klosters, a ski resort in Switzerland, where he maintains his prowess on the ski slopes. **Right** *With Patti Palmer Tomkinson, a close friend, in January 1981, and* **above** *coming to rest after a successful run on the same day.* **Opposite page, left** *The Prince at Klosters in 1978. The remaining photographs on these pages show him in fair weather and foul in 1980.*

Southend, there was really only one future for a woman and that was to marry. It was considered that she owed this to herself and the family who had brought her up and trained her for a career in the kitchen, bedroom and nursery.

That was the society Elizabeth was born into. And how times have changed since then.

Away from the drawing rooms and café society here are some of the major events that happened in her lifetime and which have affected our lives.

1901 – Queen Victoria dies.

1902 – Boer War ends.

1903 – First powered flight by Wright Brothers.

1906 – Emmeline Pankhurst launches militant campaign for women's suffrage.

1907 – Robert Baden-Powell founds Boy Scout movement.

1909 – Louis Bleriot makes first cross-Channel flight.

1910 – Labour Exchanges are established in Britain. Florence Nightingale dies.

1911 – Norwegian explorer, Roald Amundsen, reaches South Pole.

1912 – SS Titanic strikes iceberg on maiden voyage – 1,513 die. Robert Scott dies at South Pole.

1914 – First World War begins

1918 – Kaiser William II abdicates. Armistice is signed.

1919 – Albert Einstein's theory of relativity is confirmed. John Alcock and Arthur Brown make first non-stop flight across the Atlantic.

1921 – Irish Free State is set up by peace treaty with Britain.

1922 – Mussolini's Fascist movement marches on Rome.

1924 – Ramsay MacDonald forms first Labour government in Britain.

1926 – General Strike in Britain lasts nine days.

1927 – Charles Lindbergh flies from New York to Paris in 37 hours.

1928 – Women in Britain win the vote. Airship crosses Atlantic with 60 passengers.

1929 – Wall Street Crash.

1930 – R101 airship crashes in France on first flight to India.

1933 – Adolf Hitler is appointed German Chancellor.

1935 – Sir Malcolm Campbell breaks world land speed record in *Bluebird* at 301.337 m.p.h.

1936 – The *Queen Mary* makes her maiden voyage in record time to New York from Southampton. Civil War breaks out in Spain.

Prince Charles takes the helm **opposite page, below,** *or merely enjoys the fun of sailing on the ocean-going yacht Siska IV off Perth, Western Australia, during his official visit there in March 1979.* **Left and opposite page, top** *Taking part in a deep sea fishing trip during the same visit.*

1938 – The Queen Mother launches world's largest liner – the *Queen Elizabeth*. Austria annexed by Germany. Munich agreement signed.

1939 – Spanish Civil War ends.

1940 – Evacuation of Dunkirk.

1941 – Japanese attack Pearl Harbour.

1942 – El Alamein. The Dieppe Raid.

1943 – Allies land in Sicily. Mussolini overthrown and Italy surrenders.

1944 – Allied armies land in Normandy.

1945 – Victory in Europe, and Japan. Hiroshima destroyed by first atomic bomb. Clement Attlee

wins general election for Labour.

1947 – Coal industry nationalised. School leaving age raised to 15 in Britain.

1948 – Berlin Airlift.

1949 – Gas industry nationalised. Ten-power conference in London establishes Council of Europe.

1950 – Outbreak of Korean War.

1951 – Festival of Britain opened by King George VI. Conservatives win British general election.

Like two of the previous three Princes of Wales, Prince Charles has undertaken a full and exhausting tour of the United States. In the Autumn of 1977 he visited eleven major cities in less than a fortnight, and saw many aspects of American civilisation, both old and new. The old was exemplified in his visit to San Antonio in Texas **above** *whilst the new took the form of a seat, during his visit to the Houston Space Centre, in a lunar buggy which featured in the moon landings of the previous decade* **top picture.** *In between came a tour of the Texas ranch of Tobin Armstrong and his wife Anne, who was once the US Ambassador to Britain* **right** *and a cattle round-up* **opposite page** *which they had specially arranged for him.*

1952 – Britain's first atomic bomb test.

1953 – Eisenhower becomes 34th President of USA. Stalin dies. Hillary and Tenzing reach summit of Everest. Coronation of Queen Elizabeth II.

1954 – Roger Bannister first man to run a mile in under four minutes.

1955 – ITV begins transmitting.

1956 – Hungarian uprising.

1957 – First Premium Bond prizes drawn by ERNIE. First satellite launched by Russia.

1958 – Nikita Khrushchev elected to power in Russia. General de Gaulle President of France.

1959 – Fidel Castro takes over in Cuba. Jodrell Bank radios message to America via the moon. First section of M1 opens in Britain.

1960 – John Kennedy elected President of USA.

1961 – Yuri Gagarin makes first manned flight into space. Betting shops open in Britain.

1962 – Marilyn Monroe dies, aged 36. Britain's first communications satellite launched.

1963 – Great Train Robbery. President

Kennedy assassinated in Dallas.

1964 – Harold Wilson becomes Labour Prime Minister. BBC2 Television opens.

1965 – Sir Winston Churchill dies. Rhodesian Declaration of Independence, by Ian Smith.

1966 – England wins World Cup at Wembley. Aberfan colliery disaster – 116 children killed.

1967 – Six-day war in Middle East. First heart transplant in Cape Town.

1968 – Senator Robert Kennedy assassinated in Los Angeles. Russians invade Czechoslovakia.

The culmination of Prince Charles' naval career came in 1975, when he was put in command of the mine-sweeper HMS Bronington. On 1st November 1976, as Lieutenant the Prince of Wales, he took part in an exercise with other ships of the Mine Counter-Measure Squadron in the Firth of Forth. His brother Prince Andrew, who was then at school at Gordonstoun, was able to join the Bronington for the duration of the exercise **below.**

1969 – Maiden flight of Concorde. Neil Armstrong and "Buzz" Aldrin first men to land on the moon.

1970 – General de Gaulle dies. Thalidomide disaster.

1971 – Britain goes decimal.

1973 – Britain joins Common Market. Last American soldiers leave Vietnam.

1974 – President Nixon resigns over Watergate scandal. Edward Heath resigns. Labour Government takes office.

1975 – Mrs Margaret Thatcher elected leader of Conservative Party.

1976 – Harold Wilson resigns. James Callaghan takes over. Jimmy Carter elected President of USA.

1977 – Bing Crosby dies. Freddie Laker starts Skytrain service to New York.

1978 – Cardinal Karol Wojtyla of Poland becomes first non-Italian Pope for 450 years.

1979 – Mrs Thatcher first woman Prime Minister of Great Britain. Shah leaves Iran. Ayatollah Khomeni takes over.

1980 – President Reagan elected.

1981 – Attempted assassination of President Reagan. The Royal Wedding

The circumstances of the birth of Prince Charles at Buckingham Palace represented a break from tradition. For centuries it was the custom for a cabinet minister to be present at the delivery of an heir to the throne – to make sure there was no bedchamber jiggery-pokery and that a substitute child was not smuggled in by bed-warmer perhaps! Elizabeth was the first royal mother to produce a direct heir who did not have to suffer this embarrassment.

Queen Victoria is reputed to have been as imperious as ever, having just gone through the pains of childbirth,

when dealing with a representative of government on one occasion. The frock-coated gentleman said to the queen: "You have given birth to a fine healthy boy, your majesty." The unruffled monarch responded regally from her

It has now become an annual event for Prince Charles to compete at Bisley in the shooting match between the House of Lords and House of Commons. The photographs on this page and opposite **lower left** *were taken on 25th July 1980 when, reversing the previous year's defeat, the House of Lords won.* **Below** *The Prince with other members of the Lords team in front of the scoreboard at the end of the match.*

bed: "Prince you mean minister . . . prince!"

Charles' great-grandfather, George V, once said: "My father was frightened of his father . . . I was frightened of my father . . . and I'm going to see to it that my children are frightened of me."

Palace views on dealing with off-spring are, happily, more enlightened today than in the early days of this century when that Victorian-Edwardian attitude prevailed.

Charles and Philip have a very close relationship, though their personalities differ. Prince Philip is slightly aggressive, while his eldest son is gentler of character. Both father and son tend to have the same mannerisms: the same briskness of walk, that well-known

Top *Prince Charles in various moods on being invited to drive a fork-lift truck during his visit to the factory of Lansing Ltd at Basingstoke in February 1979. In October 1980 he visited BL's plant at Longbridge; he was shown the production line of the new Mini Metro* **centre right** *and addressed both management and workers afterwards* **lower right.**

habit of clenching their hands behind their backs, thrusting a left hand in the jacket pocket, and flinging their heads back when laughing. Charles once explained why they have the habit of holding their hands behind their backs: "We both use the same tailor and he always makes the sleeves so tight that we can't get our hands in front!"

All the royal sons seem to have inherited their father's sense of humour: a liking for zany, outrageous slapstick – the ludicrous rather than sharpness of wit.

The tastes of Charles and his father are generally, however, quite different. Charles enjoys music, whereas Prince Philip finds it agonising to have to sit through a concert. Charles favours solitary pastimes, while Philip is much more gregarious.

Prince Philip had considerable influence in the upbringing of the heir to the throne, however. Up to the age of eight Charles spent his time with nannies and governesses. The Queen had been following the pattern of her own childhood – and the tradition of centuries – by giving Charles a private education within palace walls. Philip changed all this, not just for Charles, but for Anne, Andrew and Edward as well.

In Charles' case, Philip, realising the restrictions of such an education, sent him to school with boys of his own gen-

Prince Charles during his hectic night of dancing at the Town Hall in Rio de Janiero whilst he was touring Brazil in 1978. Throwing himself completely into the spirit of the occasion, he was no doubt glad to cool off on the Town Hall balcony **centre right** *with one of his dancing partners.*

eration to learn how to live with other children. Dancing lessons were stopped, music lessons took a few bars rest, and, instead, Charles was taken to a playing field in Chelsea, to get into the rough and tumble of soccer, and to a private gymnasium twice a week for work-outs on climbing ropes, parallel bars and vaulting horses.

Charles was taught nearly all his physical skills by his father: Philip took him out in bitter, wintry weather to teach him to shoot among the heather around Balmoral, and Charles shot his first grouse when he was 10 years old. Philip taught his son to fish, and when he was at home he would spend an hour after tea teaching his son to swim in the pool at the palace. Charles could swim a length before he was five years old, and is now an excellent swimmer.

Father and son would occasionally have a boisterous game of football in the palace grounds, with the corgis barking round their heels. The Queen and toddler Anne might be permitted to join in the fun now and again.

The Prince was determined that his son would not have a pampered, soft life. He once noticed a servant leaping to close a door that schoolboy Charles had failed to shut. He shouted: "Leave it alone, man. He's got hands. He can go

back and do it himself."

Prince Philip's greatest influence in the early days was in bringing the royal educational style into the twentieth century. He made sure that the boys learnt independence as soon as possible, packing them off to boarding schools, where they had to stand on their own two feet, from the age of nine or ten years old. Anne, too, left the shelter of home at 13, to become a boarder at the fashionable Benenden

In 1978, Prince Charles' lengthy tour of South America included several days in Brazil. Amongst his engagements there was a dinner at the Town Hall in Rio de Janiero, which was followed by a late night dancing session. The Prince was persuaded to join a troop of exotically dressed Brazilian dancers and provided one of the most enjoyable scenes of the whole tour.

School in Kent.

The boys, at their father's instigation, were to face a tougher educational régime when they reached 13. Philip sent them to his old alma-mater, Gordonstoun, on a bleak stretch of Scotland's west coast. He had been subjected to its harsh, cold-shower system and had thought it had done him the world of good. Why shouldn't it

Charles has, however, a sensitive ear for music, plays the piano and cello, paints landscapes and holds a degree in archaeology and anthropology. Such is the sensitive side of the nature of this well-rounded man that he has also been known to say when he hears a piece of music by Berlioz: "I am so moved that I'm reduced to tears every time."

He has a tremendous thirst for danger and adventure. According to the Queen Mother: "If there was anything left to discover in the world Charles would have been an explorer."

Says the Prince: "I like to see if I can challenge myself to do something that is potentially hazardous, just to see if I can mentally accept that challenge and carry it out. I like to try all sorts of things because they appeal to me. I'm

have the same results with his own sons?

Gordonstoun was to be an institution that Andrew – who has inherited his father's ways – found easier to accept. Charles and Edward are more sensitive than their middle brother, and Charles has especially unhappy memories of Gordonstoun.

The school is mainly a collection of crude huts. Dormitories have unpainted wooden walls, bare floors, and iron beds. An obligatory cold shower has to be taken every morning, no matter what the weather. The school motto, "Plus est en vous" ("There is more in you"), heralds a harsh system aimed at stretching to the fullest both physical and intellectual capabilities.

Charles was certainly not given preferential treatment; his housemaster gave him an unsavoury task in his first term – emptying the dustbins each day. After Charles left Gordonstoun he said: "I did not enjoy school as much as I might have, but that was because I am happier at home than anywhere else."

The heir to the throne is an amazing person, with immense personal courage. Apart from being a skilled frogman, he has skippered a ship, piloted helicopters, flown jet fighters, driven tanks, trained as a tough commando and as a parachutist. If all these were not enough he is also an excellent horseman and a top class polo player.

one of those people who don't like sitting and watching someone else doing something. I don't like to go to the races to watch horses thundering up and down . . . I'd rather be riding the horses myself."

Despite frequently falling off his horses at steeplechasing, Charles made it clear that he was determined to continue competing in this dangerous sport.

"Nothing else I've ever done compares with this," he said after one tumble. He believes that steeplechasing is "a part of our way of life".

The Queen and Prince Charles have much in common. He shares her kindness and gentle qualities and, as neither of them like dramatic change, both have the same conservative attitudes. They are also aware of the continuing constitutional roles they shoulder. They sense that they not only belong to the nation and Commonwealth but are also the ongoing link of this tradition.

For his 31st birthday in November 1979, Prince Charles attended a charity concert at the Wembley Conference Centre. He met the stars after the concert, including comedian Eric Morecambe **opposite page far left** *and singer Shirley Bassey* **opposite page, left.** *Before the performance, he was introduced to Mrs Anna Realff* **right** *who presented him with a bouquet and informed him that she was 101 years of age. The Prince's reply: "All the ladies I meet these days are over 100!"* **Below** *Prince Charles chatting to one of the pop groups which performed at the concert.*

They are both frustrated actors, and often turn to mimicry to amuse the family and staff at the end of a day of being introduced to government officials or city fathers. They have a cruel ability to impersonate the more pompous of those they have met. A remarkable number of politicians or captains of industry would curb their tales of passing acquaintance with the royals if they could see the palace "cabaret" later.

Charles, who gets his love of flying from his father, has flown twice-the-speed-of-sound Phantom fighter bombers, strategic nuclear bombers and is a naval helicopter pilot trained to land Royal Marine Commandos in combat conditions. He was 20 when he first flew solo in a single-engined propeller-driven Chipmunk. According to his instructor, he had an immediate aptitude for flying. Others who have accompanied him in the cockpits of many aircraft since then all agree that he is a "natural" pilot. Does he find flying some of the exotic jet aircraft he has laid his hands on dangerous? "No, it's more dangerous crossing the road," says the daredevil Prince.

Charles also picked up his enthu-

siasm for polo from his father. It is the one great passion they have in common. Philip had taken up the game shortly after his marriage so that he could share the Queen's enthusiasm for horses.

As a toddler Charles would watch Prince Philip play, and throughout his early teens was constantly pestering his father to let him mount up and join him. Charles used to help around the stables or act as a sort of "squire", holding the polo sticks or being ready with a bottle of water between chukkas. Philip thought he was too young to take part in a game until he was in his mid-teens, so until then he taught him how to handle a pony and the difficult knack of ball control. The pair of them would ride off into Windsor Great Park for practice

Prince Charles still enjoys, after many years' participation, tough and challenging competition on the polo field. **Right** *He prepares for a game at Cowdray Park Sussex in June 1974.* **Above, and opposite page, above left** *Prince Charles shows speed and skilled horsemanship as he participates in a game at Windsor in June 1980.*

sessions.

Charles is now a better rider than his father, but, as mentioned earlier, experts say that he will never be able to match him as a polo player because, according to one of them: "Charles shows far too much consideration for

his horses and will not drive them hard enough."

Charles began playing the game at 16 and now keeps a string of ponies at Windsor – his biggest extravagance. He says: "I love the game, I love the ponies and I love the exercise. It's my favourite game." He has played all over

The Prince can often be seen spending time with his horses both before and after matches. **Below left** *He offers a titbit to one of his ponies at Windsor Great Park in July 1979.* **Below right** *On the same occasion, the Prince kits himself up before the match.* **Right** *Whilst waiting for a match to begin – Windsor again, July 1980 – the Prince rides his horses at walking pace towards the polo field.*

the world, including India, from where the game was brought to Europe by the officers of the British Raj in the nineteenth century.

With a ready sense of humour, Charles probably tries harder than other members of his family at getting down to the grassroots level. He has a genuine interest in people from all walks of life and feels that getting to know his future subjects is of vital importance.

The five years he spent in the Royal Navy were very useful to him in this respect. He not only met fellow officers from wealthy homes but also had to deal with the problems of seamen from quite humble backgrounds. He was responsible for their welfare and that could include dealing with marriage problems or telling someone the sad news that a relative had died.

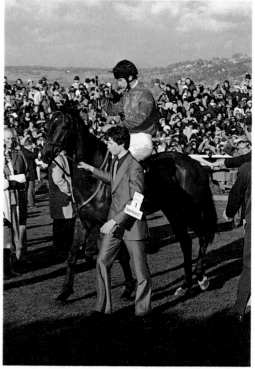

Prince Charles' first appearance as a qualified steeplechaser was at Plumpton in March 1980, when he finished second in a field of thirteen in a charity race. **Above** *He trots his horse round the paddock and outfield and gives him some brisker exercise* **right** *before the race.* **Far right, top** *Prince Charles taking one of the hurdles.* **Far right** *Prince Charles on Good Prospect at Cheltenham in March 1981, when he was thrown from his horse, though without serious injury.*

When he is about his official duties Charles likes as few barriers as possible between himself and the crowds – a security man's nightmare at times. He does not like people to be nervous about approaching him, or regarding him as a distant, god-like creature. As he once said: "I used to think 'Good God what's wrong? Do I smell? Have I forgotten to change my socks?' I realise now that I have to make a bit of the running and show that I am a reasonable human being. An awful lot of people say eventually: 'Good Lord, you're not nearly as pompous as I thought you were going to be!'"

When will Charles take over the throne? There has been great speculation about this, ranging from five years hence to as much as 40 years ahead. A frequently-discussed theory

*Prince Charles as a horseman and as spectator on the polo field at Windsor in July 1979. With him **above** were Prince and Princess Michael of Kent, and Earl Mountbatten – tragically in one of his last public appearances before his assassination the following month – applauding the team to whom Prince Charles awarded the winners cup **left and top**.*

is that the Queen will abdicate in his favour before he gets too old to bring all his youthful vigour to kingship.

When asked about his mother giving up the throne to make way for him, Charles has replied on two occasions that it could be as much as 30 or 40 years before he is crowned.

If the wait is going to be that long it could make him 60 or even well into his seventieth year before he sits on the throne. Yet the Prince insists that he sees no reason why the Queen should retire. She is healthy and absolutely on top of the job she is doing.

Should Her Majesty, as happily seems likely, live to the great age of her mother, grandmother (86) or great-great-grandmother, Queen Victoria (82) it could be the twenty-first century before Charles achieves his destiny.

(That colourful Paris weekly newspaper *France Dimanche*, has, by the way, reported the Queen's abdication at least 70 times as well as carrying more than 80 stories about her intention to divorce Prince Philip. The paper is regularly sent to Buckingham Palace by the British Embassy because the family consider it to be "amusing light reading".)

A previous Prince of Wales, Victoria's son King Edward VII, did not begin his reign until he was 58 years old, after a wasteful life trying to relieve the boredom of waiting. He was not allowed to take part in any of the affairs of State, so he turned to a profligate existence, setting a life-style that gave his name to an era.

Queen Elizabeth is at least making sure that Charles has a useful role to play, training him for the future by involving him in official duties and ensuring that he does his share of royal tours.

In September 1975, Prince Charles attended the independence celebrations of Papua New Guinea on behalf of the Queen. These pictures show him attending a pageant in Port Moresby, the capital, on Independence Day, during which he took the opportunity to meet some of the younger inhabitants. **Right** *Part of the enthusiastic native welcome accorded the Prince on his arrival.*

In March 1979, Prince Charles undertook a lengthy tour of Australia, and spent several days in Western Australia, including one in the outback where these photographs were taken: they show the three essentials for such a trip – self-sufficiency **top,** a device for keeping insects away **above** and a sense of humour **left!**

No matter how long he waits for his throne he can never be accused of being a wastrel. He has a busy schedule every working day, involving touring the world, promoting his own Principality of Wales, and organising youth schemes or bringing the palace nearer to the people with his friendly walkabouts.

The young Prince, more perhaps than others in his family, is aware that he is waiting for kingship in a changing society. He has said: "In these times the monarchy is called into question – it is not taken for granted as it used to be. In that sense one has to be far more professional than I think one ever used to be." To him, however, it is keeping pace, adapting to the new conditions, maintaining the institution as one of the strongest elements in keeping stability in Britain. Opinion polls usually show that, next to the Queen, he is the most popular member of the Royal Family.

Prince Charles, the twenty-first Prince of Wales, has set himself one task above all others before he becomes King. He wishes to learn at first hand as much as possible about the people he will govern. He also wants to experience as much of life as he can before the Crown curbs his adventurous spirit.

As Prince of Wales he is the latest in a line that includes Edward, the warrior Black Prince of the fourteenth century, the much-married Henry the Eighth, Queen Victoria's son – the fun-loving Edward VII – and the late Duke of Windsor.

His full title is His Royal Highness the Prince Charles Philip Arthur George, Prince of Wales and Earl of Chester,

The Investiture of Prince Charles as Prince of Wales: two moments from the ceremony at Caernarvon Castle on 1st July 1969: **below** *Prince Charles' speech, delivered in both Welsh and English, and* **below right** *the beginning of the Investiture proper, as he kneels before the Queen.* **Bottom left** *The portrait of*

Duke of Cornwall and Rothesay, Earl of Carrick and Baron of Renfrew, Lord of the Isles and Great Steward of Scotland, Knight of The Garter.

The titles Prince of Wales and Earl of Chester are traditionally associated with a male heir-apparent of a reigning monarch. On the death of a Prince of Wales and Earl of Chester they do not pass on to his son – they must be recreated with each reign. Cornwall and the five Scottish titles came to Charles, as eldest son of the sovereign, from the moment the Queen ascended the throne. Edward III created his son

the Prince as Colonel-in-Chief of the Royal Regiment of Wales. **Right** *Prince Charles wearing the robes and carrying the regalia of the Princes of Wales; he wears a crown specially made for the 1969 Investiture. In contrast,* **bottom right** *an informal photograph taken at Balmoral during the summer of 1972.*

Prince Charles spent much of the 1970's in the Navy and RAF, but his tours abroad have taken him to army camps as well: **above** he samples outdoor cooking during a visit to a Commonwealth country in Africa. Since he passed out of RAF Cranwell in 1971, the Prince has maintained close ties with the RAF: **far left** he piloted a helicopter at RAF Yeovilton in November 1974 – the helicopter flew the Royal Standard **opposite page, top. Left** A smile of confidence from Prince Charles as he prepares to climb aboard a Hercules aircraft for a parachute jump at RAF South Cerney in April 1978.

Duke of Cornwall in 1337, making it clear that the title should descend to the eldest sons of English rulers forever. The Scottish titles come from the fourteenth century. James VI of Scotland brought them with him when he be-

came James I of England, following the death of the first Queen Elizabeth. Charles holds them as heir to the old Kingdom of Scotland.

Unlike most of his predecessors, Charles devotes a large part of his time

to Wales and its affairs. Whether it be Welsh industry, art, music or the national rite of rugby, he gets involved.

When the Queen decided Charles should take up the title of Prince of Wales, she was determined that he should have more than just a formal link with the Principality. He learned the Welsh language – the first English

Prince of Wales to do so – and he went to the University College of Wales, Aberystwyth, to absorb Welsh culture. The Welsh language is not one of the easiest to learn and in fact is spoken by less than half the population, yet in a few months Charles mastered enough of it not only to give his investiture speech in Welsh, but also to hold a conversation in the tongue.

His popularity both at home and abroad was best summed up at his investiture as Prince of Wales in July 1969, when the Mayor of Caernarvon said "Look at him, he's the ace in the royal pack!"

Charles feels that he can make a useful contribution to the life of the monarchy and the country . . . such as his organisation during Jubilee Year, his interest in young people and the efforts he makes on behalf of Wales. He has,

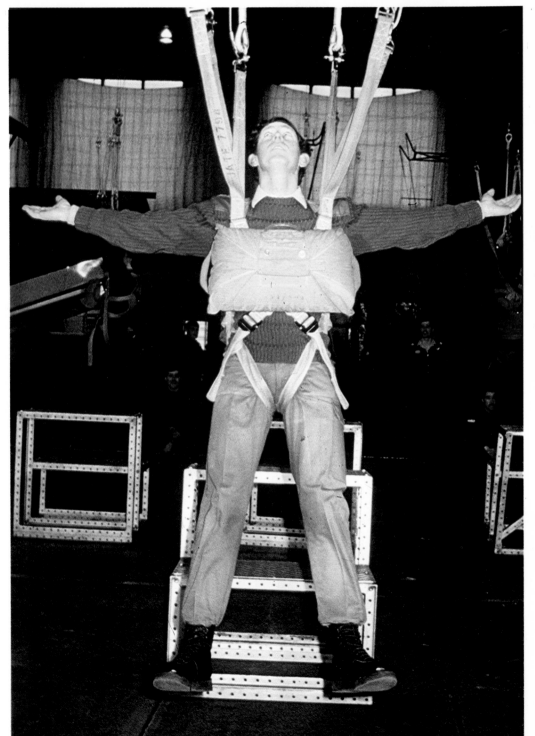

Left The Prince on a parachute course at RAF Brise Norton in 1978, and **above centre** receiving his wings after successfully completing the course. His experience in the services has enabled him to be well informed during his visits to airfields **above top** and dockyards. Chatham **above,** where he attended the rededication of his old ship HMS Bronington, in June 1980.

for instance, helped to attract more industry to the area.

Realising that he is very different from his subjects, Charles goes to great lengths to bring himself closer to those who will, one day, be his people.

Charles' spirit of adventure is such that there seem to be few things he has not tried. In the Canadian Arctic he donned a rubber suit and spent more than half an hour underneath the ice pack – in a temperature four degrees below that needed to make ice in a refrigerator.

When he was recently appointed Colonel-in-Chief of the Parachute Regiment, he was not content to accept it

Adaptable as the occasion demands Prince Charles shows determination to get his point across **above left** *as well as his ability to make friends with foreign students* **left** *and children* **above.**

merely as an honorary title. He wanted to be able to wear the wings because he had earned them. "If I'm going to be the Colonel, I'll do it properly," he said. He therefore joined other members of the regiment in a series of jumps that brought him up to combat standard. Only then would he stitch on his uniform the coveted insignia of a para-

Adapting to camels is a different matter, but Prince Charles succeeded in riding one during a horse show at Olympia in December 1979 **above:** *he remarked on "the foul smell from both ends."* **Left** *The Prince with Jimmy Savile, to whom he presented a Carl Alan Award in February 1971 – and Jimmy was suitably deferential!* **Right** *Prince Charles with Lord Mountbatten during a formal reception at Cowes, in July 1975.*

trooper. Explaining his taste for danger, he says: "It tends to make you appreciate life that much more and really to want to live it to the fullest."

The Prince has always had a bubbling sense of humour – ever since childhood. "I enjoy making people laugh," he says. "It's very useful for getting people to listen to what you are saying." Both he and Andrew like the weird comedy style of Peter Sellers and the Goons. At one very stiff regimental dinner, he sang the gibberish song made famous by Sellers, the "Ying-Tong" song. Keeping a straight face, he repeated over and over again the verse: "Ying-Tong, Ying-Tong, Ying-Tong, Ying-Tong, Ying-Tong, Tiddle-I-Po." It

certainly broke the ice around the mess table.

Soldiers in his Royal Regiment of Wales grumbled that, because they did not speak any German, they were having trouble meeting the local girls when they were stationed at Osnabrück. A few days later Charles sent them two light-hearted sheets of German-English phrases with a vocabulary limited to the pursuit of women.

At a charity cricket match he once went out to bat mounted on a pony and carrying a polo stick. When everyone was wearing name tags at a Royal Air Force dinner Charles' label said: "Watch this space."

He is gradually taking from his parents much of the burden of public appearances, official duties, and foreign touring; adopting a sort of vice-presidential role. His interests are so great that he is the president or patron of more than 140 organisations and societies, and colonel-in-chief of 10 regiments. The activities in which he gets involved range from preserving the natural beauty of Wales to blowing the trumpet for British industry.

Charles knows that he is likely to be King in a period of social, economic and political change, but he has been carefully-groomed for the task. "I worry sometimes about the future," he once said, "but I think that if one can preserve one's sense of humour, adaptive qualities and perhaps help to calm things down . . . to provide a stable appearance and approach to things, a steadying influence – all will be well".

As to his ever-interesting marriage prospects, he answered on at least one occasion to endless questions on the

Few of Prince Charles' official engagements seem to be complete without some attempt by a member of the opposite sex to plant a kiss on his cheek. The 1979 visit to Western Australia was no exception: during a morning swim **above** *he was the target of a scantily clad young lady* **above right.** *His jog along the beach afterwards* **right** *may well have served as a means of escape.*

subject: "This is awfully difficult, because you have to remember that when you marry in my position you are going to marry someone who is perhaps one day going to be Queen."

The world's most eligible bachelor eventually did what he always said he would do – marry for love.

Although there was a handful of suitable foreign princesses available Prince Charles carried out a vow he made more than 10 years earlier. "I will only marry for love."

He at last found the partner he had searched for through many years, a string of girlfriends and a mother and father hinting to him that the time had come when he should settle down, marry and stop being a regal "Action

Man" – constantly jumping out of aircraft, risking his neck or diving under water.

The traditional, arranged marriage was never acceptable to Charles. He had seen the unhappiness that those exchanges of gold rings had caused among his ancestors.

From the days when he first started to know the many girls willing to become one of the "Charlie Set" he had met many who were more than willing – prompted by their well-connected mamas – to succumb to his regal charms.

In fact, being the world's most eligible bachelor became something of a bore. He had the choice of so many women yet he never really found true love.

Throughout those confused years there were so many girls from suitably-pedigreed families who were "Charlie's darlings" for a time. They were attractive and well-connected but love never really entered his heart.

There were also many weekends spent in secluded places with girls who provided excitement, but their subsequently-discovered backgrounds killed off any hopes of marriage.

Then there were the girls, including Lady Diana's sister, Lady Sarah, who filled the role of companions – who were acceptable to Buckingham Palace and in public at Ascot – but with whom Charles did not fall in love.

After at least two years of pressure from the Queen and his father to find a suitable bride, Charles at last fell in love. It had taken a long time, but at an age when most men had already settled down with mortgages and children, the heir to the throne found someone he loved.

Lady Diana, 12 years Charles' junior, is from a family that has been close to the throne for many years. After the announcement of the engagement it was arranged for her to learn more, not just about the pomp and circumstance of a wedding but also what being a future queen entails. She has to learn of the history and training for kingship that her husband has already gone through.

The person chosen to help her into regal ways was the Queen Mother. Nearly five months of gentle lessons in

The Prince has in recent years added windsurfing to his many sports. He practises this popular activity with great determination during *Cowes Week*, when many members of his family attend the various sea-going events. These photographs illustrate his ability to handle windsurfing craft, as well as his liability to succumb to the occasional ducking.

future queenship were provided by the Prince's grandmother at her London home, Clarence House, just down The Mall from Buckingham Palace.

Lady Diana's curriculum included everything from waving to crowds to the proper way not only to curtsey – but also to acknowledge a curtsey.

Charles has the reputation of being careful with his money. Little wonder,

when running his polo stable costs him £50,000 a year alone.

His own day-to-day expenses and those of his staff come to around £100,000 a year.

At Buckingham Palace Charles lived in a three-bedroomed flatlet cut off from the rest of the building on the second floor. It was decorated in pale colours and furnished in a leathery, masculine style.

In April 1980, Prince Charles represented the Queen at the celebration of Zimbabwe's independence after almost 15 years of UDI. **Left** *The Prince salutes, with the last Governor, Lord Soames, as the Union Flag is lowered for the last time* **above left. Above** *Prince Charles, with Lord Soames, attends a banquet in Salisbury as guest of the new President, Canaan Banana and Prime Minister Robert Mugabe.*

Above *Prince Charles in a polo team during his South American tour of 1978 and* **opposite page** *posing for a photograph by the shores of a lake during the same tour.*

The bookshelves housed mainly, volumes on history, archaeology and art. The Prince was, and still is, fussy about keeping a place neat and tidy and is apt to get annoyed over clutter.

When he had the chance of an evening alone there he liked to watch comedy shows and documentaries on television or read about archaeology.

The newly-weds' country home in Gloucestershire will be a tranquil retreat away from the bustle of London, a place where Charles and Diana can relax in idyllic, secluded grounds.

The next few years will be spent learning every aspect of industry and trade, while carrying out overseas tours with his bride, and possibly taking a post in a Commonwealth country.

One of the main features of Prince Charles' tour of India at the end of 1980 was his visit to the Calcutta Mission of Mother Teresa, foundress of the Missions of Charity: **above** *the Prince arriving at the Mission and* **top right** *talking with Mother Teresa.* **Right** *Some of the many children he met both inside the Mission building and outside, where he listened to some of the moving case histories involving the homeless children who were cared for there.*

And while he jets about the world he will not cost the British taxpayer a penny.

To earn enough money to carry out his duties, pay his living expenses, cover the costs of his staff, his clothes and uniforms, his sports car, his polo ponies, his entertaining and his weekends away, Charles runs a complex but profitable business.

The main source of income is the Duchy of Cornwall which he inherited, by tradition, as eldest son of the Queen.

Its total area is 130,000 acres, which makes Charles one of the biggest landowners in Britain. Its interests are spread over Cornwall, Devon, Somerset, Dorset, Gloucestershire and Wiltshire as well as all the Isles of Scilly.

While Prince Charles was, at last, showing off to the world his bride in the garden at the back of Buckingham Palace, the Band of the Coldstream Guards marched to the front playing "Now your philandering days are over".

This song from the *Marriage of Figaro* seems very appropriate because one thing was certain – Charles was going to have to change his life-style after the Royal Wedding.

Above *Prince Charles makes a speech during his fortnight's visit, wearing the vermilion mark on his forehead – a sign of esteem.* **Above right** *The Prince visits the Jama Msjid Mosque in Delhi – wearing a straw hat, since it is forbidden to enter a mosque bareheaded!* **Right** *Prince Charles being conducted by boat around a bird sanctuary during his tour.*

According to their friends, Lady Diana had already made it plain to him before accepting his proposal of marriage that his long history of risking his neck, chasing girls, and his adventurous bachelor life was going to have to change somewhat.

Among the points that Diana and Charles discussed before the final decision to marry were those daring "Action Man" interests in risking his life . . . a number of quiet country retreats he had used in the past to meet girlfriends . . . a discreet house in Kensington where he used to meet his friends privately – including Lady Diana.

Like any future bride who has admired the virile activities of her husband-to-be before marriage, Diana had talked about Charles' constant desire to prove what a devil-of-a-fellow he was by risking his neck. His penchant for danger had also recently worried the Queen, so Diana had a strong ally at the Palace.

He had taken part in most activities that could possibly get the royal adrenalin flowing. And not all of them without nearly breaking that regal neck.

His first parachute jump during his RAF training nearly ended in disaster when he found himself descending upside down towards the sea with his legs caught in the rigging lines.

On at least two occasions he has been thrown so badly at polo that he suffered injuries from being kicked by one of his horses, including a severe blow to the head.

He once had a hoof-shaped bruise near his heart, and still carries the scar from a cut needing nine stitches near his left ear.

Just a few days before the announcement of their engagement, his favourite steeplechaser, Allibar, worth £15,000 died of a heart attack while he was riding him.

Little wonder, then, that the Queen has been saying to her eldest son for the past year: "Enough is enough, Charles. Start taking it easy."

Now she has been joined by Diana in trying to persuade him to stop taking too many chances.

Lady Diana, like the rest of the world, had known about his reputation as a ladies' man. After all, even her own elder sister, Lady Sarah, was one of the "Charlie Set" – or "Charlie's Angels" as some people called them – for two years.

It was through Lady Sarah Spencer, now married to a businessman, that

Lady Diana Spencer was dubbed "Shy Di" after these photographs of her were taken in Autumn 1980 **opposite page** *as she attempted to lead a normal daily life when interest in her friendship with Prince Charles began to grow.* **Above** *Despite heavy pursuit, Lady Diana remained cheerful, but tactfully non-committal about her liaison.* **Right** *The building in Kensington, in which her flat was situated: she shared the flat with three other girls.*

disposes of a £100,000 house he kept two miles away from Buckingham Palace in Kensington for those secret meetings with girlfriends. Lady Diana was among those he invited for quiet candle-lit dinners at this house, not far from Princess Margaret's home... and the nearest pub is called, suitably, the Windsor Castle.

In London Prince Charles' favourite hostess had always been bubbly, blonde Lady Dale Tryon, the 29-year-old wife of Lord Anthony Tryon. She was often the hostess for dinner parties at the Tryon home held in the Prince's honour before he had a wife of his own to act as hostess.

Australian-born Dale – nicknamed "Kanga" by Charles – used to accom-

Photographs on these two pages show a delightful mixture of formality and informality as Prince Charles and Lady Diana Spencer pose in the grounds of Buckingham Palace on the day of their engagement, 24th February 1981.

Charles first met Diana at one of the Spencer homes near Sandringham. But Charles barely noticed her – she was "just a 16-year-old," according to the Prince later.

At that time he was more interested in Lady Sarah.

Over the years he has had girlfriends in many parts of the world, most of whom have remained friends and have kept happy memories of their relationships – even after they went off and married other men.

From now on Lady Diana expects him to take only her to his hideaway on the Scilly Isles, and also that he

pany her husband and the Prince on fishing trips to Iceland. Charles not only liked her sense of humour, but always sought her opinion on his girlfriends, as he did that of another close confidante, Camilla Parker-Bowles, married to Household Cavalry Officer Andrew Parker-Bowles. Charles and the

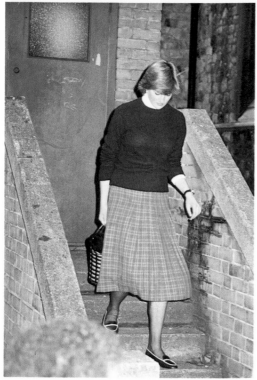

Communicating daily between her Kensington flat and the Pimlico kindergarten where she taught, was no easy job for Lady Diana as 1980 drew to a close. These pictures were taken in November, with the future bride of the Prince of Wales dutifully remaining as tight-lipped as ever.

Parker-Bowles used to hunt regularly together in Gloucestershire, and this was one of the reasons why the Prince chose as his new home, Highgrove.

Newly-weds Charles and Di will have as their neighbours Andrew and Camilla, who had often acted as the country version of Dale Tryon – a close friend able to act as a hostess and offer useful advice.

More relaxed times after her engagement. Lady Diana in happy mood at Cheltenham at the end of March 1981, particularly after receiving a daffodil from schoolboy Nicholas Hardy **above** *who then gallantly kissed his future Queen's hand.*

How will Lady Diana succeed in changing her new husband without taking away from him all the excitement that makes him so attractive?

Her father, Earl Spencer, says: "She is a very level-headed girl who knows her own mind and what she's doing. Charles is a very lucky man."

One of Diana's friends said: "She might be young, but she knows how to get her own way. She won't nag Charles or try to impose her will upon him... just like any clever woman she'll make him agree to her ways.

"They'll both be better off for it – and so happy. Diana will see to that."

After the announcement of their engagement, Lady Diana came face-to-face with another new, but sinister aspect of the changed life ahead of her – the need to always have armed protection around her at a time of terrorism and psychopathic cranks.

She was assigned two bodyguards from Scotland Yard's Royal Protection Group – one of them Chief Inspector Paul Officer, the man who saved Prince Charles when he was attacked during his navy days. Officer and another pistol-carrying colleague were to take it in turns to protect the royal bride.

Never again would she be out in the streets or even go for a walk in St James' Park without having one of 'her' policemen nearby. A total of four men would always be near when Charles

and she were together.

These security arrangements came into use when the royal fiancées went to Covent Garden for their first night out together since announcing their engagement a week earlier.

It was a private visit and they sat in the Royal box to watch an international cast headed by the American black soprano Grace Bumbry in Meyerbeer's opera, "L'Africaine".

After the performance the Prince met Miss Bumbry and Italian singers Franco Bonisolli and Silvano Carroli.

It was a fairly discreet outing, a relaxing evening with no fuss and bother. Most of their fellow opera-goers were not aware of their visit until the interval.

The couple's second night out together caused much more of a stir, however. This was when they made their first official public appearance with Diana wearing what became known as THE DRESS.

A crowd of 200 was reported to have gasped as she stepped out of a Rolls

Right *Princess Grace of Monaco attended the charity gala at Goldsmiths' Hall, London on 9th March 1981, chosen as the first official function at which Lady Diana Spencer should be present. Despite bad weather, a huge crowd turned out to see Lady Diana on her "first night".*

Royce wearing a revealing low-cut, black evening dress. The couple had joined 300 guests at London's Goldsmiths Hall for an evening of verse and music in aid of the Royal Opera House Development Fund.

Despite the stunning cleavage, Diana looked relaxed and happy, clutching a pink rose presented to her by office worker Miss Pamela Elkins.

There was a card with it, saying: "To a lovely lady – an English rose."

Jovial Prince Charles, enjoying the attention his lovely wife-to-be was getting asked Pressmen: "Have all the fashion writers finished?"

Buckingham Palace's only comment on a very un-royal outfit was: "It was something she chose herself."

But she was criticised for her dress sense from a most unlikely quarter – a fashion columnist on *The Times* no less. Prudence Glynn, former fashion editor of *The Times*, and now a columnist on the paper, made her attack in the Paris-based *International Herald Tribune*.

She called Diana "a fashion disaster in her own right". She accused her of committing a "social gaffe" by wearing such a controversial off-the-shoulder dress for her night out at the opera.

"Lady Di has a few quick lessons to learn," says Miss Glynn – in private life Lady Windlesham. "She will never again – I hope – be allowed to appear in a strapless dress for an evening at the theatre.

"Leaving aside the fact that the dress practically fell off – causing great merriment among the socialist Press, and shivers among those who know that the only secret of being well dressed is to be appropriately dressed – nobody wears a strapless dress to an occasion on which she will be seated most of the time.

"Why? Because you look as though you are sitting in a hip bath, silly!

"Never mind, it will probably be her last venture into non-royal style."

Miss Glynn also jibed at Lady Diana's "good broad shoulders descending to a

Inside Goldsmiths' Hall before the gala performance, Princess Grace of Monaco chats to the Prince of Wales **opposite page and above** *as Lady Diana looks on* **left.**

matronly bosom, essential for the support of all the ironwear incumbent in her future position.

"No Barbara Cartland heroine will be a patch on Lady Di on the wedding day. For what does it matter that this charming, high-minded English rose will be wearing everything but the kitchen sink?

"As Queen she will have to wear it every day, in broad daylight, and where better to get into the routine than at the very start of the honeymoon period."

This criticism did not seem to disturb Diana. She went back to see the man and wife team who designed the controversial dress and asked them to make her wedding gown. By going to David and Elizabeth Emanuel's salon in Mayfair's Brook Street, the royal bride-to-be broke the palace habit of choosing one of a few traditional courtly fashion houses.

"We want to keep it romantic through and through. It might not be the normal wedding colour," said David Emanuel. "Remember we are not traditional. We did one in palest pink net which was so fragile and delicate it was absolutely beautiful."

The Emanuels began by studying the background against which the wedding gown will be seen – St Paul's.

"I have to look at the steps, all the surroundings – the whole atmosphere of this vast cathedral. "We always talk it over with clients and end up in mutual agreement," said 27-year-old Elizabeth.

Added David: "We really look at the client and note the colour of her hair and skin, look to see if she has wonderful shoulders or legs, and then it just evolves. With Lady Diana it is not just a case of showing wonderful shoulders. She is wonderful all over.

Left *A smiling Lady Diana Spencer at Goldsmiths' Hall on 9th March 1981, obviously enjoying her first official night out with Prince Charles after the announcement of their engagement a fortnight before. Less than three weeks later, duty called the Prince off on a tour of Australasia, South America and the United States.* **Opposite page** *Prince Charles with the New Zealand Prime Minister Mr Robert Muldoon, during the welcoming ceremonies at Wellington on 31st March.*

"Obviously we are looking at what other people have done. The example of the Queen's wedding gown comes to mind."

They had four months up to the day of the wedding, 29 July. David said, "It is all so exciting. We are so honoured to be doing the dress."

The couple also broke another tradition in their choice of St Paul's for the ceremony. It was chosen by the future Princess of Wales simply because it is bigger than Westminster Abbey, the usual venue for Royal weddings. The Cathedral can hold several hundred more guests than the Abbey.

With the wedding taking place at the height of the tourist season, it was

This was the first occasion on which the people of Romsey had had the opportunity of seeing their future Queen Consort, and these pictures show what a good impression she must have made on them. Her experience as a kindergarten teacher proved to be a great asset when it came to meeting children and babies **top left, and above. Opposite** *The happy couple radiate joy and contentment.*

expected to be a money spinning bonanza for Britain.

Organising the event was the Duke of Norfolk. At the beginning of the year he was warned by Buckingham Palace to keep his official engagement diary free from mid-April to 31 July. The Norfolks are the official masters-of-ceremonies

In May 1981, Prince Charles formally opened an exhibition of Mountbatten memorabilia at Broadlands, and commemorated his visit by planting a tree in the grounds **opposite page.** Lady Diana Spencer was invited to help, and did so **centre picture.**

to the British Royal Family.

Before Charles went on a five-week tour of New Zealand, Australia, Venezuela and the United States he released more details of the wedding plans.

He said he was not to have a best man. Instead he would have two "supporters" to share the duty.

Prince Andrew would be one and carry the wedding ring. Prince Edward would be the other.

Sharing the duty followed the practice at previous Royal marriages, Buckingham Palace said.

It was also announced that the bride would be given away by her father, Earl Spencer, and would ride with him to St Paul's in the last of four carriage pro-

The route – to be lined by members of all three Services – would be along The Mall, Trafalgar Square south side, the Strand, Fleet Street and Ludgate Hill.

Flags were to be flown in The Mall and from Admiralty Arch – quite apart from the thousands which were expected to be fluttering less formally along the crowded route.

Other details that filtered from the Palace in the hectic days after the announcement of the engagement included news that Lady Diana's wedding ring would be made from gold mined in the Prince's own principality of Wales.

It was to be made from the same

Prince Charles and Lady Diana among the crowds at Broadlands. Lady Diana was presented with a delicate bouquet of spring flowers.

cessions. They would be escorted by mounted police.

The procession was to be for members of the Royal Family with a Captain's Escort of the Household Cavalry.

The Queen would follow with a Sovereign's Escort and then would come Prince Charles in full dress of a Navy Commander with a Prince of Wales Escort.

A first taste of Ascot for Lady Diana Spencer. Prince Charles and his bride-to-be arrive **above** at Ascot in June 1981 for the traditional drive down the course. Lady Diana wears a modest mauve-grey outfit. **Left** With Prince Charles in New York, Lady Diana's escort on the second day is Princess Alexandra. **Opposite page** Yet another escort for Lady Diana who wears a smart ensemble in the bright, sharp designs which she favours.

nugget from the gold-mine at Bontddu in Gwynedd, Wales, from which the wedding rings of the Queen Mother, the Queen, Princess Margaret and Princess Anne, were crafted.

Collingwoods of Mayfair, goldsmiths and jewellers to the Queen and makers of wedding rings for the Duchess of Gloucester, the Duchess of Kent and Princess Alexandra, were to make the ring.

Left *The Queen and Prince Philip arriving at Royal Ascot in June 1981.* **Left centre** *Lady Diana Spencer arriving with Princess Alexandra of Kent and* **above** *later on the same day.* **Bottom left** *The Queen on her way to the Royal Enclosure.* **Below** *Prince Charles and Lady Diana leave Ascot in the Prince's Aston-Martin. The following day he left for a short visit to New York –* **bottom picture** *with Mrs · Nancy Reagan on a river trip.* **Opposite page** *A selection of the 1981 Ascot fashions.* **Overleaf** *These charming and novel official portraits of Lady Diana and the Prince by Lord Snowdon were taken in March 1981.*

But the making of the cake was a triumph for newcomers to such occasions – the Royal Naval Cookery School at *H.M.S. Pembroke*, the shore station at Chatham, Kent. Chief Petty Officer David Avery, 38, had been selected as chef.

Then came the announcement of who were to be Lady Diana's bridesmaids. She was to have five. As well as five-year-old Clementine Hambro, a pupil at the nursery school during the bride-to-be's teaching days, there would be Catherine Cameron, aged six, Sarah Jane Gaselee, 10, India Hicks, 14, and keeping a regal eye on them all, 17-year-old Lady Sarah Armstrong Jones.

Lady Sarah, daughter of Princess Margaret and Lord Snowdon, was a

bridesmaid at the wedding of Princess Anne and Captain Mark Phillips – so she should know what is expected.

The other youngsters, who would also be dressed by David and Elizabeth Emanuel had known they had been picked by Charles and Lady Di but none of them breathed a word.

Little Catherine, whose mother, Lady Cecil Cameron of Lochiel is godmother to Princess Anne's son Master Peter Phillips, breathed not a word either.

Nor did young Sarah Jane, although her father Nick Gaselee who trains

Left Lady Diana Spencer with two of her pupils at the Young England kindergarten in Pimlico in September 1980. **Below and opposite** Meeting her future neighbours while visiting Tetbury on 22 May. **Below left** Prince and Princess Michael of Kent after the christening of Lady Gabriela Windsor in June.

272

horses for Prince Charles at Lambourne, Berks, admitted: "It's been a big strain for her. She had to keep it a secret at school for two weeks and she was bursting to tell everyone.

"Lady Di has been down to see us a few times and Sarah Jane is very taken with her. Prince Charles asked me about it personally and I was only too pleased to agree."

India, daughter of designer David and Lady Pamela Hicks, was named because her grandfather, Lord Mountbatten was the country's last Viceroy and first Governor General.

Two pages were selected as well: Lord Nicholas Windsor, son of the Duke and Duchess of Kent – he would be 11 four days before the wedding – and

A close friend of Prince Charles, Nicholas Soames, married Miss Catherine Weatherall at St Margaret's, Westminster, in May 1981 and the Prince attended the ceremony with Lady Diana, Princess Margaret and the Queen Mother. **Top and top right** *The bride and groom with Prince Charles after the service.* **Above, and centre pictures** *The royal guests see the newly-married couple off, as a sudden gust of wind plays havoc with the bride's veil* **above right.**

Edward van Cutsem, eight-year-old son of Mr and Mrs Hugh van Cutsem, friends of Charles.

Lord Nicholas, India, Catherine and Edward are all godchildren of Prince Charles.

Amid all the excitement of helping to plan her wedding, Diana still found time to go out and about with her fiancé in the few crammed days before he left

on his global tour.

A schoolboy stole a kiss from the Royal bride-to-be during one outing.

Sixth-former, Nicholas Hardy, boldly asked Lady Di: "May I kiss the hand of my future Queen?"

She blushed but replied: "Yes, you may." Nicholas then shyly kissed Lady Diana's fingers after gallantly handing her a daffodil. This magic moment happened during a visit by Lady Di and Prince Charles to the police headquarters at Cheltenham.

There was an anxious moment for Lady Diana on another day however, when she went to see the Prince ride in his first steeplechase at Sandown Park races. Charles took a tumble at the 18th fence.

She was in the royal box – and after giving a frightened gasp she couldn't bear to look. While Charles buried his

nose in the mud Diana buried her face in her hands. She stayed that way until a tap on the shoulder from Princess Margaret assured her that all was well.

Meanwhile, Charles was picking himself up, apparently unhurt except for a bruised and bleeding nose. His bid to win the Grand Military Gold Cup was over, after completing most of the three-mile race. Gamely he remounted his horse, Good Prospect, and rode back to unsaddle.

By this time Lady Diana was waiting to greet him with a hug and an anxious "Are you all right?"

The Prince assured her he was not badly hurt and explained what happened. "I clipped the top of the fence and came quite a cropper. A lot of horses were coming down around me, but if I want to continue to race it's the only way to learn."

Jockey Phillip Blacker, who had often ridden Good Prospect, was tipping Charles for victory until the fateful 18th fence. He said: "The Prince was riding a beautiful race. I thought it was the horse who made a mistake, not the Prince."

Charles did, at least, have one success – before the race he tipped the

eventual winner – The Drunken Duck.

When Prince Philip or Prince Charles fly, either by helicopter or in a fixed-wing aircraft, they travel in the most carefully-monitored airspace in Britain. They are given a flight path exclusive to themselves and no other aircraft is allowed to enter or cross it. That section of the sky becomes known

as the Purple Airway, out of bounds even to a plane or helicopter on a mercy mission.

Whenever they fly in Britain they often pilot one of the Royal helicopters, which, in their red livery, are a common sight over central London. Recently Prince Charles left the people he had been chatting to in Buckingham Palace to walk to a helicopter parked in the garden, in which he whizzed off in grand style to Wales for the afternoon.

On the night before the wedding of Prince Charles and Lady Diana, half a million people gathered in Hyde Park to watch a spectacular firework display, a wedding gift from the Household Divi-

Opposite page *Prince Charles, bloodied but smiling gamely, rides back to the paddock after being thrown from his horse Good Prospect at Sandown. It was the first of two falls he suffered in a month's steeplechasing.* **Top and above** *He canters his horse before the race.* **Above right** *The Prince with Princess Margaret (in fur coat), the Queen Mother and Lady Diana Spencer before the start of the race.* **Right** *Lady Diana, engaged only three weeks before, is the focus of attention from a barrage of photographers as she leaves the paddock at Sandown.*

sion. The background for the festivities took the form of a scaffolding firework palace based on a similar display held in Green Park in 1749 to celebrate the peace of Aix-la-Chapelle.

The King's Troop fired a six gun salute, beacons were lit throughout the country and fireworks exploded in the night sky to the accompaniment of music by the massed bands of the Guards Division. The whole scene, watched by an impressive array of foreign dignitaries and by the Queen, Prince Philip, Prince Charles and other members of the Royal Family (but not

Lady Diana), formed a more than fitting celebration for the Prince of Wales' last night as the world's most eligible bachelor.

On the following morning the wedding, together with all the pomp and circumstance which accompanied it, was witnessed by a crowd officially estimated at 600,000 in the capital and by a worldwide audience of 750 million. Many of those who had poured into London to be part of an historic occasion spent the night in sleeping bags and blankets or perched on every conceivable form of garden furniture in order to secure their place on the route. From 4.30am onwards, hundreds of thousands of people, many of whom had been dancing the conga with the police into the early hours of the morning, waved banners and Union Jack flags with apparently boundless enthusiasm. The Prince of Wales' procession was greeted with all the adulation epitomised in the inscription on one

The occasion when horse racing became the sport of princes occurred at Plumpton Races on 4th March 1980 with Prince Charles taking part in his first ever steeplechase. **Opposite page, top and bottom right** *The Prince riding his horse Long Wharf round before the race. The photographs on this page show scenes during the race itself, the Madhatters Private Sweepstake, in which thirteen riders took part to earn money for the Injured Jockeys Benevolent Fund. Ultimately, despite a late challenge, the Prince was unable to close the gap between himself and the winner, Derek Thompson* **right** *and had to be content with second place.* **Opposite page, below left** *The Prince with Derek Thompson after the race.*

banner wafting high above the crowd. "Prince Charles can eat three shredded wheats a day!" it announced, referring to a television commercial which claims that even Superman is incapable of so momentous a feat. Some of the bunting was more official; some of the souvenir decorations would undoubtedly have failed to meet the Lord Chamberlain's criteria for "good taste" but the underlying thought remained the same. For a brief but happy interval people from all walks of life, all creeds and commitments, were united. The milling throngs had brought all the insignia and songs of a victorious football crowd and converted them for the day into patriotism and national pride.

It was a tribute to the popularity of Prince Charles and Lady Diana that during their engagement the rumblings of discontent at the prospect of so splendid a Royal Wedding had been few and faint. The ruling Labour Group on North East Derbyshire District Council had promised to fly a red flag from the Council's flag pole on the wedding day as "a matter of principle". The Labour administration of the G.L.C. declined an invitation to the ceremony with the gracious comment, "No one elected us to go to weddings. They elected us to try to get the buses running on time", and, according to one councillor of Clay Cross in Derbyshire, when Lady Diana Spencer began her ride to St Paul's in her magnificent glass coach she would be "riding on the backs of the working class and not realising what a mess the country is in". For the people of Clay Cross, he promised, 29 July would be a day of edification, highlighted by some suitably instructive "anti-monarchist" plays, explaining to working folk and the unemployed just how wretched and resentful the monarchy ought to make them feel.

When the day actually came, however, there was little, if any, evidence of such resentment. The Queen, Prince Philip, the visiting dignitaries and Heads of State were greeted enthusiastically, so too were the many other invited guests, among them a proper number of the dignified and mighty but also a host of personal friends. At 8am the dustcarts had cleared away the piles of rubbish that had accumulated on the processional route, to the

accompaniment of shouts of encouragement from the onlookers. At 9am a brass band had begun to play outside the cathedral. The crowd joined in with "Diana", "Doing the Lambeth Walk", "Maybe it's because I'm a Londoner", "Congratulations" and even with "Charlie, Charlie, give me your answer do".

By the time Lady Diana's procession left Clarence House every square inch

Opposite *Lord Snowdon's splendidly informal portrait of Prince Charles and his fiancée, taken shortly after their engagement.* **Above** *More formally, Lord Snowdon captures Lady Diana's regal pose in this study taken at Highgrove House.* **Left** *Prince Charles' signet ring sets off the sparkling sapphire and diamond engagement ring on Lady Diana's finger.* **Overleaf** *Formal portraits of the couple before an immense tapestry at Highgrove, the house to which they will go after their return from honeymoon.*

of pavement, balcony, step, wall, tree and telephone kiosk roof was occupied. The nation held its breath for the first glimpse of the bridal gown and was kept in suspense until the bride and her father stepped out of the coach outside the cathedral.

Lady Diana had been woken early. Shortly after 6am, Kevin Shanley, her hairdresser from her flatsharing days, arrived to modify her now famous hair-

Opposite page above *The Queen and Prince Philip head the procession as they emerge from the Palace onto the concourse around the Queen Victoria Memorial* **above.** *Eight minutes later, Prince Charles and Prince Andrew follow* **opposite page below,** *and* **right** *on their way into the Mall* **top** *and* **far right.**

style for the requirements of a veil and a tiara. Barbara Daly, the make-up artist, set to work in Lady Diana's Clarence House dressing room to apply only the lightest of make-up designed not to detract from the bride's "pretty natural blush".

Inevitably, the early visitors to

Clarence House also included David and Elizabeth Emanuel, designers of The Dress. "We want to make her look just like a fairy-tale princess", David Emanuel had promised when it was announced that they were to be granted the commission for the royal wedding dress, and the first glimpse the waiting

world had of her through a cloudy mass of mother-of-pearl spangled tulle, held in place by the Spencer family tiara, had all the mysterious quality of a fairy-tale. When the dress was finally revealed, as Lady Diana stepped from the Glass Coach, the richness of the lace and the hand embroidered mother-of-pearl sequins and seed pearls, the layers of tulle and the taffeta bows together with a 25-foot train spoke not only of romance but also of grandeur.

Tradition had been adhered to. The lace, according to an announcement from Buckingham Palace, was old, the taffeta, woven from the life's labours of British silkworms, was new, the tiara, a family heirloom, was borrowed, and a small blue bow was sewn into the boned waistband of the dress. Further-

more, just in case all this did not ensure sufficient luck for the "bride of the century", a tiny 18-carat gold horseshoe studded with diamonds was also stitched into the dress, although the Palace did not reveal precisely where.

The low-heeled shoes were made from matching ivory silk top-stitched in a diamond pattern and in the centre of each diamond was stitched a tiny mother-of-pearl sequin. On the front of each slipper was a large, gold-embroidered, pearl – and sequin – decorated heart, trimmed with gathered lace in the manner of a Victorian valentine.

The bouquet was also steeped in sentiment and symbolism. A gift from the Worshipful Company of Gardeners of London, it was designed and made by David Longman, whose father made the Queen's wedding bouquet in 1947. The flowers were all fragrant and all British: golden Mountbatten roses to commemorate the man Prince Charles regarded as his honorary grandfather, gardenias, orchids, stephanotis, lily-of-

the-valley, white freesia and traditional myrtle and veronica cut from bushes at Osborne House which, in their turn, had been grown from cuttings from Queen Victoria's wedding posy.

The bridesmaids, with something of a pre-Raphaelite air, wore fresh flowers in their hair to crown their ivory taffeta and lace dresses enlivened with broad satin ribbon sashes.

When, therefore, Lady Diana began her long walk up the aisle of Sir Christopher Wren's masterpiece, to the sound of the Trumpet Voluntary, her

entry was nothing if not dramatic. The photographers tucked away in the Cathedral's baroque cornices were not denied a spectacular visual display. Inside St Paul's Beefeaters, Gentlemen at Arms and Military Knights of Windsor added to the colour already provided by an eye-catching array of hats and the whole scene was off-set by what Prince Charles himself had rightly promised would be a feast of music. Purcell, Britten, Elgar, Vaughan Williams – the Best of British re-sounded in one of the most effective concert halls in London. Trumpets, hymns, orchestras and choirs all reflected the Prince of Wales' love of music.

On this occasion, Sir David Will-cocks, Director of the Royal College of Music assisted Christopher Dearnley, the Cathedral organist. The Cathedral Choir, the Choir of the Chapel Royal, the

Opposite page: Top left *Chief brides-maids India Hicks and Lady Sarah Armstrong Jones, who is seen following the bride into St Paul's. The Queen and Queen Mother turn to wave as they enter the Cathedral with Prince Philip and Prince Edward.* **Left** *Lady Diana turns to check that all is well as she ascends the steps. The pictures* **this page** *show the early arrival of the bridesmaids, and the beginning of Lady Diana's long walk up the nave on the arm of her father* **top and bottom left** *followed by her attendants* **centre.**

London Bach Choir and the augmented Covent Garden Orchestra all combined to lead the singing of the hymns and the anthems, some of which were specially composed for the ceremony. To highlight an already outstanding musical presentation the soprano soloist, Kiri Te Kanawa was invited to sing during the signing of the register.

The service itself represented an unprecedented drawing together of the Churches. The presence and participation of a number of denominations made it a more ecumenical service than any previous Royal Wedding. Apart from Dr Runcie, Cardinal Basil Hume, Roman Catholic Archbishop of Westminster, and the Right Rev. Andrew Doig, Moderator of the General Assembly of the Church of Scotland, read the prayers. Mr George Thomas, Speaker of the House of Commons and a leading Methodist read the first lesson. A dynastic event was endowed with yet another dimension.

"Here", said the Archbishop of Canterbury in his address, "is the stuff of which fairytales are made: the Prince and Princess on their wedding day"... "There is an ancient Christian tradition", he reminded his congregation, "that every bride and groom on their wedding day are regarded as a royal couple. To this day in the marriage ceremonies of the Eastern Orthodox Church crowns are held over the man and the woman to express the conviction that as husband and wife they are kings and queens of creation." All of us are given the power to make the future more in God's image and to be "kings and queens" of love – was his

message – "We as human beings can help to shape this world".

If the great and historic performance was also moving, however, it was because if every human being has the potential for kingship, then at the same time kings and queens are also human, and this momentous occasion showed the heir to the throne and his bride to be no exceptions. When it came to making her wedding vows, the bride took someone called "Philip Charles Arthur George to my wedded husband, to have and to hold from this day forward". Her

The superbly rich splendour of the interior of St Paul's matches the historic occasion as **right** *Lady Diana, dressed in ivory silk with a veil and train spangled with mother-of-pearl and sequins, follows the clergy towards the Choir.* **Top** *She approaches the specially constructed platform, which effectively extends the chancel, and at which Prince Charles waits with his supporters Prince Andrew and Prince Edward. Having reached this point, she stands before the Archbishop of Canterbury* **opposite page** *with her father on her left and her husband-to-be on her right.*

inversion of the first two of Prince Charles' prolific string of Christian names, early in a service at which the couple were visibly nervous and overcome by a profound sense of occasion, was quickly followed and softened by a slip on the part of the Prince.

As he placed the ring on the bride's finger, the bridegroom, whose experience of public engagements, if not of marriage, began in the year his wife-to-be was born, announced solemnly; "with this ring I thee wed, with my body I thee honour, and all thy goods I share with thee".

Outside St Paul's, and all along the processional route to Buckingham Palace the crowds were listening to the service on radios and portable tele-

Far right With the Prince and his bride now married, the first part of the wedding ceremony is over and the royal couple sit for an address by the Archbishop. Then, during the singing of Parry's anthem "I Was Glad" they rise right and follow the Archbishop to the High Altar for prayers above. Opposite Another superb view of a significant point in the service: the Prince and Princess stand before the Altar, which is fashioned in Sicilian marble and overhung by the huge ornate cupola bearing the figure of Christ in Majesty. Top right After the signing of the Register, the newly married couple walk back down the nave towards the West door of the Cathedral.

vision sets. On every spare inch of space they sat, eating sandwiches and generally recovering from an early morning start, but when the moment came for Prince Charles to say "I will", great cheers resounded. When his bride said "I will" also, the cheers were even louder and when both the bride and groom were shown to be susceptible to human frailty, the crowd took the

couple tumultuously to their hearts. "I pronounce that they be man and wife together", announced the Archbishop of Canterbury, and outside the Cathedral the radio listeners shouted unanimously, "Three cheers for the Prince and Princess of Wales".

When the bride came out of the registry with her veil at last thrown back, the Prince and Princess of Wales walked down the aisle to Elgar's Pomp and Circumstance, and the Queen followed on behind. As the Prince and his new bride emerged from St Paul's they were pelted with confetti, rice and rose petals. The Church of England had poured the treasures of its liturgy and its music at the feet of the royal couple and now it was the turn of the expectant crowds to offer their tributes.

The newly-weds' carriage led the procession back to Buckingham Palace to be met by an ecstatic reception, and as the carriages circled the Victoria memorial the Queen also received enthusiastic acclaim. As she was driven past, this time in the company of Earl Spencer, the onlookers burst spontaneously into the National Anthem. Those who were concerned that Queen Elizabeth II might be upstaged by her young daughter-in-law need not have worried. As the three-quarters of a million people pressed down the Mall to witness the traditional balcony appearance, the singing and shouting was not only for the rulers of the future but also for the reigning monarch.

The Prince and Princess of Wales, and the Queen and the Duke of Edinburgh, appeared three times on the palace balcony. The regulation time for balcony appearances is three minutes, after which attention is supposed to wane, but the Royal Family were visibly

The moment the crowds outside the Cathedral, and the several hundred million throughout the world who watched the wedding on television, had waited for – the first public appearance of Britain's new Princess of Wales on the arm of her husband. **Top** *The bride's triumphant wave to the wildly cheering crowds.* **Right and opposite** *Both partners radiating happiness as they descend the steps towards their waiting carriage.*

moved by so unbridled a demonstration of affection and the crowd held them each time for five minutes. Then the immediate family of the bride and groom, together with the pages and bridesmaids, disappeared from public view for a somewhat belated wedding breakfast. All that remained was for the new Prince and Princess of Wales to ride away at four o'clock for Waterloo.

When they emerged, 20 minutes late, it was in a coach festooned with blue-and-white balloons, each bearing the arms of the Prince of Wales, and with a

The long journey back to Buckingham Palace for the Prince and Princess of Wales was accompanied by a continuous and tumultuous roar of delight from the crowd. These photographs show how pleased the new Princess was with the warmth of her reception as the royal couple's procession left the precincts of St Paul's Cathedral. They were driven in the 1902 State Postillion Landau in which Prince Charles and Prince Andrew had ridden to the service.

cardboard sign which was obviously not the handiwork of the royal sign writer but which announced quite clearly that they were "Just Married".

At Waterloo Station the luxurious private coach of British Rail's Southern Region Manager waited to transport the newest royal couple to Broadlands where they would spend the first days of their honeymoon, before flying to Gibraltar to join the royal yacht *Britannia*. In the sitting-room of the royal carriage were two orange sofas, three posies of red, white and blue flowers, a radio, a bowl of fruit and a

bottle of champagne. The carriage had been overhauled and repainted for five weeks prior to the wedding to ensure an appropriate start to a royal honeymoon. The meticulous planning and preparation had not been to no avail and the conclusion of a 90-minute journey to Romsey offered privacy behind the unbreached and unbreachable wrought iron gates of Broadlands, where in 1947 the Queen had begun her honeymoon.

Opposite page above *An uncharacteristic view of a section of the 650,000 spectators lining the route as they wait patiently for the procession to pass.* **Above** *A respite for police and mounted militia before the Royal Family returns from St Paul's.* **Top** *The carriage bearing the Duke of Edinburgh and Mrs Peter Shand-Kydd.* **Centre right** *Salutes and cheers for the Queen Mother as she passes by St Clement Danes. Her carriage is followed by the landau in which Princess Margaret, Princess Anne, Captain Mark Phillips and Viscount Linley ride* **right,** *travelling towards St Mary-in-the-Strand.* **Opposite page below** *Sarah Gaselee and Clementine Hambro enjoying their ride back in Queen Alexandra's State Coach.*

Jubilant balcony scenes as the bride and groom appear **opposite page above** with their bridesmaids and pages – from left to right, India Hicks, Edward van Cutsem, Clementine Hambro, Lord Nicholas Windsor, Sarah Gaselee, Lady Sarah Armstrong Jones and Catherine Cameron. **Opposite page below** The Queen joins her son and daughter-in-law. **Centre right** The moment that captivated all who saw it: the famous 'balcony kiss'. **Bottom right** A close-up of the newly-married couple. **Bottom** Alone on the balcony, the Prince and Princess wave as the vast crowd cheers ecstatically.

Overleaf Lord Lichfield's formal group photograph showing the bride and groom, their bridesmaids and pages, together with members of their families. Two of the bridesmaids complete an irresistible picture as they stand with their toes turned in in the manner of little girls the world over.

Not quite waiting in the wings – more likely popping his head round the curtains – and impatient to get fully involved in public life, is Prince Andrew, the Queen's second son.

If Charles tends to take after his mother in his personality, Andrew is truly a chip off the old block. He is a strapping six-footer, having all the exuberance of youth, as well as the fearless, sand-paperish characteristics of his father. With his striking good looks, he is also, much to his delight, being dubbed by the media as the new royal "pin-up boy".

He is more extrovert than Charles, yet has the Queen Mother's crowd-pleasing charm. He is very open and frank, and fond of using sometimes

excruciatingly corny jokes to break the ice with people he meets.

From early on he was a boisterous child; even as a toddler he would drive the palace staff mad with his mischievous ways and determination to get his own way every time.

As soon as he was out of the nursery Prince Philip set him on the same path as brother Charles 12 years earlier; gymnastics, riding and swimming – activities which Andrew took to with more enthusiasm than Charles did at the age of five. He only needed about half-an-hour to get the hang of swimming and was soon racing down to the palace pool with his father.

By the time Andrew went to Gordonstoun, at the age of 13, the staff were claiming that it was less Spartan than in Charles' day. Showers were no longer compulsory in winter, and girls had been admitted to the school as an experiment in co-education. A great value was still placed on the hardiness of life, however, and Andrew accepted the whole thing with zest. He wrote glowing letters home after only a few months there.

With an aggressiveness inherited from his father it was to be expected that he would land himself in the odd quarrel, and masters recall that he was good with his fists. He became what

Royal guests, including the Duke and Duchess of Gloucester **opposite page centre** *arriving at Claridge's for the State Banquet given by King Khalid of Saudi-Arabia during his State Visit to Britain in June 1981.* **Top** *The King talking to the Queen before the banquet.*

Gordonstoun likes to turn out, a good, all-rounder in the British public school tradition – someone who was good academically yet could still wield a straight bat on the sports field. He fitted in easily with the tough régime of Gordonstoun.

He has enormous physical energy and courage, and is now developing into a greater daredevil than his eldest brother.

By the age of 18 he had already proved himself a tough opponent on the rugby field, a first-rate yachtsman, an excellent skier, an almost reckless ice-hockey player and a qualified glider pilot.

Flight Lieutenant Peter Bullivant, the man who trained Andrew to glide while at Gordonstoun, recalls: "He learnt fast, really fast. I am not saying that because he is a prince. It really is so. The only thing that stopped him from getting his licence as a glider pilot in a record time up here in Scotland was the fact that we had to wait for his 16th birthday. He was ready for it within weeks, and to celebrate his birthday he went solo for the first time."

The Queen and her advisers have

always thought it essential for the royal sons to spend some period of their education in the Commonwealth.

Charles went to Timbertops in Australia and the experience was not only successful in cementing Commonwealth relations but it also brought out all the best that we now see in Charles. He often says: "I grew up in Australia."

It has become one of his favourite countries, which he always enjoys visiting and he regards it as a second home.

Canada was to be the place for Andrew. Lakefield College, about 100 miles east of Toronto and a school which had an exchange scheme with

Like his elder brother, Prince Andrew has shown an inclination to serve in the armed forces, particularly in the RAF and Royal Navy. **Below** *With Prince Charles, Prince Andrew underwent a short course in parachute jumping at RAF Brise Norton in 1978. In April of that year* **right and far right** *he made a series of jumps from an RAF Hercules at South Cerney RAF Station in Gloucestershire. Despite one or two heavy landings, the Prince came through the exercise without injury.*

He could not resist making clear his reputation as a comedian soon after reaching Lakefield. He told 16-year-old Peter Dance, the boy taking his place at Gordonstoun: "It's like a prison out .there. Like being cooped up in a wartime camp like Colditz. The mattresses are a thin layer of old straw. The beds are hard as iron. The food is terrible." It was a perturbed Peter who headed across the Atlantic, where, fortuitously, his fears proved groundless.

Andrew had been taught to ice skate when he was seven years old but ice-hockey at Lakefield was a new experience. At first he had to take some mighty spills, leaving him with a mass of bruises.

When he arrived at Lakefield there was a reaction among some of the boys there who declared that they would "push in the royal nose". On the ice-rink Andrew came up against experienced schoolboy players in this roughest, and sometimes dirtiest, of all sports. He seized the initiative right from the beginning and laid about him with such verve that the referee warned him about "rough play". One of the survivors of the onslaught said admiringly later: "He is no English gentleman – he plays dirty."

Andrew made the most of his half year in North America. He did not stay solely in Canada. On one occasion he travelled with a party of his schoolmates 600 miles in a chartered bus to Pittsburgh to watch the *Pittsburgh Penguins* play ice-hockey. He was fascinated by what he saw on the journey, constantly asking questions about the

Gordonstoun, was chosen for the Prince.

The six months spent there by Andrew, with his love of the outdoors and hardy, physical activities, became more like a holiday than an educational chore. He improved his skiing on the snow-covered hills around the school, and went on an adventure trek and canoeing expedition in the wild north of Canada.

Prince Andrew entered the Navy as a midshipman in August 1979, and passed out of Dartmouth in March 1980 **top right.** *On that occasion, his mother, the Queen, visited Dartmouth to inspect the parade, and is seen* **top left** *passing just behind her son.* **Centre left** *Prince Andrew, who shares Prince Charles' interest in polo – but as a spectator and not a participant, with his brother at Windsor in 1980. Prince Andrew has already begun to undertake tours abroad: in July and August 1979 he accompanied his parents* **left** *on their tour of East Africa.*

Pictured above Prince Andrew with the Queen and Prince Philip taking a lively interest in the events at Badminton in April 1978. **Far right** Captain Mark Phillips takes his horse successfully through the water-splash, but **opposite page, top** comes a cropper second time round, in the 1972 event. **Right** Moment of departure as Captain Phillips and his horse find one of the fences too challenging during the 1980 event.

American way of life. At Pittsburgh he spent two nights in a local hotel – heavily guarded all the time by his personal detective, and a Mountie sent from Canada.

The Queen wishes to keep Andrew out of the public eye until he finishes his education, but he is gradually being brought to the fore. His first big, formal occasion was at the Montreal Olympics when he was among the royal party at the games.

He is mad about sport, and at Montreal he, alone among the royals, wanted to see every sport he could. When his parents returned to their quarters Andrew insisted on staying around to watch whatever sport was still going on.

One of Andrew's greatest ventures so far was to become a fully-trained parachutist. His cool courage was noticed when he took the 10-day "para" course with the Royal Air Force in the spring of 1978. He was not given any special privileges because he is a prince – he had to go through all the arduous training and take the same risks as the other members of the crack Parachute Regiment who were with him.

Left *Nearly a nasty accident as Princess Anne, competing in 1980, tried to keep control of her mount.* **Right** *Captain Phillips manages to keep reasonably dry – upper picture – as he takes his horse through the water-splash in 1972, but – lower picture – it's an early bath for Princess Anne.*

was great – I can't wait to get up again." Was he scared? "Yes, of course – if you're not scared and nervous you'll do something stupid," he answered.

What will happen to Andrew next? He may go to university but a career in the Royal Air Force or Royal Navy seems certain. He may experience them both, as Charles has done. Whatever he does, neither Andrew nor his lifestyle will be boring.

Now that Charles has taken the big step into marriage the role of "royal girl-chaser" seems to have been taken over by Andrew, who was given the nick-name "Randy Andy" from the age

During one of his early jumps from a Hercules aircraft at a thousand feet over South Cerney in Gloucestershire, the slipstream of the plane flung him into a spin, twisting his parachute rigging into a tangle. He jerked and bounced his body on the end of the 'chute until it was free, made a text-book landing and said calmly: "That

extremely courteous and aware.

"I guess he is attractive to women. He really liked to be where there were women, I think because they didn't give him a rough time.

"When he was at the home of the people acting as his guardians in Canada he tended to go into a room where the ladies were, while I went into a room with the men.

"Whether they are grandmothers or little girls, he always gravitated

As Queen of Canada, Her Majesty opened and attended the 1976 Olympics at Montreal. **Above** *A broad smile from the Queen during the opening ceremony.* **Left** *Faces in the crowd: the Queen with Prince Andrew and Prince Philip, amongst the spectators.* **Above left** *A gloomy outlook, as the Queen, Prince Andrew and the Prince of Wales watch the equestrian events in heavy rain.*

towards the ladies and was utterly charming to them. He knew they weren't trying to analyse or compete with him."

Andrew once said to some friends: "I don't think I've ever been in love with anyone."

"Except yourself," countered a girl companion, which brought a broad smile from Andrew.

Andrew obviously delights in his own image of a rather racy adventurer, a bit of a lad with the ladies, and having film-star good-looks.

He has never been as shy as Charles, who has always seemed conscious of a great responsibility eventually to be borne. He has inherited the briskness of manner of his father.

Says one of his contemporaries: "He can be blunt to the point of rudeness,

of 16, when he began dating girls during his half year of education in Canada.

His first proper girlfriend was a local girl, blonde Sandi Jones, who first met Andrew when she was his official hostess at the Olympic Games in Montreal in 1976.

She said recently: "He is a real character who always tries to make people laugh. He loves girls.

"When he lets his hair down he is just like any teenager on the block.

"In public he knows he has to play his role and be a prince. Then he is

Right *Princess Anne, who took part in the 1976 Olympics, discusses the equestrian event with Prince Philip.* **Below right** *A quick word of encouragement from the Queen for Princess Anne, as Prince Edward looks on.* **Below and bottom right** *The Queen with her three sons wait for Princess Anne's turn to compete.* **Bottom picture** *The Queen keeps a keen eye on the afternoon's events, with her camera at the ready.*

particularly about protocol or boring red tape. And he has a stinging wit when he wants to use it."

Inevitably, much of the public's interest in Andrew has centred on his reputation as the sailor with a girl in every port. His amorous adventures, many of them no doubt harmless enough, have earned joking references to "Andy's Harem".

His "dates" are legion, showing a preference for stunning models rather than dukes' daughters – looks before lineage.

Since leaving Gordonstoun and joining the Royal Navy he has dated Caroline Seaward the beauty queen, the 21-year-old models and cousins Gemma Curry and Kim Deas, and Carolyn Biddle, beautiful daughter of a wealthy American family.

Says one of his first girlfriends: "He is just an ordinary sort of guy who likes to have fun with his girlfriends."

Fun, in fact, seems to be high on his list of priorities.

He enjoyed hugely his first shore leave in Florida at a topless bar, though the resulting publicity couldn't have pleased his parents.

The royal pin-up role amuses him too.

He stands a strapping 6ft tall, has a 39 inch chest and a 32 inch waist. Clear-eyed, clear-skinned, clean cut.

He admires Charles's "Action Man" achievements and keenly competes with his brother at everything from

bestowed on the second son of the monarch, but that is unlikely to entail many duties.

But he has already started to see State papers on a regular basis.

He has shown all the signs of a new maturity in the transition from boyhood to manhood – from a self-willed, exuberant boy whose catalogue of prank-playing, including whoopee cushions for unwitting guests, bubble-bath in the palace pool, and even

Opposite *A forest of hands greets the Queen as she disembarks from her aircraft at Blantyre, at the beginning of her State Visit to Malawi in July 1979. The welcoming group of colourfully dressed girls wore robes bearing the portrait of their President as they danced on the tarmac* **above right. Top** *The Queen with President Banda of Malawi during her three day visit. Two days before arriving at Malawi, she had visited Tanzania:* **above** *arriving at Dar-es-Salaam and being escorted by President Nyerere. Part of the same tour of East Africa that year included a visit to Botswana, during which the Queen, Prince Philip and Prince Andrew attended a garden party at State House* **right.**

wind-surfing and skiing to parachute jumping.

As a hopeful helicopter pilot he must continually meet the rigorous fitness requirements of the Navy. He qualified as a helicopter pilot in April 1980.

Andrew's life over the next 10 years will concentrate on his Naval career.

He can look forward to becoming Duke of York, a title traditionally

knotting the bootlaces of palace sentries, to a forthright young man with an active career ahead of him.

He has never been enthusiastic about intellectual matters, choosing a service career rather than Cambridge, but he has a dogged determination to succeed which will stand him in good stead.

Edward shows a keenness for football, rugby and cricket and he has started to go sailing with Andrew in the

waters around Gordonstoun.

Although Andrew and Edward have taken up sailing, one of their father's favourite hobbies, Charles never developed the same enthusiasm for it as Prince Philip. Neither do they seem to follow the same tack when they are afloat, as Charles once recalled: "I remember one disastrous day when we were racing and my father, as usual, was shouting. We wound the winch harder and the sail split in half with a sickening crack; father was not pleased! Not long after that I was banned from the boat after an incident cruising off Scotland. There was no wind and I was amusing myself taking pot shots at beer cans floating around the boat. The only gust of wind that day blew the jib in front of my rifle as I fired. I wasn't invited back on board . . ."

Two highlights of the Royal Tour of East Africa undertaken by the Queen, Prince Philip and Prince Andrew in July and August 1979. **Top** *The Queen with Mr Kenneth Kaunda of Zambia on her arrival in Lusaka when she received a beautiful bouquet of flowers from an impeccably dressed young lady (opposite page).* **Above** *The Queen with Prince Andrew, whose first official tour abroad this was. The royal party also visited Malawi and met President Hastings Banda,* **centre left** *who accompanied them during an inspection of the guard of honour* **left.**

Prince Charles and Prince Philip do, however, both enjoy shooting. Charles is keen on the gun and his standards are as high as those of his grandfather, George VI, who was rated one of the finest shots in the royal household. Charles and Philip go shooting at Sandringham for pheasant and partridge, and in North Yorkshire and Scotland for grouse. One weekend at Sandringham Charles and Prince Philip, together with a few friends, bagged 600 birds between them.

Sitting among the congregation at the service in St Paul's Cathedral in the summer of 1980, to mark the Queen Mother's Birthday, was Lord Snowdon.

It was typical of the Queen Mother to have Princess Margaret's former husband at the ceremony, because she always was, and still is, very fond of him.

Her daughter Margaret, with her well-publicised, eventful life, has never had the easiest path as far as her emotional involvement with men is concerned.

If ever a girl, then a woman, needed an understanding and compassionate mum to turn to it has been Princess Margaret, 50 years old in August 1981, and still causing eyebrows to be raised.

Fortunately for her tempestuous daughter and her confused affairs, the Queen Mother was always there when

Top photographs *The Queen arriving at the Aldwych Theatre for a performance of the Comédie Française in the early 1960's* **left;** *the Queen Mother with Princess Margaret at the Royal Opera House in February 1978* **centre;** *and the Queen and Prince Philip attending a Claridge's banquet given by the visiting President Gowon of Nigeria in June 1973* **right. Above** *Princess Margaret at the film première of "Valentino" in October 1977.* **Right** *The Queen attending the première of the epic film "Waterloo" in London in October 1970.*

needed, but never interfering unless asked to do so.

All she has ever wanted for her daughter has been happiness. It would be wrong to say that the Queen Mother has a favourite between her two children, but those close to her say that she has always had a softer spot for Margaret Rose.

The mature judgement she has always brought to bear on her youngest daughter's activities was needed when the Princess, then in her early twenties, fell ecstatically in love with the handsome RAF fighter pilot, Group Captain Peter Townsend, who had been chosen as an equerry to King George VI.

As the world now knows, it was a

Left The Queen Mother chats with the stars after attending the Royal Film Performance at the Odeon Leicester Square, March 1981. **Below left and below** The Queen talks with Barbra Streisand after the Royal Film Performance in March 1975. **Bottom left** Princess Anne after the première of "Little Lord Fauntleroy" at the Haymarket Cinema in February 1981.

love that had tragic and painful results.

Attitudes have changed since Margaret wanted to marry Townsend, but 25 years ago everything seemed to be against them. He was a commoner, he was more than 15 years her senior, and he had already been married and had children.

The Queen Mother was very fond of Peter Townsend and appointed him to her own household after King George VI died. She is still friendly towards him and they have met occasionally over the years since the enforced break-up of his romance with Margaret.

In his autobiography, Group Captain Townsend, now a businessman living in France and Belgium, says: "My admiration and affection for Queen Elizabeth was, like everybody's, boundless – all the more so because beneath her graciousness, her gaiety and her unfailing thoughtfulness for others she possessed a steely will."

Whether or not she tried to use this strong willpower and influence of hers to help Margaret and Townsend find

happiness, the Government and other royal advisers were against the match.

Despite the wishes of the Queen Mother and the Queen, the powers that be insisted that the affair be ended. He was sent abroad to an exile which lasted more than two years. The lovers were kept apart, but they continued to exchange letters and 'phone calls during that period.

A few weeks after Margaret's 25th birthday, the Queen Mother brought the pair together again at her London

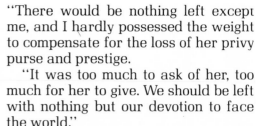

"There would be nothing left except me, and I hardly possessed the weight to compensate for the loss of her privy purse and prestige.

"It was too much to ask of her, too much for her to give. We should be left with nothing but our devotion to face the world."

Neither the Queen nor the Queen Mother put pressure on Princess Margaret at this delicate time. They made it clear that she had a free choice. While her mother listened to her

Top *A formal wedding group after Princess Margaret's marriage to Lord Snowdon on 6th May 1960. The group includes the best man, Dr Roger Gilliatt, and Princess Anne — at nine years of age, the chief bridesmaid. Princess Margaret's first child was born on 3rd November 1961 and was christened David Albert Charles. He is*

*seen **above** with his parents returning to Kensington Palace after his baptism at the end of November. **Below left** Princess Margaret with both her children in 1966: her second child, Lady Sarah Armstrong-Jones, was born on 1st May 1964. **Above left** Princess Margaret with her Lady-in-Waiting.*

home, Clarence House. She left them alone for the evening to see if they could sort out a commonsense solution to their problem.

Apart from Townsend's unsuitability as a prospective husband for a princess, there were also other snags to their relationship. If Margaret went ahead and married the man she so desperately wanted, she would have to renounce all her rights to the throne, retire from royal life and forfeit her official "salary" from the Civil List – worth at the moment around £60,000 a year.

Remembering the decision they had to take together, Townsend wrote:

younger daughter pouring out her soul hour after hour, she realised that there was only one real decision to be made – in the atmosphere of those days.

With great reluctance, Margaret took the step her friends say she has regretted ever since. On 31 October, 1955, Margaret and Townsend were left alone again by the Queen Mother at Clarence House so they could say a final farewell.

An hour later Princess Margaret issued a statement that referred to such matters as "being conscious of my duty to the Commonwealth" and "mindful of the Church's teaching that

Christian marriage is indissoluble".

It was all dressed-up in high-handed phrases, but what really mattered was the sentence: "I would like it to be known that I have decided not to marry Group Captain Townsend."

The great romance was over, finished for ever... but the pain of parting was softened by the Queen Mother's shoulder always being there to cry on.

Four years after that break Princess Margaret fell in love with another commoner, fashion photographer Tony Armstrong-Jones. This was a time when photographers did not have the "in" image they have today and there are some in royal circles who claim that Margaret deliberately turned her back on better-connected suitors to defy those who had caused her so much heartbreak earlier.

Margaret and Tony used to meet secretly in a small cottage alongside the river in London's dockland. It became their own special home, where, among discreet neighbours, they used to have very close friends around for dinners, cooked by the Princess on a small stove.

The Queen Mother knew what was going on and hoped that this second great love of her daughter's life would have a smooth passage.

Thankfully it did. All that she had been denied five years earlier came true for the Princess on 6 May, 1960 with a wedding in Westminster Abbey that had all the traditional royal trimmings.

Margaret adored her husband and began to enjoy the company of his artistic friends, ranging from fashion designers to film stars such as Peter Sellers and Liza Minelli. Their home in Kensington Palace soon took on a Bohemian air, with all-night parties attended by the sort of guests not normally invited to royal homes.

The marriage went well, even though Margaret was against Tony making a living and career away from court circles. He was not prepared just to live off his wife – a decision that impressed the Queen Mother, who admired his independence.

But, after 10 years together, and despite both being devoted to their two children, their love for each other began to turn sour. It became an open

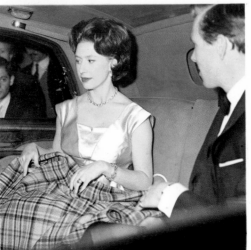

Above *Princess Margaret and Lord Snowdon are accompanied by the Lord Mayor of London, Sir Bernard Waley-Cohen, as they enter St Paul's Cathedral for a service in May 1961.*
Right *Two months later, and after the announcement that she was expecting her first child, the Princess and her husband return to Kensington Palace after an evening at the ballet.*

secret among their friends that they were spending more time apart than together.

With their son and daughter away at

boarding schools, the need to stay together seemed unnecessary. They are both quick-tempered and their rows became too frequent.

Lord Snowdon moved into a house of his own a mile away and they began to lead separate lives. In March 1976 the inevitable happened – they announced their separation, which was followed by a divorce.

Throughout this time, and since, the Queen Mother stayed in touch with Lord Snowdon, as guide and sympathetic adviser. She tried to ease the harshness of their breaking-up, especially for the children, Viscount Linley,

who was 15 at the time, and his 11-year-old sister, Lady Sarah Armstrong-Jones.

Lord Snowdon has remarried, but he and the children still go to visit grandma. She has no bitter feelings towards him, and although still supporting her own daughter during her latest romantic escapades remains what she has always been... the ideal mother-in-law.

The Princess and Lord Snowdon had what today is called a "quickie" divorce, with neither of them being present in court. It took just one minute and 53 seconds to end the fairy-tale

marriage of the Princess and the photographer. The no-fuss, Mrs Jones-style, divorce was sandwiched in a list of 28, which included a barmaid and a cleaner.

The sunshine marriage which began with all the pomp of the Westminster Abbey ceremony ended on a dull May day in 1978 in Court 44 of the High Court Queen's Building – opened, ironically, by the Queen 10 years earlier.

Above, and top *Princess Margaret in ebullient mood at an Exchange Teachers' Garden Party at Lancaster House in 1978. After 1978, the Princess lost weight, and by March 1981* **left** *she was at her most elegant when attending the Royal Film Performance at the Odeon Cinema, Leicester Square.*

Princess Margaret was still convalescing "somewhere in the country" with a stomach illness, and was not expected to carry out any public duties for at least a month.

Lord Snowdon was at home in his elegant white house in Launceston Place, Kensington.

Like the glittering wedding, the divorce went off smoothly, without a hitch. The Princess and Lord Snowdon were 20th on the list. Just another two names... "H.R.H. The Princess Margaret Rose, Countess of Snowdon v. Armstrong-Jones A.C.R., Earl of Snowdon."

The judge, 71-year-old Roger Blenkiron Willis, asked: "Is there any party or any person present to show cause why a decree should not be pronounced?" There was no reply. He then asked whether there was "anybody to say anything on costs?" Again, there was no reply and the judge announced: "Very well. I pronounce decree nisi in accordance with the respective registrars' certificates." Then the judge moved on to other court business. It was all just routine.

The 47-year-old Princess's divorce had gone through like that of any other wife and mother on the day's list.

Lord Snowdon had met Mrs Lindsay-Hogg several years earlier when they worked together on a BBC documentary film. She was a production assistant and a year before their marriage they worked together again on a documentary in Australia.

This was at a time when Princess Margaret's name was beginning to be linked with that of Roddy Llewellyn, the 31-year-old son of Olympic star, Colonel Sir Harry Llewellyn.

Mrs Lindsay-Hogg was previously

Above *Princess Margaret looking radiant at a performance of the Royal Ballet in March 1981.* **Right** *In the days before her divorce, she is accompanied by Lord Snowdon at another Royal Ballet performance, this time in New York in May 1974.* **Far right** *Princess Margaret visited Hollywood in November 1977 as part of an extensive tour of the USA. Here she meets the stars of "Starsky and Hutch"–David Soul (right) and Paul Michael Glazer.*

married to film producer Michael Lindsay-Hogg, but that ended in divorce in 1971.

The number of relatives now involved in royal duties is a tremendous help to the Queen. They are of different age groups and personalities, have a wide range of interests and are, therefore, able to take part in a breadth of royal involvement she could never hope to achieve alone. Apart from the

Photographs of Princess Anne and Captain Mark Phillips taken during their engagement in the late summer of 1973. **Opposite page** *The gentle touch: the couple on a bridge over a stream in the grounds of Frogmore House, Windsor, and* **below left** *enjoying the idyllic scene from a waterside bench there.* **Left** *An effective study in diffused light.* **Below** *The couple with one of Princess Anne's dogs pose for one of the many official photographs, released a few days before the wedding in November 1973.*

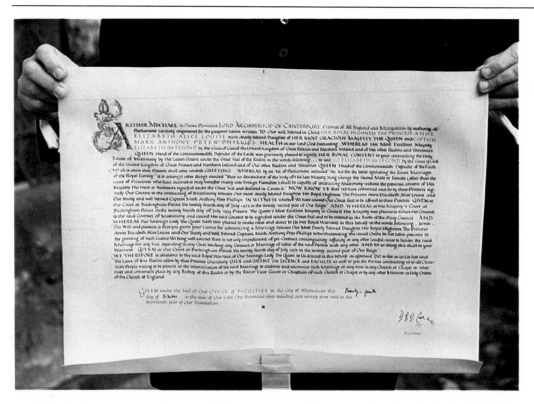

demands on her time, there are some activities which would be out of character – yet the other recruits can fit in very easily. Prince Charles, for example, is a natural choice for something dangerous or adventurous, whilst Princess Alexandra and her husband, the Honourable Angus Ogilvy, a successful financier, are perfect for links with the business community.

What might be called a mini-court now exists around the Queen. First in the complicated order of who should represent her on official duties is, of course, Prince Philip, followed by Prince Charles.

Until Prince Edward and Prince Andrew reach an age when they too can play their full part in royal duties, Princess Anne and husband, Captain Mark Phillips, are most important in the royal line.

Princess Anne never felt that she was in second place to Charles as she grew up, because they have always been so close and she was never overshadowed. It is not in her nature, anyway, to be a shy, blushing violet. She takes after her father, with a forceful personality, a slightly abrasive attitude to life and a determination not to be bossed around.

All the royal sons and daughters are great home lovers. As a group they are closer to each other and their near relations than most other families these days. Their happiest moments are when they are together. Whether at Buckingham Palace or one of the other royal homes, they are a tight little group that finds a welcome relief from the pressures around them. When the cheers and flagwaving have ended, they still have each other.

30th May 1973. On the day following the announcement of their engagement, Princess Anne and Lieutenant Mark Phillips walk in the grounds of Buckingham Palace for a camera-call **left.** *The marriage of prominent members of the Royal Family is usually authorised by Royal Licence, and the photograph above shows the beautifully hand-scripted licence recording the Queen's consent to Princess Anne's marriage and requiring that arrangements for it be put in hand.*

Royal witnesses to Princess Anne's wedding at Westminster Abbey on 14th November 1973: **below left** The Queen with the Queen Mother, Prince Charles and Prince Andrew are driven to the ceremony; **left** the Queen Mother and Prince Charles; **below** Lady Sarah Armstrong-Jones, the bridesmaid, and Prince Edward, the page. **Below right** Princess Anne, accompanied by her father, the Duke of Edinburgh, on her way to the Abbey for her wedding.

said at the time of her silver wedding anniversary: "A marriage begins by joining man and wife together, but this relationship between two people, however deep at the time, needs to develop and mature with the passing

They value one another, and protect one another. If any one of them is abroad, he or she keeps in constant touch by telephone or letter. None of them do anything without discussing it first with the others.

During the tragedy of the break-up of her marriage, Princess Margaret was helped through the experience by her family. The Queen and Prince Philip took a sympathetic interest in what was happening not merely because of a constitutional responsibility, but because they wished to offer filial comfort.

Their concern was also extended to Lord Snowdon and the couple's children, Viscount Linley and Lady Sarah Armstrong-Jones.

The Queen best summed up her attitude towards family life when she

years. For that it must be held firm in the web of the family relationships, between parents and children, between grandparents and grandchildren, between cousins, aunts and uncles. If I am asked today what I think about family life after 25 years of marriage I can answer with simplicity and conviction, I am for it."

It has been difficult for Princess Anne to fit into the romantic public-relations role of "Princess Charming". She has never wanted to be a plastic figure satisfying the demands of a Hollywood-style image of a princess.

Inside Westminster Abbey on 14th November 1973. **Upper left and above** *Prince Philip escorts his daughter up the nave of the Abbey.* **Left** *Princess Anne and Captain Phillips, with best man Captain Eric Grounds, stand before the Archbishop of Canterbury. The family of Captain Phillips is on the left of the Princess, whilst the Royal Family stands on the right.* **Opposite** *After the solemnization of the marriage, the couple stand before the altar, and Prince Edward and Lady Sarah Armstrong-Jones remain at the foot of the chancel steps.*

She has made it clear from her teenage days that she is an intelligent human being in her own right who wishes to be accepted for what she is, rather than for what fairy-tale dreamers may wish her to be.

Left *Princess Anne and Captain Phillips kneel before the altar in Westminster Abbey for the saying of prayers after the solemnization of their marriage.* **Below** *After the signing of the register, the Royal couple emerge to make obeisance to the Queen before proceeding arm in arm* **opposite page** *towards the West door, on their way* **above** *to the carriage which will take them back to Buckingham Palace.*

She was born on a sunny August day in 1950 at Clarence House, 18 months before her mother succeeded to the throne. Anne, the only one of the children not to be born in Buckingham Palace, is fourth in line after her brothers.

The strong steel-fibre of her backbone soon began to show itself when she was barely a toddler. Prince Charles, the sensitive child, would go into a shell after any harsh words of discipline, while Anne virtually ignored attempts at chastisement and continued on her own merry way.

It is not surprising that someone who is such a formidable opponent in horse-riding events today did not bother much with dolls, preferring a tree-climbing, mud-pie, tomboy childhood. She liked playing with and looking after the Queen's famous corgis and soon followed her mother's enthusiasm for horses.

(The Queen has around 10 corgis, all

of whom are descended from one named Susan, who was so popular with her that she took her on honeymoon. Whenever she is at any of her royal homes, the Queen makes sure she is free around 4.30 each afternoon to feed her dogs, which now include black labradors, with a mixture of meat, dog biscuits and gravy.)

Such was Anne's fiercely independent spirit that she disliked staying at home while her brother went away for his education. Eventually Anne was allowed what she had been demanding for so long when, at the age of 13, she was sent to boarding school. After school, and by the time she reached 18,

*Formal wedding groups after the marriage of Princess Anne to Captain Mark Phillips on 14th November 1973. Prince Edward and Lady Sarah Armstrong-Jones acted as page and bridesmaid, and amongst the foreign Royalty in the large group **top** was ex-King Constantine and Queen Anne-Marie of Greece, Crown Princess Beatrix and Prince Claus of the Netherlands, Crown Prince Harald and Princess Sonja of Norway, and Prince Juan Carlos and Princess Sophie of Spain. **Opposite page** Princess Anne leaves Westminster Abbey on the arm of her husband after the marriage ceremony.*

trend-setter. She was at her happiest in private with her family, especially when indulging in their country-life activities. Riding became, and still is, the activity that overshadows all her other interests.

From childhood she was always a courageous and natural horsewoman and the older she got the better became the quality of animal her mother and father provided for her. "Anne only seemed to live when she was on one of her ponies or, later, on a full-size horse," a former member of the court said recently. To her, riding was a perfect way in which she could establish herself in international competition as someone to be reckoned with for her own skills – not because she was a member of the Royal Family.

During her early days among horses she was reluctant to learn the finer points of riding expertise. The monotonous repetition of training bored her, as did the nuisance of having to look after the animals. Because she wished to excel in the field, however, she eventually agreed to learn the skills of horsemanship – efforts which have since paid off with the number of national and international awards she has gained.

After the usual girlish round of local gymkhanas, the Princess entered what could be called the Big League of the horse world in 1971, the formidable, Badminton three-day horse trials. This is a complicated test presenting both horses and riders with every possible demand, from dressage to a tough cross-country obstacle course and show jumping. Anne came through this and other tests magnificently and as a result was chosen to represent Britain in international events, including the 1976 Olympic Games in Montreal. She tackled the 36-fence cross-country course with her usual courage but halfway round she fell. Although shaken and lying on the ground for several minutes she re-mounted and finished the course, but it was of little use. She had too many faults to help the British team, which, in any case, had a bad running all round in that year's Games.

Away from the show ring the Princess involves herself in charity work. She works very hard as president of the Save The Children Fund and is

Anne clearly showed she was not only a product of the palace, but also typical of her era – the swinging 60s and early 70s. She seemed to make it clear from the very start in her public life that she valued her independence and felt she should be able to do whatever she wished without succumbing to pressures. She was a typical girl of her time.

She set a style of her own during her late teens and early 20s as far as fashion was concerned, favouring delicate ruffled formal dresses which were not too way-out, or at the other extreme, the ubiquitous sweaters and jeans. Once again, showing her determination to be seen and appreciated as herself, rather than as the result of image-making, she did not try to become what was unnatural to her – be a "swinger" or

the patron of a charity close to her heart, the Riding for the Disabled Association, to which she devotes a lot of her time.

Anne, unlike her brother, had never been the subject of much gossip or speculation on romance. She had few boyfriends and it was through her love of horses that she met someone who could share her life.

She first met Captain Mark Phillips when she went with the Queen Mother to a reception, in the late summer of 1968, for Britain's team in that year's Olympic Games. She had just left school

and was not on anyone's marital list, but over the years they saw more of each other on the horse-show circuit. Mark, a dashing young Army sub-altern, was a member of the British equestrian team which won gold medals at the Munich Olympics in 1972, which Anne attended as a spectator.

They soon began to spend a lot of time together outside the show ring and after a year of secret courtship, their engagement was announced by Prince Philip, in May 1973, during a family "get-together" to celebrate the 50th

anniversary of the Queen Mother's wedding.

The son of a country-squire businessman and the daughter of a Queen married on a chilly November morning that year. Anne became for the first time a fairy-tale princess as, in her wedding dress, she drove with her father in a glass coach, through streets lined with thousands of well-wishers, to Westminster Abbey. The coach had been used by her mother and father on their wedding day and Anne's long veil was held in place by a tiara that the Queen had also worn for her wedding. Before the wedding Mark said: "I just love everything about her."

Mark, who is two years older than Anne, comes from a long line of military men and a family who live very much in

Princess Anne's long equestrian career has taken her to every major eventing ground in Britain, and to many in Europe and the Commonwealth. **Above** *Taking a fence in practice at Aldershot in 1970.* **Top right** *Seated on her horse, and* **right** *in action at Amberley Horse Trials in March 1973.* **Above, far right** *Another practice round, this time before the trials at Stockley in March 1974.* **Opposite page** *The Princess clears an obstacle at Silvermere, Surrey in April 1980.*

the country style in a sixteenth-century manor house in Wiltshire. After their marriage Anne became a soldier's wife, living with Mark in quarters at Sandhurst Military Academy, where he was an instructor, but their original interest in riding did not die. They became a regular and popular couple at riding events throughout Britain and abroad.

The varied public and private life of a very active Princess Anne has drawn close public interest ever since she came of age. Her early sporting activities included sailing at Cowes, which she latterly spiced with a deft touch of marine fashion **opposite page,** with Prince Philip during Cowes Week in August 1970. She is renowned for her chic dress sense on formal occasions **right,** during a visit to Beacon School, Crowborough, near Tunbridge Wells, in October 1978 and for her regal appearance on State occasions such as the Opening of Parliament **top,** in November 1975. Interest in her foreign tours has been maintained at a high level: **below** with Prince Charles and President Kenyatta in Kenya in February 1971; **bottom left** with her husband, Captain Mark Phillips in Thailand in July 1979. **Below right** The Princess and Captain Phillips leaving St Mary's Hospital, Paddington after the birth of their first child in 1977.

Four years almost to the day after their wedding, Princess Anne gave birth to her first child, Peter. She set a number of breaks from royal tradition. She decided to go into a public hospital, St Mary's in Paddington, in one of the grimmer suburbs in London, and young Peter became the first baby so near the throne to be born in hospital. After his birth, both Anne and Mark insisted that Peter, named after his paternal grandfather, should not be given a title – another royal first.

Anne completed the picture of the happy country family when she gave birth on May 15 1981 to the Queen's first grand-daughter. It took nearly a month before deciding on a name for the child – the unusual Miss Zara Anne Elizabeth Phillips.

The strange first name for the little girl who became sixth in line to the throne is a version of a Greek Biblical name meaning "Bright as dawn".

Since the arrival of their children

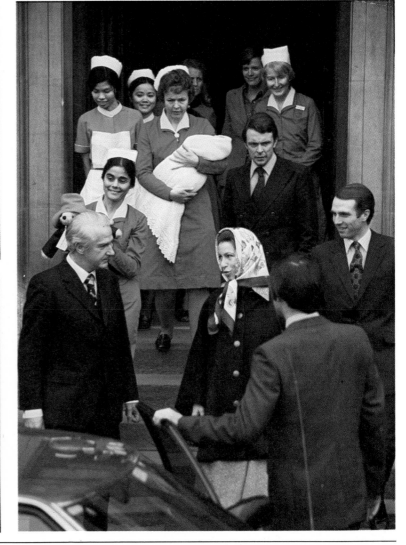

Anne and Mark have begun to set up a home of their own in magnificent Gatcombe Park in Gloucestershire, a stone-built mansion built in the eighteenth century which stands in 730 acres. It was bought for them at a price of three-quarters of a million pounds by the Queen. It is a considerable change from their first home after marriage which was rented Army accommodation costing £8 per week.

Now that they have begun to lay the foundations for a new branch of the family, Anne and Mark look to a future as farming folk and estate owners.

Mark has left the Army, with regret, because his marriage was a drawback to any promotion he could expect to the top ranks of his career. Any officer in the British Army today has to have experience in Northern Ireland, in combat conditions. Because the hus-

The photographs on these pages show a few of the many occasions when Princess Anne has taken part in horse trials all over the country. **Above** *Princess Anne on Doublet during the Badminton Horse Trials in April 1971.* **Left** *The Princess mounted on the Queen's horse Columbus, on which Captain Mark Phillips has scored many successes.* **Opposite page** *Three pictures of Princess Anne during the horse trials at Locko Park in Derbyshire in August 1980.*

band of the fourth in line to the throne, was such a prime target for a specific terrorist attack or kidnapping, he would never have been allowed to go there. The only alternative for Mark, who did not wish to stay for ever at the bottom of the military tree, was to resign his commission.

There are many dangers that the royal security men cannot ignore, especially as far as Mark and Anne are concerned.

They were the targets for a violent kidnap attempt one spring evening in 1974 when they were driving along the Mall to the palace after being guests of honour at a film show. A 26-year-old man, Ian Ball, subsequently found to be mentally unstable, swung his small family car in front of the royal limousine, forcing it to stop, and came out waving two guns. He came face to face first of all with the incredibly brave royal bodyguard, Scotland Yard Inspector James Beaton, whom Ball shot in the chest. The policeman drew his gun, which jammed after one shot but, though wounded, he still tried to tackle the attacker and did not give up the fight until he collapsed on the

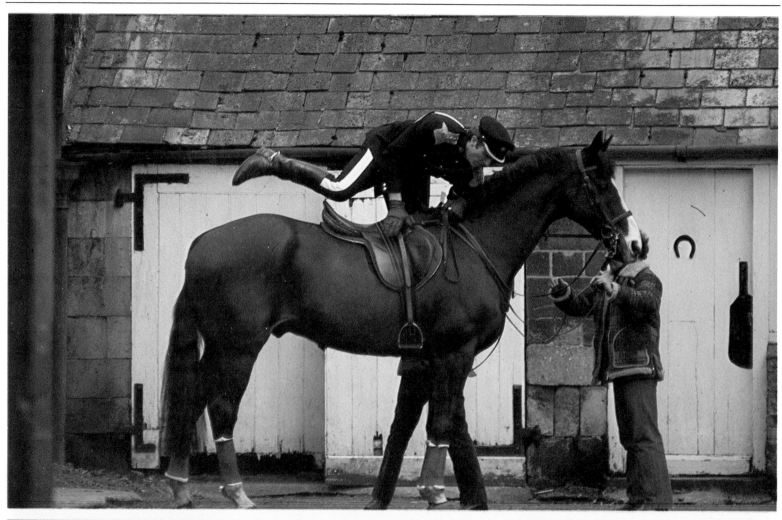

Captain Mark Phillips dismounts after taking part in a 3-day event **opposite page, above.** *For many months in 1977, when her first child was born, Princess Anne had to be content with being a spectator, rather than a competitor, at horse trials:* **opposite page, below** *at Chatsworth in October 1977, just one month before her confinement, and* **right** *with Captain Phillips at Brigstock Horse Trials in March that year. Husband and wife competing together* **below** *at Hickstead in July 1974 and* **below centre** *Osberton, Notts in August 1973.* **Bottom picture** *Princess Anne taking photographs at the Munich Olympics in August 1972.*

ground having been wounded twice more. How he ever survived his wounds is remarkable.

Next to be shot was the royal chauffeur, Alexander Callender, who was wounded in the chest as he tried to grab the gun. A third victim was a Fleet Street journalist, Brian McConnell, who jumped from a passing taxi and tried to persuade Ball to hand over the gun. McConnell was severely wounded by a shot in the chest. By now more people, including police, had reached the scene and Ball fled into nearby St James' Park, where he was brought down by an unarmed constable. Police later found adequate evidence that Ball intended to kidnap the Princess and demand a £3 million ransom. He was sent to a security hospital "without limit of time".

Mark and Anne are now concentrating on building up and administering the Gatcombe Park estate, where, apart from breeding high-quality cattle, they intend to train horses for show jumping and competition. The house has a fine row of recently renovated stables.

An indoor training ring will be used for year-round work with the horses, and the estate is nicely placed for riding and hunting. It is in the area of one of the finest hunts in England, the Beaufort, and not far away from the venue of the Badminton Horse Trials.

Anne is competing as hard as ever and she is still a keen huntswoman.

Being the only girl in the Queen's family, Anne has to cope with more than usual pressures and, in addition to being herself, she has always had to remember her position as a member of the Royal Family. It was not easy merely to grow up, fall in love and have children like anyone else and yet Anne has coped with it all superbly, never forgetting the role she has to play.

The admiration for the Princess and her husband, Captain Mark Phillips, that exists throughout the world was best demonstrated one balmy evening at the airport on the Caribbean island of Barbados when the couple flew in to begin their honeymoon. Three of the best calypso bands in the West Indies had rehearsed a selection of music to greet them and thousands of happy islanders packed the airport perimeter and reception area shouting their good wishes and carrying banners with such slogans as "Have a good time Anne

baby!" or "Well done Mark!"

The route from the airport to the capital and main port, Bridgetown, was lined with more flag and banner-waving crowds – all pleased to see at last the Queen's daughter they had heard so much about. This is the sort of reception, though sometimes less boisterous, that the Princess receives wherever she goes, at home or abroad.

*The Royal Family's habitual interest in the Badmington Horse Trials has long been intensified by the participation of Princess Anne and her husband. These pictures were taken in 1974, when both the Princess **left and below left** and Captain Phillips **above** took part. **Below** Recording the event were the Queen, the Queen Mother and Princess Alexandra's son, James Ogilvy.*

One of the hardest working members of the "outer court" is the Duke of Gloucester, a cousin of the Queen, who is ninth in the order of succession. A family tragedy brought him closer to royal duties. As Prince Richard, the second son of Elizabeth's late uncle, he never expected to inherit land, riches or the responsibilities of links with the monarchy. By nature he is a quiet, affable man, rather shy, and one who

Top *Princess Anne and friends take a walk round the course at Amberley near Cirencester in March 1973.* **Above left** *The Princess on her horse, looking confident of her chances of success at the Show.* **Far left** *Looking somewhat more anxious, Princess Anne watches her husband competing* **above** *at Bigstock in March 1977.* **Left** *Captain Phillips on Columbus at the Tidworth Horse Trials in May 1975.*

The strongly sympathetic nature of the Duchess of Kent is evidenced by these two pictures: **above** enjoying a chat with a Chelsea Pensioner at the Founders Day Parade in 1980, and **left** as Patron of the Not Forgotten Associ- ation, she presides at the annual Christmas party at Buckingham Palace Mews, and listens attentively to an old soldier, in December 1980.

always wanted a secluded life away from pomp and ceremony. He had studied architecture at Cambridge, and always intended to make his own, unob- trusive, way in the world. He met his wife, Birgitte van Deurs, the daughter of a Danish lawyer, at a tea party while he was at university. She was studying English at a Cambridge language school. Both of them tended to be modest in their ways, so they never wanted a big fuss made of their wed-

Far right *The Duchess of Kent arriving with the Duke at a film performance in London in March 1966.* Above *The Duke and Duchess attending a function at the Dorchester Hotel in May 1967.* Below *They arrive at Claridge's for a State Banquet given by the Grand Duke of Luxembourg in June 1972.* Right *The Duchess wore this elegant gown at the Queen's Silver Jubilee Gala in June 1977.* Above right *The Duke and Duchess arriving at the Houses of Parliament for the State Opening of Parliament in November 1977 – just over a month after she suffered a miscarriage whilst expecting her fourth child.*

ding three years later in 1972. Instead of a traditional royal affair in Westminster Abbey, the marriage ceremony, and chosen church, matched the simple sort of life they both prefer. It was a village wedding in the thirteenth-century church at Barnwell in Northamptonshire, the ancestral home of the Gloucesters. Such was the restrained simplicity of the occasion that Richard's mother, the Duchess, arranged the flowers in the church.

Richard and the blonde Birgitte seemed all set for an unsophisticated life as a working couple – he as an architect and she in business – when his elder brother, Prince William, was killed in a plane crash. The tragedy happened only two months after their wedding. William, a dashing sort of fellow with a fondness for fast cars, aircraft and a hectic existence, was destined to inherit the estate and the position so close to the throne. He had trained as a diplomat with the Foreign Office and was well-used to public life, but a light aircraft he was piloting suddenly swooped to the ground soon after take off and burst into flames.

Two years later, in 1974, the old Duke died and Richard and his new wife were thrust into a public role they never sought. In spite of this they now play their full part in carrying out royal duties.

Another wife who was never trained for such a task, but who has taken to it with great aplomb, is the Duchess of Kent, the graceful companion of another of the Queen's cousins. She was born Katharine Worsley, daughter of Sir William Worsley, a family of York-shire country stock. Katharine had met the Duke when he was serving with his cavalry regiment, the Royal Scots Greys, not far from her home, Hovingham Hall in North Yorkshire.

She was at first reluctant to commit herself to marriage with the young Duke, because it would mean becoming

so closely linked with the throne. Eventually she accepted that the restrictions of stately life would have to be coped with, and they married in York Minster in 1961. Since then she has taken on more than her fair share of the

---

Princess Alexandra of Kent, one of seven cousins of the Queen on her father's side, was married to the Hon. Angus Ogilvy, second son of the Earl of Airlie, on 24th April 1963: **above left** *driving, with her brother, the Duke of Kent, to her wedding at Westminster Abbey. She has two children: James, born on Leap Year Day 1964,* (**below, left,** *with his mother after his chris-tening in April 1964) and Marina, born on 31st July 1966. The Duke of Kent, who is the elder of her two brothers, married Katharine Worsley in York Minster on 8th June 1961. They have two sons and a daughter, Lady Helen Windsor* (**below,** *with her parents, attending the wedding of Lady Elizabeth Anson in July 1972).* **Left** *The Kents among the Royal Family as they leave St George's Chapel Windsor after the Christmas service in 1970.*

royal work-load and, for someone not born in a palace, has taken to the life with all the charm and expertise of a princess.

A princess who was born to the job, but married in reverse, so to speak, is Princess Alexandra, the vivacious daughter of the late Duke of Kent and Princess Marina of Greece. "Alex" met a man who was far from the royal crowd, the Honourable Angus Ogilvy, son of the twelfth Earl of Airlie, but essentially a young, thrusting business-man making his way in the City of London. Because he is heavily com-mitted to his career in finance, the couple have a very efficient working relationship as far as official duties are concerned. Princess Alexandra meets a busy diary generally working alone, except when it would normally be expected that a husband and wife should be together – at dinners, premières, weddings and church ser-vices, for example.

The Princess always seems to be so happy with life and has a ready smile whenever she appears in public – qual-ities that have made her one of the best-liked of the Queen's relatives.

Among the new royals also taking their full share of family duties are Prince Michael of Kent, younger brother of the Duke of Kent, and his wife Marie-Christine, known as Princess Michael of Kent.

By marrying the tall and elegant blonde, Prince Michael not only kept alive links with the European nobility in the style of Victoria, but also caused considerable controversy. Austrian Baroness Marie-Christine von Reibnitz was not only a Roman Catholic, but also a divorced woman. She had previously been married to London merchant banker Thomas Troubridge.

The Duke and Duchess of Kent are keen tennis fans, and the Duke is President of the All England Tennis Club. **Above, left** *The Duchess with ball boys at Wimbledon in July 1979.* **Left** *The Duke congratulates the Men's Singles winner, Jimmy Connors, after his victory in the 1974 Wimbledon tournament.*

Under the terms of the Act of Succession of 1700, members of the royal family are forbidden to marry Roman Catholics. Getting round this was made possible by Michael renouncing his right of succession to the throne, but not denying the same right for his descendants. The Queen was happy with this arrangement, but the Anglican Church would not marry the couple because the Church of England opposes the re-marriage of divorced people in church.

This obstacle was presented even though the prince and his wife-to-be had agreed to bring up their children as Anglicans.

A further complication then arose because under the 1949 Marriage Act members of the Royal Family cannot marry in England and Wales in a civil ceremony at a register office.

They decided on a Roman Catholic wedding in Vienna at the church where Marie-Christine's grandmother and great-grandmother had been married, but then The Vatican came up with more problems. Because the children of mixed marriages had to be brought up as Catholics, the Pope would not grant a dispensation in this case.

This complicated love story eventually found a happy ending when the pair were married at a civil ceremony in Vienna town hall on June 30, 1978. Among members of the Royal Family who attended was Princess Anne, though the Queen was not officially represented.

Since then, Prince Michael has given up his career in the Army and settled down with Marie-Christine at Nether Lypiatt Manor not far from the homes of Princess Anne and Prince Charles in Gloucestershire. They have two children, a boy and a girl.

No monarch in the history of the British Crown has met so many of her subjects as Queen Elizabeth II. She has achieved this by a series of jet-paced tours at home and in the Commonwealth countries.

She is not only a Queen of the United

Opposite page, far left *Prince Michael of Kent and his fiancée, Baroness Marie-Christine von Reibnitz, photographed in front of the gate of Princess Alexandra's home Thatched House Lodge, in Richmond Park, in May 1978, shortly before their wedding.* **Opposite page, bottom** *The Prince and Baroness arriving at the Town Hall in Vienna for their marriage on 30th June, and leaving again afterwards.* **Opposite page, above right** *The newly-weds in evening dress, attending a celebration ball in Vienna on their wedding night.* **Above** *Prince and Princess Michael emerge from the Town Hall after the civil ceremony.* **Above, left** *With some of their guests, including (left to right) the Duke of Kent, Princess Alexandra and the Hon Angus Ogilvy, and Lady Helen Windsor.* **Left** *Also among the guests were Earl Mountbatten of Burma, Princess Anne and Princess Olga of Yugoslavia.*

build or to keep alive, political links with other nations. The Queen paying a visit to a non-Commonwealth country is a gesture of friendship from Britain. The highly-successful week the Queen and Prince Philip spent in West Germany, during the early summer of 1978, was partly Britain letting her Common Market partner know she enjoyed having them as neighbours.

Not only does the Queen and the rest of her family find any visit to the United States enormously interesting, they

Kingdom but also rules over, or has allegiance paid to her by, nearly 20 nations throughout the world, from Australia to Trinidad and Canada to Tonga. Hardly any corner of the Commonwealth has not been visited in the past 25 years at least once by her or a member of her family.

In addition, the Queen and Prince Philip have a new function – as well as cementing Commonwealth ties they are also salesmen for Britain and British exports. Much of their work overseas is now linked with export promotion, a job they do well. During a highly-successful tour of Japan in 1975 a West German diplomat said to one of his hosts at a British Embassy reception: "You've got the best salesmen in the world in your Queen and her husband . . . we can't match them."

A royal tour also helps, either to

The marriage of Prince Michael of Kent **top left,** *in Vienna in June 1978 to Baroness Marie-Christine von Reibnitz introduced into the Royal Family a new Princess who has become noted for her elegance and flair for fashion* **opposite page.** *She wore this eye-catching hat* **far left** *at a Variety Club Ladies' Luncheon at the Savoy on 8th July 1980, and again for her private trip to Paris at the end of that month. Her frequent changes of hair-style include the plait – reflecting her Austrian origins – which she sported at a BBC Symphony Orchestra Concert at the Royal Festival Hall in October 1980* **left** *and* **above left** *with Prince Michael and their first child, Lord Frederick Windsor, who was born in April 1979.*

also get a special thrill there because they are welcomed as America's own very special "royals". The Queen's links with the United States go back to the days when she went there for the first time with her husband shortly after their marriage. President Truman wrote to her father: "They went to the hearts of all the citizens."

Arranging a tour can sometimes take as long as two years. Before the formal invitations and acceptances are exchanged there are usually months of diplomatic discussions. When dates have been fixed, an advance team is sent from Buckingham Palace about three months ahead. They check on security, the programme, pass on to the

host nations matters of special interest to the royal guests, and even make sure that blood of the correct groups will be available. A confidential medical report is also sent to hospitals near the royal route so that a member of the party can be quickly and efficiently treated in an emergency.

Wherever the Queen goes in the world she does not drink the local water but insists on having only British Malvern water, the pure spring water that many people mix with whisky. The Queen takes dozens of bottles of the spa water around the world with her, not to mix with alcohol, but because she does not wish to upset her tummy. She cannot afford to go down with an illness while touring.

Despite having her regular supply of Malvern water, the Queen still has to taste some strange foods when she is abroad. A local delicacy that might be considered a treat to the natives of one country is not always easy on the palate

of one who is used to simple, English cooking. Prince Charles reckons that he and his family have had to plough their way through so many strange concoctions that they all have cast-iron stomachs.

He and his relatives usually manage to express approval and nod happily when required to taste, in public, some rare drink or foods, but on at least one occasion Her Majesty could not prevent her distaste from showing.

This was in Kyoto, the fascinating, ancient capital of Japan, during the royal tour of the country in 1975. The

The Duke of Gloucester at the time of his engagement to Birgitte van Deurs early in 1972 **far left.** *As Prince Richard, he unexpectedly became heir to the Dukedom when his elder brother, Prince William, was killed at the age of 30 in a flying accident, just two months after acting as Prince Richard's best man at his wedding at Barnwell in July 1972* **above and opposite page, left.** *Richard succeeded as Duke of Gloucester on his father's death in 1974.*

traditional tea ceremony is something the Japanese treasure and take pride in, though the product of this complicated ritual can taste bitter and sickly to newcomers to the art.

A bowl of tea was offered to the Queen and Prince Philip by one of the best tea-makers in Japan. The Queen accepted the greenish-coloured, tepid liquid in the appropriate manner. This meant first of all turning the bowl round to admire the decorations around the side, and then tasting the contents. She looked, tasted – then almost retched as, with a grimace on her face, she handed the bowl back to the tea-maker and gave the Prince a warning that he would have to suffer as well.

The Royal Yacht *Britannia* is frequently used at home and abroad as a floating Buckingham Palace. The Queen does not share her husband's love of the sea, however, and finds travelling on board ship distinctly upsetting. Because of this she prefers to fly to wherever the ship is anchored and usually only sails any distance on board when she is in calm waters.

Britannia, first launched in 1953, costs £10,000 a week to run whilst at sea, but only half that amount when she is in dock. She has a permanent crew of 21 officers and 256 ratings, all of whom are entitled to wear the coveted insignia "Royal Yacht Service". There is no need for punishment for any misdemeanours among the crew – any trouble means a return to normal naval service.

When the Royal Family travels by air they usually go in one of the aircraft of

The new Duke and Duchess had their first child, Alexander, Earl of Ulster, in October 1974: **opposite page, centre** *Alexander's christening at Barnwell in February 1975. Their second child, Lady Davina Windsor, was born in November 1977:* **right** *the Duke and Duchess leave St Mary's Hospital, Paddington with Davina and* **above right** *scenes from her christening at Barnwell the following year, when she wore the long lace robe which had been made for Queen Victoria's eldest child in 1840.*

the élite, Queen's Flight, which is based at Benson in Oxfordshire. This distinctive fleet, painted bright red, includes three twin-engined Andover medium range airliners and two Wessex helicopters. They are manned and serviced by a 100-strong team and the operation costs around £1,000,000 a year to run.

If the Queen, by an unlikely chance, should suffer from overcrowding at Buckingham Palace, she can still turn for space to a total of 20 royal homes and palaces in Britain. Including the recently-acquired country houses of Prince Charles and Princess Anne, that is the number of residences linked with the sovereign.

There are palaces which have not had a member of the ruling family in them for centuries but which are part of the nation's heritage. There are also buildings, large and small, which the family do not merely regard as part of the trappings of their function but as homes.

The royal homes and palaces used regularly are: Buckingham Palace, Kensington Palace and Clarence House in London; Windsor Castle, Royal Lodge, Windsor, and Fort Belvedere, Windsor; Sandringham House in Nor-

Sandringham House is one of the Royal Family's private residences, purchased by the future King Edward VII 120 years ago. It is here that the Queen and her immediate family come, after spending Christmas at Windsor, to celebrate the New Year and take a short break before resuming duties from Buckingham Palace. Its ornate decoration belies its essentially homely character: like Balmoral, it is a place where little official business is done. **Above** *Two views of the long narrow salon.* **Left** *The dining room with its interesting but restful murals.* **Below left, and opposite page, lower** *The main drawing room, which houses a portrait of Queen Alexandra (below) when Princess of Wales.*

folk; Chevening House in Kent; Gatcombe Park in Gloucestershire; the Palace of Holyroodhouse, Edinburgh; Glamis Castle in Angus; Balmoral Castle and Birkhall in Aberdeenshire; and the Castle of Mey in Caithness.

Palaces associated with the throne but not used by the sovereign these days in London are: The Palace of Westminster (the Houses of Commons and Lords); Westminster Hall; Lancaster House; Marlborough House; St James's Palace and the Tower of London.

Buckingham Palace originally belonged to the Dukes of Buckingham, until the property was bought by George III for £21,000 in 1762. It was smaller then, and most of what we see today was built in the hundred years following the Crown's acquisition.

George III and his wife, Queen Charlotte, purchased it originally as a retreat from nearby St James's Palace, which was then the official home of the sovereign. It still is, to some degree, because ambassadors are accredited to the "Court of St James" . . . although

they present their credentials at Buckingham Palace.

George and Charlotte regarded it as a family home to which they could escape from the affairs of State, and it was not until George IV came to the throne that the decision was made to turn it into a grand palace. That great Regency architect John Nash was called in to organise the transformation, but the King died before it was ready for occupation. So did his successor, and younger brother, King William IV. The first monarch to use Buckingham Palace as a permanent official home was Queen Victoria, who moved her court into the building in 1837. It has become not only a London home for the Queen and her family, but also a busy office block – a government department administering Crown affairs.

It must have the most photographed balcony in the world. That raised terrace above the main entrance is traditionally used by a sovereign to appear before the crowds at times of

major celebrations. Victories, coronations, weddings and births have all been marked by the familiar line-up of royal hand wavers looking down on the revellers below.

Members of the public can now admire some of the marbled and scarlet décor inside by visiting the art exhibition in the Queen's Gallery. This used to be the private chapel where royal babies were christened, and monarchs and their families and staff occasionally worshipped. Only a small part of

The Queen ended her four-day State Visit to Italy in October 1980 with an audience with Pope John Paul II. This was her third visit to the Vatican, although she has been there only twice as Queen. After the Pope had greeted the Queen **top** *and the Duke of Edinburgh* **left,** *they posed for photographers in the Pope's study* **opposite page,** *exchanged words of welcome and thanks* **above left,** *and presented each other with gifts* **above.** *The audience lasted just over an hour.*

the chapel remains – the rest was destroyed by bombs in the Second World War. (During that war Buckingham Palace was damaged nine times by bombs, or the forerunner of today's guided missiles, the flying bombs.)

The Queen decided that the old chapel should be rebuilt as an art gallery where her private collection could be put on display. The work was

Top right *The Queen leaves Concorde as she arrives in Bahrein on the first day of her 3-week tour of the Gulf States in February 1979.* **Centre right** *with Prince Philip, she watches a folk dancing display during her visit to Kuwait. Her important State Visit to Saudi Arabia later that month included a visit to the races near Riyadh* **above** *and a massive desert banquet* **right.** **Top left** *The royal barge bringing the Queen from the Royal Yacht Britannia to the State of Oman.*

completed in time for opening in 1962. All the profits from visitors to the gallery, as well as income from the days when the public are allowed around Sandringham, Windsor Castle and Balmoral, are given to charities.

Buckingham Palace and Windsor Castle now belong to the nation, but Balmoral and Sandringham, used by the family nearly three months of each year, are among the private estates of the Queen.

Balmoral and nearby Birkhall, which is the Queen Mother's favourite retreat, are places where they can relax as a group more easily than anywhere else. They can move around the heathered countryside without being bothered too much by sightseers, and most of the villagers are familiar old faces to them. In Scotland they become "lairds", wearing kilts of Royal Stuart

tartan or the special Balmoral tartan which is a weave of black, red, grey and lavender.

Sandringham consists of 20,000 acres of windy, agricultural land in North Norfolk, where the family gathers for a month after spending Christmas at Windsor Castle. It is used as a place to invite friends from London for informal country weekends, and as a centre for Prince Philip and Prince Charles when they organise their shooting parties.

Windsor Castle is regarded mainly as a weekend home, although it has one

Left *The Queen is greeted by the Amir of Qatar as she disembarks from the Royal Yacht to begin her visit there.* **Below** *Prince Philip keeps his distance as, with the Crown Prince of Bahrein, he visits the Salman Falconry Centre.*

troublesome problem . . . the noise from aircraft taking off from nearby Heathrow, one of the world's busiest airports.

Gatcombe Park, the new Gloucestershire home of Princess Anne and Captain Mark Phillips, is a sheltered estate amid the Cotswold Hills. It has 530 acres of farmland and 200 acres of woods, plus a lake stocked with trout.

Prince Charles's home, Chevening, near Sevenoaks in Kent, is a 250-year-old mansion among 3,000 acres of park and woodland. It has 24 acres of landscaped gardens and a four-acre lake. It was the home of generations of the Earls Stanhope, a family that devoted itself to public service. When the seventh earl died without an heir in 1967 he left it to the nation, hoping that Charles would take up the offer. He also left £250,000 for the repair and maintenance of the house.

A modern touch that Charles has brought to the eighteenth-century atmosphere is hi-fi music. He has loudspeakers in every room.

Among the newest of royal homes is the love-nest of the newly weds, Charles and Diana.

Prince Charles found it by house hunting with an estate agent's brochure just like many young men with marriage in mind.

His search took him to a Georgian house behind wrought-iron gates in Gloucestershire.

"This looks interesting," he said, as he crunched up the gravel drive with a man from Humberts, the up-market auctioneers.

Charles wandered through the house with its four beautifully-appointed reception rooms, nine bedrooms and six bathrooms. Then he tramped round some of its 346 acres.

It took him less than an hour to make up his mind.

"I'll have it," he said. And the Highgrove Estate at Doughton, near Tetbury, then the home of Tory MP Mr Maurice Macmillan, became royal property for the princely sum of £800,000.

By Diana's standards the house is small. Her father's Elizabethan home near Northampton is far grander.

But she was delighted with Highgrove when she saw it for the first time.

Lady Diana told friends: "It's perfect. I couldn't wish for a nicer

house."

The Royal Family's personal wealth is almost incalculable, even excluding priceless paintings, stamp collections and other treasures.

The Queen was said to be worth £44

Left *The Queen arrives to attend a folk dancing display during her visit to Kuwait. Although she wore western dress for this part of her tour, her clothes for the Saudi-Arabia visit had to take account of local custom:* **bottom picture and opposite page, below** *She is greeted by King Khalid and members of his Court on arrival at Rijadh airport; and* **below** *wearing a long day dress she confers with the King in, for her, most unusual surroundings.*

million when she came to the throne in 1952, inheriting the Royal Family's personal fortune. The figure has multiplied several times since then and is now probably around £100,000,000. All of this has been preserved in land and property and invested in the best blue chip companies all over the world.

All their money is handled by the long established bank, Coutt's. Shares are bought by a group of well-informed City stockbrokers.

The official salaries of the family are paid by Parliament through what is

Left *During her visit to Qatar, the Queen was taken on an excursion into the desert where she was entertained to a picnic lunch by the Amir.*

known as the Civil List. On Budget Day 1981 they received a 12 per cent "pay rise".

Total Civil List allowances for the Royal Family rose from the previous year's £3,791,350 to £4,249,273, an increase of £457,923.

But the Queen refunded an extra £21,273 to the Treasury, leaving a net increase of £436,650.

The Queen's own allowances went up by £359,700 to £3,260,200.

The Queen Mother: £32,100 to £286,000. Prince Philip: £18,050 to £160,000.

Princess Anne received an extra £11,550 to give her £100,000.

Prince Andrew was awarded £20,000.

As usual, the Queen carries out a varied programme of engagements during her tour of the Gulf States in February and March 1979. She visits a general provisions store in Bahrein **above** *and attends a camel tournament in Saudi Arabia* **right and far right.** *As she arrived in Qatar* **above right** *she was met by many boatloads of well-wishers who came by whatever means they could to see her* **opposite page, top.**

Princess Margaret's allowance went from £87,750 to £98,000 – a £10,250 increase.

Other allowances were: Princess Alice, Duchess of Gloucester, £40,000 (a £5,000 rise); the Duke of Gloucester,

£78,000 (£7,500); the Duke of Kent, £106,000 (£11,500); Princess Alexandra, £101,000 (£11,200).

Two-thirds of the money received by the Queen is used to pay her staff of 350.

With due respect for Saudi Arabian traditions relating to womens' dress, the Queen wore this long outfit when she arrived **below** to attend a race meeting near Riyadh. **Bottom** The Queen with Prince Philip and the Crown Prince during the playing of the National Anthems at the meeting. **Bottom left** Young girls dance to folk music before the Queen in Saudi Arabia. **Bottom centre** The royal yacht Britannia, which took the Queen from country to country during her extensive journey.

Besides her Civil List allowance, the Queen receives profits from the Duchy of Lancaster.

These are areas of land and properties which make up vast estates throughout Britain known as Crown Lands. Much of the property is in the North of England, but there is a fair-sized chunk of valuable sites in London.

The value is beyond measure in a time of inflation, but the annual profit is estimated to be around £1,000,000.

The Government pays for the upkeep of royal residences. Buckingham Palace costs £1,485,000 to maintain, of which £177,000 is spent on electricity, gas and water.

Windsor Castle is almost twice as costly at £2,718,000. Because the Royal Family use it for just a few months each year the bills for gas, water and electricity have recently been kept down to £148,000 a year. The annual running costs for St James's Palace, which incorporates the Queen Mother's home Clarence House, the Duke of Kent's London residence, York

must do the Queen's bills for food and alcohol each year are an estimated £250,000. She drinks very little, but there must obviously be some very thirsty, as well as hungry, official guests at Buckingham Palace receptions.

Perhaps it's fortunate that royal estates like Balmoral and royal parks like Richmond provide a regular supply

Opposite page, above *The Queen arrives at the racecourse in Bahrein with the Amir – he is also pictured* **far left** *awaiting the Queen's arrival the previous day.* **Opposite page, below** *Admiration from Bahrein girls in traditional costumes as the Queen visits the Muharraq Museum there.* **Left** *The Queen with King Khalid of Saudi-Arabia: she always wore a long dress when in his presence.* **Below left** *On her arrival in Qatar, the Queen inspects a guard of honour.* **Below and bottom picture** *The Queen attending a banquet given by the Amir of Qatar at the Rayyan Palace.*

House, and an office for Princess Alexandra, are £763,000.

Princess Margaret's home, Kensington Palace, costs £438,000.

The Government also takes care of some of the bills for the Queen's Scottish palace, Holyroodhouse and Sandringham and Balmoral, both private homes of the Royal Family.

With all the official entertaining she

of Angus beef and venison to royal kitchens.

Additional expenditures covered by the Government are annual running costs of £2,000,000 for the royal yacht *Britannia* (it recently had a £5,000,000 refit) . . . £2,500,000 for the Queen's Flight . . . £400,000 for the royal train . . . £1,000,000 for royal tours . . . and £500,000 to cover the costs of royal

In the second week of his visit to New Zealand, Prince Charles visited Tokoroa where he was garlanded with strings of shells by a dancer from the Cook Islands. He was visiting the local sports stadium and spent much of his time there talking with some of the thousands of children who had gathered to see him **below left. Below** The Prince inspects a naval guard of honour during another of his engagements in New Zealand, and **opposite page** a look that seems to resent the constant presence of photographers at a time when, because of his impending wedding, public interest in the Prince was at its height.

130,000 acres, which makes Charles one of the biggest landowners in Britain. It is a mixture of farms and country homesteads, old terraced houses, shops and even pubs, spreading west from London.

Outside London his tenants include sheep farmers on Dartmoor, Cornish tin miners, and daffodil growers in the Scillies. In Cornwall he has an oyster farm which produces a million tasty morsels every year.

It is often mistakenly thought that the money that goes to the Queen and her relations is just spending money; income to be frittered away on caviare and fast cars. This money is, in fact, used to pay their staffs and cover the costs of official duties. Whenever the Royal Family has a pay rise, this is to meet the increases in costs of living of their staffs.

police protection.

Charles has no State salary so he takes on other tasks to raise enough money to carry out his official duties. He heads an organisation which administers his Duchy of Cornwall estates.

Latest figures for 1980 showed that his income rose from £306,382 in 1979 to £536,013.

Most of this was spent on salaries, at Civil Service rates, for a private secretary, treasurer, clerks, valet and secretarial staff. The Duchy's accounts for 1980 showed that income – from rents, sale of wood, farm receipts, dividends and interest and other sources totalled £3,147,259.

Outgoings totalled £2,596,814 – leaving a balance of £550,445, about half of which is paid to the Treasury in lieu of income tax.

The bulk of the Duchy's income – £2,011,066 – came from rents.

The Prince's spending on his personal interests, such as riding, comes from his private income, part of his inherited wealth.

The total area of the Duchy is

On June 6th, 1981, Prince Charles took the salute at the second rehearsal for the annual Trooping the Colour ceremony. There are normally two or three rehearsals each year, which provide an opportunity for the participating battalions to go through their paces and for those spectators who did not manage to obtain tickets for the Trooping proper to get a hint of the spectacle involved.

The line of succession to the throne is: Prince Charles; Prince Andrew; Prince Edward; Princess Anne; her son Master Peter Phillips and daughter Zara; Princess Margaret; her son Viscount Linley and daughter, Lady Sarah Armstrong-Jones; The Queen's cousin, the Duke of Gloucester; his son the Earl of Ulster and daughter, Lady Davina Windsor; the Queen's cousin, the Duke of Kent; his elder son, the Earl of

St Andrews; his younger son, Lord Nicholas Windsor and his daughter, Lady Helen Windsor; the Queen's cousin and sister of the Duke of Kent, Princess Alexandra; her son, James Ogilvy and daughter, Marina Ogilvy.

Unique traditions and glorious pageantry keep the monarchy alive with a ceremonial splendour seen nowhere else in the world.

Whether it be the pomp of the State Opening of Parliament or the simple

The 1981 ceremony of Trooping the Colour **left** *was marred by the incident in the Mall when six blank shots were fired at the Queen as she rode to Horse Guards Parade. She quickly recovered her composure* **above** *though looking distinctly ill at ease* **opposite page.**

After the shooting incident, the Queen looks tense **opposite and above** *as do Prince Charles and Prince Philip* **above right.** *But it was all smiles on the Palace balcony afterwards* **top** *where Lady Diana Spencer appeared for the first time. Lord Nicholas Windsor, Lady Davina Windsor and the Earl of Ulster are the three children.*

giving of the specially-minted silver Maundy Money coins to old people every year, the Queen carries everything off with a style that has millions gasping with admiration.

The Royal Family enjoys dressing up for a great occasion: the chance to drive through banner-hung streets, and to take part in ceremonies that are

living proof of the continuity of rule.

One of the highspots of the royal year for the Queen is Trooping the Colour, or the Queen's Birthday Parade. Being a monarch she is allowed to have two birthdays each year – her natural anniversary (April 21) and an official one, which usually falls on the first Saturday in June.

This is the day when 1,600 officers and men in her five regiments of foot-guards and two regiments of horse-guards, march and trot on Horse Guards Parade, off Whitehall, in intricate patterns that require six weeks rehearsal. There is a twisting movement of the mass bands that is so

began in 1805 and it has continued annually ever since. The Queen has made a point, throughout her reign, of leading her troops off the parade ground and along The Mall. She rides side-saddle on a police horse that has been trained to behave placidly amid all the din of the military bands and the cheering and shouting.

One of the most important constitutional functions Her Majesty performs each year is the State Opening of Parliament. This is the occasion when it is formally accepted that it is "Her Majesty's Government". After a procession through the streets from Buckingham Palace to Westminster she sits before the robed Peers in the House of Lords and reads a statement outlining HER government's intentions in the way of legislation in the coming year. It is a ceremony going back to the days of

As Colonel-in-Chief of three Army Regiments, Princess Anne undertakes several engagements every year with detachments of the Army both at home and abroad. **Left** *She inspects a guard of honour in October 1971 and* **top left** *talks to members of one of her regiments during the Sovereign's Parade at Sandhurst in June 1973. The remaining pictures on this page and opposite show Princess Anne being shown round a Scorpion tank during her visit in November 1969 to the 14th/20th King's Hussars at Paderborn in West Germany.*

complicated that it can never be written down on paper – the skill is handed down by word-of-mouth through generations of drill sergeants.

Parading regimental colours goes back more than 200 years to when the flag would be carried among the soldiers on the eve of a battle so that they could recognise it as a rallying point amid the smoke, fire and slaughter.

Ceremonially parading the colours of a guards battalion – embroidered with battle honours – before the sovereign,

William the Conqueror, who told the bishops, earls and barons of his day what he expected them to do. Although the Queen's Speech is couched in such terms that it appears she is instructing the Government what to do, it is, in fact, a policy statement prepared by the

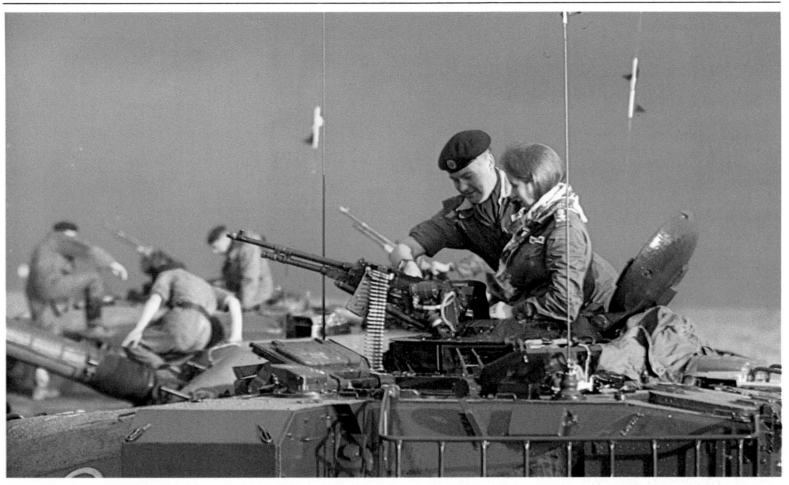

Prime Minister. Members of the House of Commons are also allowed – on this one day – to stand at the door of the Upper House to hear the speech.

It is the Queen, of course, who confers the great honours of Peerage and Knighthood at ceremonies held mainly at Buckingham Palace, but she often dubs a knight with her sword during tours abroad. She has also been known to perform the act of knighthood with a close friend, privately, at one of the royal homes, and in 1967 she tapped round-the-world yachtsman Sir Francis Chichester on the shoulders alongside the Thames at Greenwich. Formal investitures are held 14 times a year in the State Ballroom at Buckingham Palace. The velvet-covered stool on which the recipient kneels has been used for this purpose for 60 years.

The greatest honour the Queen can bestow is her personal Order of the Garter. There are only 24 Knight Companions, at any one time, who have the

privilege of wearing the garter insignia on their left breast with the inscription "Honi soit qui mal y pense" (Shame on him who thinks evil of it). King Edward III used these words after he picked up the blue garter of Joan, Countess of Salisbury, when she lost it while he was dancing with her in April 1348. He said this to silence snickering courtiers . . . and from this has come the oldest order of chivalry in Britain.

Taking part in much of the royal pageantry are some of the more colourful of the Queen's escorts, the Yeomen of the Guard. They wear bright red costumes that have not changed

The Queen is escorted by the Canadian Prime Minister Pierre Trudeau **left** *at an American football match at Hamilton, Ontario, during her visit to Canada in Summer 1978.* **Below** *A section of the huge crowd in the stadium as the Queen arrives.*

During 1977 the whole world joined in the celebration of the Queen's Silver Jubilee – the twenty-fifth anniversary of her accession to the throne.

Millions of people came to Britain from all parts of the globe to witness or to take part in the festivities. Those who could not be there cabled good wishes

The Queen **left** *acknowledges the cheers of the supporters as she is led by Mr Trudeau to the Royal box, with Prince Philip, who accompanied her on the tour.* **Above** *The Queen in conversation with one of the officials.*

or sent letters in almost every known language.

The Queen and her family made special efforts, however, to greet the Commonwealth with fast, exhausting tours overseas.

The beginning of that incredible year was a six-week-long visit by Her Majesty and Prince Philip to the South Pacific, New Zealand and Australia.

After a brief stop in Samoa to board the royal yacht *Britannia* they spent a few days in Tonga and Fiji. In Tonga they were greeted by the giant, 28-stone King, His Majesty Taufa'ahau Tupou IV, who treated them to a feast of roast

since the days of Henry VIII, who founded the corps. It is the oldest military regiment in the world. To join this exclusive band of bodyguards a man has to have served at least 22 years in one of the services, reached a non-commissioned or warrant officer rank, have a good conduct medal and must have fought in at least one campaign. Although they no longer carry out these functions, but hold the titles as a mark of honour, four of them are "Yeoman Bed Hangers" while

another four are "Yeoman Bed Goers". The jobs were created by King Henry, who trusted nobody. Their original duties were to check the curtains hanging round the royal bed for any possible assassins and to turn the straw mattress to search for hidden knives or swords.

They now have the no less important duty of walking alongside the Queen on ceremonial occasions, carrying pike-staffs.

wild pigs, lobsters and exotic fruits.

One of the highlights of the visit to Fiji was the greeting, out at sea off Suva harbour, by hundreds of small boats, and the boarding of the *Britannia* by local chiefs in colourful, warrior-like costumes.

Warriors of another kind met the royal party at the start of their two weeks in New Zealand. Maoris massed in front of them – shouting their frightening war chants – and performed a mock battle.

The Queen's fondness for "walkabouts" – just wandering among the people – proved very successful in bringing her closer to delighted crowds. In one of her speeches she even tried speaking a little Maori.

During Jubilee Year the Queen received many thousands of gifts, from rich and poor, governments and business organisations, but few gave her as much pleasure as the horse she was presented with at a Parliamentary reception in Canberra when her

Australian journey began. Visibly pleased, she told the Australians: "I thank you all for this imaginative and exciting Jubilee gift."

In two very hectic weeks the royal pair went to every state in Australia, going out of their way to try to meet as many people as possible – not just the officials at banquets and formal lunches, but the children and their parents lining the streets.

Engagements during the Queen's tour of Canada in August 1978 included a Sunday Church service **centre left** *followed by an official signing ceremony* **opposite page above** *and a chat with the crew of the engine on which she and the Duke of Edinburgh had travelled* **above left.** *There was also a tour of the headquarters of the Royal Canadian Mounted Police:* **opposite page, below** *posing with officials, and* **below** *showing her usual keen interest in the horses, at the stabling quarters.*

The Queen was barely back in Britain at the end of March before she set out on a back-breaking four months of visits and ceremonial duties.

This included reviewing the three services, in particular the Royal Navy, whose ships were joined by vessels from other nations in a spectacular display of sea power off Spithead in the Solent.

The last time so many warships had gathered in ranks for Her Majesty was 24 years earlier, in the same anchorage, after her coronation. The ships this time were smaller, but with modern weapons the firepower was greater.

Not to be outdone, the Royal Air Force put on a dramatic fly-past of jet fighters and bombers at their Finning-

ley base in Nottinghamshire which ended with 22 aircraft swooping over in formation in the shape of a "25".

To receive the Army's tribute the Queen and the Prince went to West

*The Queen **left** arriving at one of the ports of call during her visit to Canadian provinces in 1978: she disembarks from an aircraft of the Royal Canadian Air Force. Two of the evening engagements during the 12 day tour were a banquet **below left, and opposite** and a dinner given by the Canadian Prime Minister, Mr Trudeau **below and bottom left.** On both occasions the Queen wears a Canadian Order on her evening dress.*

Germany, where the Rhine Army roared past in tanks, armoured troop carriers and helicopters.

On the eve of the official Jubilee Day – 7 June – the whole country was, almost literally, set alight. The Queen put a flame to a bonfire near her home at Windsor Great Park which sparked off a chain that spread the length and breadth of Britain.

The following day, watched by millions throughout the world on television, one of the greatest processions through London since the coronation took place. The Queen, with Prince Philip, drove in the 216-year-old Golden Stage Coach from Buckingham Palace two miles through the centre of London to St Paul's Cathedral for a service of thanksgiving.

Lining the route were military bands

and thousands of troops, and the streets were packed with nearly a hundred thousand rainsoaked flag wavers from all over the world, many of whom had camped overnight in the rain.

Leading the mile-long procession was a troop of scarlet-clad Royal Canadian Mounted Police, while behind them were coaches and open carriages carrying Statesmen and all the Royal Family – except one – Prince Charles, who, looking dashing in the tall bearskin and crimson jacket of a colonel-in-chief of the Welsh Guards, rode as an escort alongside his mother and father on a sleek black horse that had just been given to him by the Mounties – a horse he nearly fell off at St Paul's, because someone had put the dismounting block on the wrong side.

Above *Princess Anne enjoys a lively exchange of views with a Chelsea Pensioner during her visit to the Royal Hospital on Founders Day, 1972.* **Far left** *A fuller view of the grounds during the Founders Day ceremony.* **Left** *The Queen greeting Princess Anne warmly as they meet for the Academy of British Film Awards ceremony in March 1976.*

"It wasn't nearly as disastrous as I had thought," said Charles, on television later.

The sun came out, at last, by the end of the cathedral service, and the Queen and Philip walked through the streets of the City of London to a banquet held in the fifteenth-century Guildhall.

In one of the most significant speeches of her reign the Queen said at

copter, which was necessary for security reasons, and her first visit to Northern Ireland since the outbreak of the sectarian fighting. She and Philip also took along Prince Andrew, as if to let the troubled population know that

Left *Who has the most colourful robe? Princess Anne meets a Commonwealth contingent at a London reception.* **Below left** *The Princess with actor Peter Barkworth at a Theatre award ceremony in London.* **Bottom left** *She meets the stars of the James Bond film "Live And Let Die" in July 1973.* **Below right** *With Captain Mark Phillips, she attends a ball at Cowes during Cowes Week in August 1975.* **Bottom right** *Attending a preview of "Oklahoma" at the Palace Theatre in 1980.*

the Guildhall: "When I was 21, I pledged my life to the service of our people and I asked for God's help to make good that vow. Although that vow was made in my salad days, when I was green in judgement, I do not regret nor retract one word of it."

That tumultuous day ended with one of the biggest firework displays ever seen along the banks of the Thames. All the multi-coloured rockets were cleverly matched to music, by Handel, which was relayed over loudspeakers.

The Queen achieved two firsts during August . . . her first trip in a heli-

Prince Charles spent Lady Diana's 20th birthday at Newcastle to open the exhibition "Learning to Live" organised by the Local Council for the Disabled. By his express command, a large contingent of disabled people were grouped in the forecourt of Buckingham Palace on his wedding day, to enable them to be amongst the first to see the new Prince and Princess of Wales.

the Royal Family had not forgotten them.

In farewell words of encouragement she said: "I look forward to the day when we may return to enjoy with the people of Northern Ireland some of the better and happier times so long awaited and so richly deserved."

At the end of the summer Her Majesty finished her Jubilee tours with a visit to Canada.

This, then, is what the world regards as its first family – even citizens of countries with their own monarchies still look to the British Royal Family with admiration and affection.

They cover four generations and are a living link going back to the Victorian Age – 80 years of glorious pageantry behind them and every indication of a greater future ahead.

As the man said: "They're such a nice family to be with."

Bibliography

Much of the material for this book has come from private papers and books that are now so old that they are preserved only as collector's items. There were some books I referred to, however, which are still in print or can be found by diligent searching. For those readers wishing to learn more about the Royal Family the following should prove invaluable...

ANDREWS, ALLEN, The Follies of King Edward VII, Lexington Press 1975

ASHDOWN, LUCY M., Princess of Wales, John Murray, 1979

BUCHANAN, MERIEL, Queen Victoria's Relations, Cassell and Co, 1954

CATHCART, HELEN, Anne and the Princesses Royal, W. H. Allen, 1975

CATHCART, HELEN, The Queen Mother Herself, W. H. Allen, 1979

COOLICAN, DON, Royal Family Album, Colour Library International, 1978

COOLICAN, DON and LEMOINE, SERGE, Charles: Royal Adventurer, Pelham/Crown, 1978

CULLEN, TOM, The Empress Brown, The Bodley Head, 1969

DUFF, DAVID, Victoria Travels, Frederick Muller, 1970

DUFF, DAVID, Elizabeth of Glamis, Frederick Muller, 1973

DUFF, DAVID, Eugenie and Napoleon III, William Collins, Sons and Co, 1978

EDGAR, DONALD, The Queen's Children, Arthur Barker, 1978

EDGAR, DONALD, Prince Andrew, Arthur Barker, 1980

FRASER, ANTONIA, The Lives of the Kings and Queens of England, Weidenfeld and Nicolson, 1975

FISHER, GRAHAM and HEATHER, Consort, The Life and Times of Prince Philip, W. H. Allen, 1981

HIBBERT, CHRISTOPHER, The Court of St James's, Weidenfeld and Nicolson, 1979

HINDLEY, GEOFFREY, The Royal Families of Europe, Lyric Books, 1979

HOLDEN, ANTHONY, Charles, Prince of Wales, Weidenfeld and Nicolson, 1979

JUDD, DENIS, Prince Philip, Michael Joseph, 1980

LACEY, ROBERT, Majesty, Hutchinson, 1977

LAIRD, DOROTHY, Queen Elizabeth, The Queen Mother, Hodder and Stoughton, 1966

LANE, PETER, The Queen Mother, Robert Hale, 1979

LIVERSEDGE, DOUGLAS, Queen Elizabeth II, Arthur Barker, 1974

LIVERSEDGE, DOUGLAS, The Queen Mother, Arthur Barker, 1977

LONGFORD, ELIZABETH, Victoria R.I., Weidenfeld and Nicolson, 1964

MARTIN, CHRISTOPHER, The Edwardians, Wayland, 1974

MATSON, JOHN, Dear Osborne, Hamish Hamilton, 1978

MONTGOMERY-MASSINGBERD, HUGH, Burke's Guide to the British Monarchy, Burke's Peerage, 1977

PICKNETT, LYNN, Royal Romance, Marshall Cavendish, 1977

SINCLAIR, DAVID, Queen and Country, J. M. Dents and Sons, 1979

STRACHEY, LYTTON, Chatto and Windus 1921, Penguin 1978

TALBOT, GODFREY, The Country Life Book of the Royal Family, Country Life Books, 1980

TALBOT, GODFREY, Queen Elizabeth, The Queen Mother, Country Life Books, 1978

VICTORIA, QUEEN, Leaves from a Journal, Andre Deutsch 1961

WHITLOCK, RALPH, Royal Farmers, Michael Joseph, 1980

First published in Great Britain 1981 by **Colour Library International Ltd.**
© 1981 Text: **Colour Library International Ltd.,** New Malden, Surrey, England.
© 1981 Illustrations: **Keystone Press, Serge Lemoine** and **Camera Press.**
Colour separations by FERCROM, Barcelona, Spain.
Display and text filmsetting by Focus Photoset & The Printed Word, London, England.
Printed and bound in Barcelona, Spain by JISA-RIEUSSET and EUROBINDER.
All rights reserved.
ISBN 0 906558 74 3
COLOUR LIBRARY INTERNATIONAL

D.L.B. 30797-81